Nationhood, Migration and Global Politics

NATIONHOOD, MIGRATION AND GLOBAL POLITICS

An Introduction

RAYMOND TARAS

EDINBURGH
University Press

Edinburgh University Press is one of the leading university presses in the UK. We publish academic books and journals in our selected subject areas across the humanities and social sciences, combining cutting-edge scholarship with high editorial and production values to produce academic works of lasting importance. For more information visit our website: edinburghuniversitypress.com

Edinburgh University Press Ltd
The Tun – Holyrood Road
12(2f) Jackson's Entry
Edinburgh EH8 8PJ

Typeset in 10.5/12.5 Goudy by
Servis Filmsetting Ltd, Stockport, Cheshire

A CIP record for this book is available from the British Library
ISBN 978 1 4744 1342 8 (webready PDF)
ISBN 978 1 4744 1341 1 (paperback)
ISBN 978 1 4744 1343 5 (epub)

Contents

Boxes, figures and tables

Boxes

Figures

Tables

Chapter One

Reinventing nationhood

From nation to nationhood

States may today be best defined less by the nation or nations residing in them and more by the notion of nationhood. Nationhood is a term that posits how complex, diverse societies have become characteristic in an age of global migration. Conversely, like all maladapted structures, nations have outlived their usefulness and have become anachronistic.

Panarchy concerns the study of all things. It suggests that 'cascades of change are reshaping natural and human systems around the globe'.[1] Structures, like nations, become outmoded: 'A disturbance that exceeds a system's resilience breaks apart its web of reinforcing interactions.' At a critical moment, 'Early in the renewal phase, the system is up for grabs.'[2] In a social system undergoing cascades of change, powerful new groups may seize control of particular institutions. That maps out what has been happening to the nation.

I argue that the meaning of the 'hood' contained in 'nationhood' is misleading. The Urban Dictionary defines the hood as 'a place where plenty of shit goes down like gangbangin', drug dealin', killin', a place where you wouldnt want to be'. The word first appeared in 2005, its origins lying in what have been called American ghettoes: using the vernacular, these are Brooklyn and parts of Queens and the South Bronx in New York; Philadelphia; Southside Houston; and South Central Los Angeles, among others.

The shift to nationhood as the frame to understand the contemporary state is more than just a paradigm shift. It abandons ideas of monoculturalism and assimilationism that were previously demanded of society and which had insisted on blind loyalty by immigrants to the majority culture. Nationhood was being nudged from a primordial, ethnic understanding of the nation towards a civic one where, regardless of ethnicity, people could become law-abiding citizens.

From the 1990s on, the much-lauded civic nation concept has run the gamut from loosely knit multicultural structures of community to compactly organised forms of social integration and cohesion. In the latter case, outsiders or strangers – primarily recent influxes of immigrants – were expected to conform to a receiving society's norms and values.

Nations and nationhood have, for the most part, been used interchangeably, rarely in opposition to each other. No decentring and distinctive focus on the hood making up nationhood has emerged. In contrast, distinctions are made between, say, the state, nationalism, national identity, national character, patriotism and chauvinism. Nation and nationhood invariably appear synonymous, overlooking the possibility of drawing meaningful distinctions.

Nationhood should mean something different from the nation. It can suggest a communitarian perspective in which traditional, ethnically based nations are fused with recent immigrant populations. This can occur when certain conditions are met; in migration parlance it encompasses immigrant integration. The result can produce post-ethnic nationhood.

Put differently, nationhood signifies the process of expanding the nation when otherwise different people, not constructed ethnically, share some combination of language, religion, norms, values, faith, culture, identity and ideals. Unity out of diversity is a worn-out cliché used in many parts of the world, but nationhood reinvents this idea when it manages differences so as to produce a felt and experienced whole. However, it may fall short of forming an *organic* whole comprising a postmodern relationship of pasted-together fragmented parts. What differentiates nationhood from related concepts is, then, enlarging the nation so that it consists of different integrated ethnic parts.

The notion is not as new or radical as it may appear. It builds on ideas already circulating in migration research. For example, an assertion is made that 'There is no such thing as homogeneous nation-states in Europe but until this is understood more clearly by EU Member States, anti-migrant sentiments and racism will continue.'[3] Nationhood is a term not as loose and malleable as civic nation but it requires a degree of social integration needed to make people feel they belong (Box 1.1).

This book examines whether immigrants are treated as belonging to the state and forming part of its nationhood. It suggests what is new and valuable in breaking from established canonical thinking about nationalism studies and shifting the focus to nationhood. A number of writers considered here do stretch the nationhood concept in imaginative and reinvented ways.

The focus in this chapter is on migrants arriving in receiving societies. It is also a phenomenon that has undergone significant change as attitudes towards strangers have hardened as a result of multiple causes. I explore key concepts related to nationalism studies, including an inherent Eurocentric

> ## Box 1.1 Nationhood misunderstood
>
> In Elena Ferrante's novel, *The Story of a New Name*, the protagonist decides to read a book about, of all things, nationhood. But she puts it down quickly and goes to sleep – 'the book vanishes', as she puts it. Yet it may have been what was written in the book that turned her off: Federico Chabod's view of the nation as 'naturalistic' in contrast to Europe as cultural process founded on moral solidarity. Elena mutters at the end, *No, no, questo non suona bene* – 'no, no, that doesn't sound right.'
>
> Source: Elena Ferrante, *The Story of a New Name* (New York: Europa Editions, 2013). Her reference is to Federico Chabod, *L'idea di nazione* (Bari, Italy: Gius Laterza & figli, 1961). He equated nation, again, with nationhood, perhaps evoking her comment, *No, no, questo non suona bene*.

bias. The identity of the state, remade through nation branding, is analysed. Distinctions and conflations in migration research, such as that between refugees and economic migrants, are investigated. The blowback to minority rights resulting in the emergence of majority rights is highlighted.

What are migrants, the subject of this study? The term refers to

> all people on the move who have yet to complete the legal process of claiming asylum. This group includes people fleeing war-torn countries such as Syria, who are likely to be granted refugee status, as well as people who are seeking jobs and better lives, who governments are likely to rule are economic migrants.[4]

The real world of migration politics follows in the next two chapters. Chapter 2 parses the weight of secularism, race, religion and language in migrants being considered for notional membership in nationhood. Unlike citizenship, which is a certificate issued by the state attesting to the fulfilment of all legal requirements expected of citizen applicants, nationhood is ceremonial, symbolic and, perhaps more tellingly, about belonging to a host society.

In Chapter 3, I address the importance of social integration and the social cohesion that results in a receiving society. Today there is blowback, with critics suggesting that integration is the least that migrants can do to become a part of society; learning an official language is one of the most basic expectations. Social cohesion is the result of successful immigrant integration but it remains an uncommon occurrence.

The last six chapters are case studies, three from the northern hemisphere – Russia, the UK, the US – and three from the south – India, South Africa, Peru.

A NON-WESTERN CRITIQUE OF CONCEPTS

There are too many concepts related to nationalism to do all of them justice. Let me therefore begin by considering writers outside of the Western tradition who are critical of the dominant European paradigm of the nation.

In *The Location of Culture*, Homi Bhabha criticises all forms of nationalism derived from the European experience and instead features the in-between life that he calls the third space, *l'espace entre-deux*. Here we find syncretism, cultural hybridity, multiculturalism, liminality, and space situated on the margins of our societies. The phenomenon termed *migrance* emerges, highlighting the status of postcolonial populations who serve as metaphors for displacement. Bhabha reverses the colonial injunction to be like us – *soyez comme nous* – and satirises its absurdity.[5]

For Seyla Benhabib, liberal democracies must pass a test of moral conscience in their treatment of aliens and foreigners. Three principles must be heeded:

1. Members of cultural, religious, linguistic and other minorities cannot possess lesser degrees of civil, political, economic and cultural rights than the majority: that is, egalitarian reciprocity.
2. An individual must not automatically be assigned to a cultural group by virtue of birth but has the right to change it: that is, voluntary self-ascription.
3. An individual's freedom to exit the ascriptive group must be unrestricted: that is, freedom of exit and association.

Minority rights therefore outweigh majority rights: 'Universal human rights transcend the rights of citizens and extend to all persons considered as moral beings.'[6] Instead of ridiculing the idea of being like us, Benhabib offers no guarantees that a majority culture can be found within the panoply of ever-changing minority rights. Some of her ideas are now under renewed challenge by majority rights advocates, as discussed later.

For Gayatri Spivak, postcolonial theorists are well positioned to question Europe's civilisational exceptionalism. She noted the vague, limited formation of nationalism in the global south, such as India. She asked an important nationhood-related question:

When and how does the love of mother tongue, the love of my little corner of ground become the nation thing? I say nation thing rather than nationalism because something like nations, collectivities bound by birth, that allowed in strangers gingerly, have been in existence long before nationalism came around.[7]

Singling out the exclusionary character of European philosophy, Spivak denounced 'how Kant foreclosed the Aboriginal; how Hegel put the other of Europe in a pattern of normative deviations and how the colonial subject sanitized Hegel; how Marx negotiated difference'.[8] Even in an age of postcoloniality, Eurocentrism presented an obstacle to understanding philosophy.

Writing around the same time, Dipesh Chakrabarty weighed in on the 'first in Europe, then elsewhere' Eurocentric assertion. In his introduction to *Provincializing Europe*, he affirmed how 'No major Western thinker has publicly shared Francis Fukuyama's "vulgarized Hegelian historicism" that saw in the fall of the Berlin wall a common end for the history of all human beings.'[9]

Chakrabarty held in relief actual European practices: 'The European colonizer of the nineteenth century both preached this Enlightenment humanism at the colonized and at the same time denied it in practice.'[10] Furthermore, 'Historicism, and even the modern, European idea of history, one might say, came to non-European peoples in the nineteenth century as somebody's way of saying "not yet" to somebody else.' What did this mean? 'Not yet civilized enough to rule themselves,' he explained.[11]

Partha Chatterjee cautioned that the roads to nationalism West and East have diverged. In the West, the nation took advantage of linguistic, educational and professional competence to develop a progressive civilisation. In the East, however, ancestral cultures were not adapted for this purpose, particularly when 'those standards have come from an alien culture'. The essential question was, then, 'for a regeneration of the national culture, adapted to the requirements of progress, but retaining at the same time its distinctiveness'.[12]

Chatterjee insisted that Asian and African nationalisms differed from the West not on matters of identities but on paradigmatic questions. Notably, Eastern nationalists divided culture into spiritual and material dimensions. The crucial distinction was between the colonial and the modern state: 'the notion that colonial rule was not really about colonial rule but something else was a persistent theme in the rhetoric of colonial rule itself'. Moreover, in Eastern thought, nations and imagined communities were concepts difficult to combine, and no amount of Western conceptual stretching, the author suggested, could turn them into intersecting ideas.[13]

Andre Gunder Frank's *ReOrient* was a further effort to decentre Europe. His goal was to provide a 'holistic universal, global, world history – "as it really was"', which would turn 'Eurocentric historiography and social theory upside down by using a "globological" perspective'.[14] Gunder Frank, too, rejected the Eurocentrism inherent in the works of European philosophers such as Karl Marx, Max Weber, Arnold Toynbee and Karl Polanyi. Similar to Spivak, he wished to construct a 'different paradigmatic perspective' that would again place Asia, not Europe, 'at the helm of history'.[15] In 1998, the author was convinced that the centre of the world economy was returning to the Middle Kingdom – China.

Many of these critical writers were dubious about the liberal nature of Eurocentrism. Claims that it represents the civilisational repository of tolerance, inclusion, human rights – the array of values encapsulated by the term universal values – were nonsensical. Eurocentrism applied processes of othering to assign people to an ethnic hierarchy. For these writers, European fears are again becoming tangible: distrust of rootless migrants, Roma, Jews, Turks, Russians: in other words, all things categorised as Orientalism.

Eurocentric bias

Does nationhood suffer from a Eurocentric bias? A specialist on nationhood who triggered renewed interest in the concept in the 1990s focused his study on Europe: more precisely, *Mitteleuropa*. In *Nationalism Reframed: Nationhood and the National Question in the New Europe*, Rogers Brubaker proposed several key concepts in nationalism research but relegated nationhood to a word derived from its cognate, the nation.

Examining the cultural and historical roots of what he called nationhood in France and Germany, Brubaker concluded that the nation in France was equated with the institutional and territorial frame of the state. The French therefore defined nation as a form of political unity, synonymous with *la république*. In Germany, on the other hand, nationhood and citizenship were primarily ethno-cultural, based on common descent, blood and ancestry. Nationhood was the word used to depict respective pathways of the nation.[16]

Brubaker held that French and German national self-understandings (roughly parallel to nationhood) contrasted civic with ethnic approaches to membership in a nation. 'If the French understanding of nationhood has been state-centered and assimilationist, the German understanding has been Volk-centered and differentialist,' he noted.[17] These were products of centuries-old traditions of nationhood in the two countries, shaped by distinct geographical, cultural and political conditions.

Brubaker was concerned, therefore, with parsing forms of nationalism rather than retooling nationhood. He emphasised how *nationalizing nationalism* originated in formerly marginalised ethnic groups who insisted on being seen as a core nationality partaking in legitimate ownership of the state they live in.

Nationhood needs us to nudge it along, and Brubaker did that, if in a different context, in an article he published in 2004:

> nationhood is not an ethnodemographic or ethnocultural fact; it is a political claim. It is a claim on people's loyalty, on their attention, on their solidarity. If we

understand nationhood not as fact but as claim, then we can see that 'nation' is not a purely analytical category. It is not used to describe a world that exists independently of the language used to describe it. It is used, rather, to change the world, to change the way people see themselves, to mobilize loyalties, kindle energies, and articulate demands.[18]

He interpreted nationhood as a political claim: 'What does it mean to speak "in the name of the nation"?'[19] As political claims, nationhood could 'develop more robust forms of citizenship, provide support for redistributive social policies, foster the integration of immigrants'. It is integration of immigrants that comes close to approximating my view of nationhood.

Managing diversity and achieving social cohesion rank high as the goals of nationhood. Social cohesion means positive outcomes derived from immigration policy, such as productive economies. Citizenship and belonging are ways to accelerate social cohesion.[20] In turn, multiculturalism and interculturalism are models for producing managed diversity. Finally, postnationality, transnationalism and supranationalism are terms describing states where the nation is no longer the focus of identity.

A fundamental question that political theorists ask is whether nationhood should be a prerequisite for liberal democratic government. In theory, it is nationhood that mobilises citizens to distribute social trust in a society. 'Absent nationhood, electoral systems fracture, are manipulated by the wealthy, ratify dictatorship, descend into violence, succumb to military coups, or become paralyzed by ethnic bloc voting.'[21]

Nationhood, then, is built on a liberal democratic system but does not necessarily reproduce it. Russia, China and Iran, critics claim, are nations without nationhood precisely because they are undemocratic and illiberal. But system of government is not an attribute of nationhood any more than territory is. In that case, nationhood should be decoupled from democratic politics.

Reinhard Bendix regarded the extension of citizenship to members of widening communities, including migrants, as the trademark of successful nation building.[22] Nationhood is much the same, mirroring the process of bringing together people from a different heritage and moulding them into a communitarian whole.

The cornered state

The literature on the making of nations, nationalism and national identity is vast. Nationhood combines essentialist features of nations – ethnicity, religion, territory, shared experience, language – with integrated immigrants. But the story begins with the state. The state was once unchallengeable in the age of divine rights of kings, of dynasties and of sovereignty. Even before the Westphalia pact was concluded in 1648 and attributed sovereignty to particular nations, the Council of Constance in 1416 marked a caesura where bidding and bargaining over the nation had become paramount. The lines were drawn:

> It is difficult to imagine more impressive evidence for the national question in medieval Europe. Here were delegations from all over the Continent struggling for recognition of their independent national status, voting in national blocs of interest and debating the meaning of the national concept. In this debate they invoked blood relations, language, common customs, and shared history, on the one hand, as well as territory, systems of government and law and voluntary participation, on the other.[23]

Territorial autonomy also yielded political integration. In 1555 the Augsburg formula to end the massacres of Catholics and Protestants in Europe was enshrined: *cuius regio, eius religio* – 'who rules decides which God his subjects worship'.[24] Over the next five centuries a snakes-and-ladders approach to the nation developed. Some states went out of existence, others were remade under different names, new makeshift ones were created, and wars great and small changed state boundaries. Among the commonly identified functions of the classical state were providing for peace and prosperity at home while protecting the values, identity and territorial integrity in interstate relations.

When large-scale immigration into a state occurs, many of these functions may be affected. But the state usually insists on its right to carry out its primary function – controlling its borders (Box 1.2). Sociologist Zygmunt Bauman remarked that the nation–state had acquitted itself decently in terms of independence and autonomy. But it 'is demonstrating daily its singular unfitness to act effectively under the present condition of planet-wide interdependence of humans'.[25] As examples, 'By stopping people from poorer countries moving to richer ones ... borders perpetuate global inequality, and by turning natural resources into private property divided between nation–states, they prevent meaningful collective action to tackle climate change.'[26]

Inequalities *within* a society are inextricably linked to those found in international society:

> all of the pressures that result from international migration are also generated by migration within a country's borders. Linguistic and cultural differences, scarce public resources, unequal distribution of wealth: all of these exist within as well as between nation–states. So why limit controls to international borders? Why not prevent people from Solihull moving to London and putting pressure on the rental market? Should we build a wall around North Wales to prevent further dilution of the Welsh language?[27]

8

Box 1.2 The state's last chance to flex its muscles?

Erecting border walls in a world denying their importance is now an indisputable fact:

in 1990 just 15 states had walls or fences at their borders; by 2016, nearly seventy did. In the past such defenses were set up principally because of conflict between neighboring states (North and South Korea, for instance, or India and Pakistan), but today's border defenses are primarily focused on civilians, aimed at stopping unwanted or 'irregular' migration. It isn't just in the West: barriers proliferate in Asia and Africa too. These defenses, supported by a military infrastructure of patrols and surveillance, come at a price. According to the International Organization for Migration, forty thousand people died attempting to cross a border between 2005 and 2014.

Source: Daniel Trilling, 'Should We Build a Wall Around North Wales?', *London Review of Books*, 39, no. 14, 13 July 2017, p. 16.

In an age of globalisation, arguments to augment the role of the state are today unfashionable and unconvincing. Three decades ago, Theda Skocpol had already made the case for regaining state autonomy so as to affect policy changes.[28] But there were limits: 'This is the part of the state that is constantly seeking privileges that only God can have. The state wants to become an all-pervading, omniscient, and supreme arbiter.'[29] Especially relevant to migration, the question arises: if the state abandons its traditional gatekeeping functions, which institution *will* maintain social order, adopt policies promoting economic development, avoid capital flight, preserve majoritarian values and identities, and keep borders salient?

Since 1945, a two-pronged attack has undermined the state. First, the postwar bipolar world required that countries engage in either bandwagoning or balancing behaviour with a superpower. Few states enjoyed the luxury of having full sovereignty. Dictators, despots and tyrants aligned themselves with one or other of the superpowers. It was not always the case that oppressive regimes invariably backed the USSR and democratic ones the US.

The second blow to the state system occurred when the bipolar system ended. The era of globalisation took flight, first with efforts at free trade (even if the Multilateral Agreement on Investment failed in 1998); then with multiple, unfettered trade and investment treaties (the European Union (EU) was a case in point); and finally with a slowdown caused by increased protectionism and defence against the Trans-Pacific Partnership (TPP) and Transatlantic Trade and Investment Partnership (TTIP).

The irony is that the more globalisation that has taken place globally, the more desperate nations are to brand themselves as unique and distinct.

NATION BRANDING

Amy Chua has persuasively outlined how exporting free market democracy can breed ethnic hatred in many countries, particularly in developing states. Her logic is incontestable: free markets concentrate starkly disproportionate wealth in the hands of an ethnic minority who are resented for that. Market-dominant minorities become objects of hatred. Simultaneously, democratic expansion empowers the impoverished majority to lash out at them, some-times unleashing ethnic cleansing, even genocidal vengeance.[30]

The ethnic minorities that Chua studied were the Chinese in Southeast Asia, Croatians in the former Yugoslavia, Whites in Latin America and South Africa, the Indian population in East Africa, the Lebanese in West Africa, and Jews in post-communist Russia. Despite her stinging critique of the consequences of economic disparities, she claimed still to be a friend of economic globalisation.

But market economies that create profound inequalities between haves and have-nots has become a sophisticated tool in the hands of nation brand-ers, and Melissa Aronczyk has exposed the many internal contradictions in the commerce of whitewashing disparities. In her view, 'Nation branding maintains and perpetuates the nation as a container of distinct identities and loyalties, and as a project for sovereignty and self-determination.' A nation's culture and territory are given marketable, monetisable values. The end result is commodification of the nation, in which economic experts 'give them the license to determine what values, attitudes, behaviors, and beliefs are superior to others'.[31]

A transnational promotional class (TPC) develops from the 'there is no alternative' (TINA) argument to globalisation. This class consists of 'a group of diverse actors devoted to maintaining the legitimacy of the national form for a range of profit-generating purposes'. The contradiction becomes evident: a national form is enwrapped in globalisation. The hocus-pocus of spin defending inescapable globalisation is regarded as exogenous and beyond our direct control.

The TPC combines public and private sector resources for fiscal advantage. They project images of legitimacy and authority in, for example, legitimising trade deals at the cost of increasing a country's balance-of-trade deficits. They spin positive foreign public opinion about a country – a form of soft power. What follows is not a level playing field but a way to 'maintain and reinforce historical inequalities and reify paternalist and neocolonial assumptions'.[32]

This is where populism steps in. Brubaker explains the phenomenon:

The opening of national economies to immigrant labor is part of a broader set of economic transformations that have created opportunities for populists to speak in the name of 'ordinary people' against 'those on top' and against outside forces seen as threatening 'our' jobs, 'our' prosperity, and 'our' economic security. The litany is familiar: sharp increases in inequalities, the regionally concentrated collapse of manufacturing jobs, the accelerating cross-border flows of goods, services, and investments as well as labor, and the shifting of risks and responsibilities to individuals through neoliberal modes of governance.[33]

These phenomena are cross-regional processes so Aronczyk asks what it may mean to *claim* to have a national identity. Its benign quality is invariably stressed: 'a nation's brand is meant to offer a version of nationalism rooted in the unifying spirit of benign commercial "interests" rather than in the potential divisions of political "passions"'. As she puts it,

> the future of the nation consists of finding a 'lucrative role' to play within a globally integrated economic system. Under the rubric of global nationalism, national identity is acknowledged more in terms of its fitness for capital attraction than for its cohesive or collegial properties; that is, cohesiveness and belonging are seen to follow from the nation's fitness for capital attraction, as state polices are mutually configured to favor economic growth as the engines of citizens' well-being.[34]

Nation branding organised by the state seeks to reclaim a unique, distinctive and inimitable *national self*. In a knock-on effect, it also promotes belonging and social cohesion. The commodity of *diversity* stands out: culture converted into marketable resources trades on the currency of diversity. In her six case studies, all countries market diversity.

The author is damning about invoking such sweeping claims: 'this making and marketing of diversity is a fundamentally flawed project, one that celebrates difference only insofar as it corresponds to patterns of consumption'. Indeed, it comprises 'A fantasy of diversity in which the only kind of diversity that matters is one that is defanged for purposes of global trade'. It is skin deep: 'It encounters social difference without social consequences.'[35] Diversity is fake news in that it does not produce nationhood.

Segregation, radicalism, illiberalism and xenophobia may, paradoxically, be the consequences of bogus diversity. Its schismatic character is true for Canada, for instance. Celebrating 150 years of Confederation, a 2017 nation branding exercise, presented on posters with the heading 'Canada is nice', featured visible minorities appearing to adore White Canadians. Even Canadians felt uneasy about nation branding portraying them as benefactors of minority adulation.

Nation branding makes special demands on individuals in a particular country and becomes a cultural, personal, emotional and devotional experience. It requires a person's loyalty, allegiance and belonging. The

11

country-of-origin effect expects special loyalty from the nation doing the branding. Pride in German automotive technology seemed obvious, until German manufacturers started cheating on emissions tests.

In concluding her cross-national research project, Aronczyk takes up the theme of nationhood:

> Theorists of nationalism have conveyed that 'idioms of nationhood' emerge from a number of corners and in a variety of registers: from the 'felt' nationalisms of communities, classes, and social movements to the 'official' registers of state organization, conscription, and education.... The idiom of nationhood at stake in the phenomenon of nation branding, the 'other' who is made to matter for the nation, is the amorphous figure of the 'global'.[36]

Global entails forgetting about the nation and ignoring ethical and moral standpoints about what it really means to be national. In this way, the market becomes natural, while the nation or state is not.

Which immigrants?

If nation branding seeks to reassure, forced migration is used to describe people who are on the move precisely because of fears about their security. Alexander Betts observes how 'refugees are not only a consequence of insecurity and conflict but may also contribute to insecurity and conflict'. He focuses on how refugees may exacerbate conflict:

> refugees and internally displaced persons may, if they are not provided with adequate protection and durable solutions, become a barrier to the development of peace-building initiatives. They may disrupt post-conflict reconstruction and peace building as returnees with property and rights-based claims, through remaining militarized groups in exile, by remaining outside of peace negotiations, postponing possibilities for repatriation, or refusing to renounce violence.[37]

Forced migration is a case in which the independent variable is security and the threats to it, the dependent variable is the migrant. Migrant numbers would not be as overwhelming as in recent years if it were not for persons compelled to escape xenophobia. Forced migration is a compelling reason why nationhood should be expanded to incorporate asylum seekers.

On the other hand, the freedom to emigrate without being forced to do so should not be discounted. Bob Marley's epic 'Exodus' refers to free movement – that is, the 'Movement of Jah people':

> Open your eyes and look within,
> Are you satisfied with the life you're living?
> We know where we're going, uh!
> We know where we're from.

We're leaving Babylon,
We're going to our Father land.

The lyrics reference a 'Back to Africa' movement in the US and other former slave states around the 1920s. Its premise was that Africans preferred to be ruled by their ethnic kin rather than by societies with slave-owning histories. It is hard to imagine a 'roots movement' now, even if many migrants are misled by their migration experience. The contrary is more often true: refugees claim they face persecution, even death, when they return to their fatherland.

A recent offshoot of migration research focusing on mobilities of return brings us back to 'Exodus'. Its purview is the movement of people back to places that are designated as home. It has seldom been the focal point of robust analysis and, like supranationalism and postcoloniality, appeared to be assigned to oblivion, until its importance has again been recognised.[38]

WHICH REFUGEES?

European states have not agreed on a migration policy, even on asylum seekers,[39] yet estimates put the number of migrants hoping to enter Europe from various countries as high as 8–10 million. The distinction between asylum seekers and economic migrants has grown more liminal.

Speaking for many migration specialists in 2017, the French Interior Minister contended that public opinion was increasing in its hostility to welcoming migrants. As he put it, 'If one does not draw the distinction between the right to asylum and other motives for migration, it will be the right to asylum that will be put into question.' In other words, those justifiably claiming refugee status will be overwhelmed by those simply seeking work. He stressed that France 'welcomes everyone who flees wars and persecutions, but we distinguish refugees from those where migration stems from other jurisdictions, notably economic. Therefore welcoming is important, but also organising returns.'[40]

Does the Universal Declaration of Human Rights ratified by the United Nations (UN) General Assembly offer the protections – indeed, the right – 'to enjoy' asylum (Article 14.1), promised by the 1951 Convention Relating to the Status of Refugees? Complicating matters further, there may be a difference in protections offered under international refugee law, and rights and standards of treatment offered by international human rights law.[41] In Europe, countries differ over offering asylum: countries extending full rights limit the number of refugees who receive them, while others admit many asylum seekers but limit the benefits they receive. In short, the trade-offs are not just between refugee and economic migrant applications, but also between refugees with full entitlement and those without.[42]

13

Shifts in the reception of migrants can also be subtle. Security expert Andrew Michta noted how 'Europeans' initial calm, goodwill, and even enthusiasm for the new arrivals and manifest *Willkommenskultur*, or welcoming culture, have given way to growing public anger.' Migrants have become a divisive subject: 'No other issue drives political realignment in Europe more directly today than the growing public anger over governments' inability to stop the flood, process applications in a timely manner, and return those whose asylum applications have been rejected.'[43] The middle ground between supposed populists calling for a halt to migration and enablers invoking the international rights of migrants has caved in.

Overall, the UN reported in 2016 that 'The number of international migrants – persons living in a country other than where they were born – reached 244 million in 2015 for the world as a whole, a 41 per cent increase compared to 2000.'[44] This total included forced migration – about 20 million refugees fleeing from conflict, discrimination, disease, and disasters of all kinds. The other 200 million plus were economic migrants, those subsumed under family unification (a UN mandate), climate refugees and unspecified numbers.

The state's function of controlling its territory has become precarious, then. As a result, states today are defined less by the nation or nations in them and more by the idea of nationhood: their decision to expand the national community by integrating newcomers from different countries. Nationhood also requires abandoning the ethnic and ethnicised model of the nation and opting instead for demographic diversity. When skilfully managed, it can result in a felt and experienced whole.

WHO GETS WHAT, WHEN, HOW

Contemporary states manage ethnic differences in radically different ways. Some promote a sense of belonging for persons now resident in these societies, while others favour a given ethnic group and privilege it to the exclusion of others. It is a thin line between instilling belonging and encouraging nationhood, and feeling excluded from it, risking alienation or even radicalisation. Surveys can tell us which groups enjoy full inclusion in nationhood and who does not. Let me briefly examine a 2015–16 report on discrimination and racism against migrants in Europe.

Based on national questionnaire responses in twenty-six EU member states, the study identified groups subject to exclusion. The European Network Against Racism (ENAR), which carried out this research, stressed how anti-migrant political discourses were becoming hateful and had an impact on racialised migrants. Most of the blame was placed on far-right groups cultivating Islamophobic, anti-migrant and anti-EU reactions, but

ENAR made clear that it was becoming increasingly difficult to differentiate between groups organising anti-migrant protests and individuals perpetrating violent, racially motivated crimes.[45]

Discrimination takes many forms. One is the labour market that includes outright discrimination against migrants, restrictions associated with migration status, non-recognition of migrant qualifications, and the language migrants speak. These produce an employment gap between migrants and nationals. Desperate to find work, many fall victim to exploitation. Without a labour market opposed to discriminatory practices based on race or status, social inclusion remains problematic for racialised migrants.[46]

But there is a different attitude which displays little or no attachment to nation and nationhood. Craig Calhoun points to cosmopolitanism as an irresistible force that divides elites and public: 'Today, cosmopolitanism has considerable theoretical advantage. It seems hard not to want to be a "citizen of the world".'[47] Attitudes indifferent to nationhood used to flourish in imperial capitals and trading cities, and some still exist in cities with a colonial past. Cosmopolitan citizens hold themselves up as the epitome of multicultural modernity. They differentiate themselves from people rooted in monocultural societies. Postnational cosmopolitan politics, it seems, offer a sure path to neoliberalism, its economic standard bearer. This group stands aside from forms of racialised discrimination.

Another tendency is found within the migration advocacy community. It believes that migrants have never been better off. Unprecedented global migration, it holds, has given immigrants the edge. They boost a country's net reproduction rate, guarantee tax revenue streams, lower labour costs, sometimes through a race to the bottom, and provide a reserve army of unskilled labour. Historian Walter Laqueur contrasts the limited resources set aside for immigrants a hundred years ago with the more recent coddled approach:

> There is, to begin with, the scale of immigration. Only tens of thousands came to Western Europe 100 years ago, not millions. They made great efforts to integrate socially and culturally. Above all, they wanted to give their children a good secular education at almost any price. The rate of intermarriage was high within one generation, and even higher within two. No one helped them. There were no social workers or advisors, no one gave them housing at low or no rent, and programs such as Sure Start (a British equivalent of Head Start) and 'positive discrimination' had not yet been invented. There were no free health service or unemployment benefits. There were no government committees analyzing Judeophobia and how to combat it.[48]

Laqueur does not explain why migrants became pampered, but a reason cited by a so-called migration industry is that corporations and big business invariably support migration for their own economic interests, not out of compassion for migrants.[49]

Since immigration gives a country the opportunity to expand the nation, many Western states – and non-Western ones too – lend support to it. But sometimes states and their leaders refuse to accept immigrants in order to safeguard their national identity; discourage ethnic kin from another country to move in and change the demographic equilibrium; pursue economic autarchy, protectionism and sovereignty; or some other reason.

Ernest Renan's idea of building a nation one day at a time – 'The existence of a nation is a daily referendum' – is never truer than when building nationhood. In such a case, state policy is diurnal, a response to the daily pressures of enlarging a nation.[50] It is guided by inclusionary attitudes that subsume both policy preferences and societal attitudes.

The first step in forging nationhood involves incorporating migrants in the receiving society. Both policies of multiculturalism and interculturalism promise such inclusion.[51] But social integration, discussed in the next chapter, is more circumspect about giving such assurances. Which states, then, take advantage of the opportunity to expand nationhood? What is the cost of preserving ethnic identity, especially for a small nation? Can it lead to policies excluding migrants in order to preserve *le sang pur*? Larger nations have more wiggle room to expand nationhood, especially those having track records as receiving societies.

Today about 80 per cent of countries are multinational. They often harbour historic national and ethnic communities born and bred in their country. In Europe, for example, Jews and Roma are such historic minorities. Indigenous nations (examined in Chapter 3) also have a prior claim on rights and property. As a result, political leaders often feel that new migrants are an addition to the queue.

Managing diversity is a complex policy process. It can lead to failure when, for example, specific regions of the country are neglected. Some leaders are mindful of neocolonial attitudes embedded in a society. They may express concern about internal migrants arriving in cities having little in common with the regions to which they move. Nationhood can be wrecked by ethnic schisms, breakouts of social conflict, even secessionist movements. Holding it all together is the delicate task of nationhood builders.

For migration studies, a crucial issue is whether immigrant communities reject assimilation on the terms set by dominant majorities. Sticking together – a natural reaction that cements bonds within groups of migrants rather than networking outside them – can lead to normative clashes. The term 'two solitudes' was coined by writer Hugh MacLennan in 1945 to describe the separate lives led by Canadians and Quebeckers,[52] but today in hyper-diverse societies we may speak of three or more solitudes.

Majority groups, along with minorities who are Indigenous, communitarian or immigrant, are after the same thing: who is to get what, when and how.[53] Politics decides how resources are allocated and immigrants are one voice seated at a big table.

TYPOLOGIES OF THE NATION

Today most definitions of nation and national identity outline specific ethnic and religious affiliations, use of particular languages, and cultural pathways in order to determine the peoples subsumed by them.[54] The first wave of nation-building scholars typically stressed the elective character of creating a nation and placed emphasis on the centrality of primordial factors.

Historian Eric Hobsbawm demonstrated how nationalism in the first part of the nineteenth century was associated with political liberty and progressive ideals. But for the last twenty-five years of the nineteenth century, it had become usurped by religiously and linguistically exclusionary, sometimes violent, movements that celebrated a nation's glory and insisted on identity, order and stability for it.[55] Language and religion shaped national struggles: 'Most of the aspirations for statehood in nineteenth-century Europe were in terms of ethnic nationalism based on language; and linguistic claims were often based on a legitimating connection with religion.'[56]

For most of the twentieth century, nationalism was linked to irredentism, border disputes, illiberalism, racism and oppression of minorities. Religious differences served as their deep structures. The struggle for national self-determination after World War I produced momentous changes, many of them benign and constructive. President Woodrow Wilson's Fourteen Points was a formula for managing the collapse of the Austro-Hungarian, Prussian and Turkish empires. It brought independence and the remapping of postwar European borders, itself the source of incessant conflict: for example, Poland and Czechoslovakia fought a series of little-known border wars from the time they became independent states in 1918.

After World War II in Asia and Africa, liberation struggles persisted in Indonesia, the British Raj, Vietnam and neighbouring colonies, as well as the British, French and Portuguese dominions across Africa. The rise of independence movements in post-Soviet republics after the Cold War in 1989 became the latest phase of sovereignty claims. Unfortunately, the vestiges of postcolonialism in many of these states have never entirely disappeared.

Scholarship on nation building acknowledged the positive role played by claims for territorial, religious and language rights in the creation of national communities. For Carlton Hayes nationality was primarily cultural and only incidentally political,[57] whereas for Elie Kedourie it was essentially political[58] and for Dudley Seers economic – affirming a state's autonomy from the global economy.[59]

An organic approach to nationality was provided by Hans Kohn.

17

Group attributes contributing to nationality included such factors as 'common descent, language, territory, political entity, customs and traditions, and religion'.[60] Writing in 1927, Ernest Barker provided a comprehensive, robust definition of the nation, as enmeshed in the Western tradition:

> A nation is a body of men, inhabiting a definite territory, who normally are drawn from different races, but possess a common stock of thoughts and feelings acquired and transmitted during the course of a common history; who on the whole and in the main, though more in the past than in the present, include in that common stock a common religious belief; who generally and as a rule use a common language as the vehicle of their thoughts and feelings; and who, besides common thoughts and feelings, also cherish a common will, and accordingly form, or tend to form, a separate state for the expression and realization of that will.[61]

The primordial school of nation building – the baseline of this research – recognises the significance of objective markers of identity such as language and religion. It also acknowledges subjective shared identity based on objective cultural factors. Anthony Smith, for one, referred to shared group attributes such as religion, language, dress, music, crafts, laws, customs and institutions. But he recognised the centrality of psychological feelings of common solidarity with other group members.[62]

In contrast to primordialism, instrumentalists regard ethnicity as 'a tool used by individuals, groups, or elites to obtain some larger, typically material end'.[63] Ethnic identity gains social and political significance when ethnic entrepreneurs, whether in response to threats or opportunities, manipulate ethnic symbols to forge political movements seeking collective ends.[64] This type of politicised ethnicity is the creation

> of elites, who draw upon, distort, and sometimes fabricate materials from the cultures of the groups they wish to represent in order to protect their well-being or existence or to gain political and economic advantage for their groups as well as for themselves.[65]

Instrumental nationalism is summed up in the observation made by Napoleon Bonaparte that only two forces unite men: fear and self-interest. Hostility towards strangers and to the project of nationhood may be a crude way in which fear and self-interest are combined. All political leaders may therefore be entrepreneurs. To be sure, a corrective was advanced by Nelson Mandela, who challenged the mantra that there is nothing to fear but fear itself.

> No one is born hating another person because of the color of his skin, or his background, or his religion. People must learn to hate, and if they can learn to hate, they can be taught to love, for love comes more naturally to the human heart than its opposite.[66]

18

The school of constructivism that dominates academic thinking today emerged in the 1990s. It rejects the notion that either ethnic identity is a natural phenomenon or it is an instrument manipulated by ethnic entrepreneurs for individual or collective political ends. It contends that ethnic identities are durable social constructions, the products of human actions and choices rather than biologically given ideas.

Max Weber, a writer who put emphasis on the social construction of ethnic identity a full century earlier, regarded human groups as those who believed in the myth of a common ancestry that laid the foundations for a community.[67] Ethnic membership by itself 'does not necessarily result in ethnic group formation but only provides the resources that may, under the right circumstances, be mobilized into a group by appropriate political action'.[68] People draw on historically symbolic myths originating in stories, music, art, drama and rituals to reveal how these symbols of ethnic identity need to be appropriated and internalised by individuals before social action can be undertaken.

Comparing nation-building schools suggests how primordialists, instrumentalists and constructivists are all concerned with the role of culture in the formation of ethnic identity. But key areas are still left out. For example, in *Multiculturalism without Culture*, Anne Phillips argued that cultural stereotypes of women are not really about culture at all.[69]

The seamier side of nation building – ethnocentrism, xenophobia, exclusion, intolerance – can be lethal. French historian Pierre-André Taguieff was unable to say which approach was worse: 'On the one hand, then, rejection, hostility, aversion – *xenophobia*; on the other, creating distance, cultural deafness, the inferiorization of "others" than us – ethnocentrism.'[70] These factors share in common a total rejection of the nationhood principle.

KULTURNATION AND NATIONHOOD

Old school approaches to the study of nationalism displayed only a passing interest in the role of language or religion in the making of a nation; a will to exist seemed more vital. Historian Hugh Seton-Watson believed that 'A nation exists when a significant number of people in a community consider themselves to form a nation, or behave as if they formed one.'[71] Arnold Toynbee concluded that nationality is 'nothing material or mechanical, but a subjective psychological feeling in a living people'.[72] Sociologist Émile Durkheim defined nationality as 'a group whose members wish to live under the same laws and form a state'.[73] Renan condensed the nation to 'a daily plebiscite', although 'expanded nation' might be the preferable term.[74]

But for political scientist William Safran it is not subjective qualities, a will, or the plebiscitary nature of nation that is important but something more concrete. 'Language and religion are related; both have deep structures and both are regarded as constitutive aspects of "primordialism" in the sense that individuals are born into one, the other, or (in most instances) both.'[75] Precocious political nations such as France, England and the US epitomised this fusion: 'In these three states, a process of domestic political transformation generated the nation as a community of politically aware citizens equal before the law irrespective of their social and economic status, ethnic origin and religious beliefs.'[76]

The presence of religious and linguistic communities becomes salient when we encounter the idea of a *cultural* nation. If the political nation underscores subjective criteria – individual will, a we-feeling, shared values – its cultural counterpart stresses the spirit of community anchored in 'objective criteria such as common heritage and language, a distinct area of settlement, religion, customs and history'.[77]

The rise of the *cultural nation* is associated with the historical experience of countries in Central and Eastern Europe where nation formation took place largely independently of state structures. The distinctive characteristic of a cultural nation was that it emerged before the formation of a state, and its transition to a political nation entailed politicisation, including the emergence of statist ideas within it. Many first-generation scholars of the nation originated from here:

> It is hardly a coincidence that nearly all the founding fathers of the modernist school in the study of the national phenomenon – historians and sociologists such as Hans Kohn, Karl Deutsch, Ernest Gellner, Eric Hobsbawm, and Elie Kedourie – were immigrant refugees from the horrors of the 1930s and '40s.[78]

These first-wave academics viewed much of continental Europe through the eyes of the *Kulturnation*. The nation–state was created around the *Volk*, which had a sense of shared descent (whether real or mythic), history, customary practices, religion and language. Still, there was something patronising, inferior – perhaps even 'Orientalist' – in Western European scholars conceptualising Eastern Europe as this egregious cultural nation.

Secular and multilingual societies in the West have been regarded as the result of centuries of political evolution guided by state institutions and encapsulated by forms of civic nationalism – a big-tent nationalism inclusive of all residents within state borders. Azar Gat, an Israeli political scientist who may know something about 3,000-year-old civilisations, has contrasted civic and ethnic nationalisms:

> Ostensibly, civic nationalism is defined as belonging to a political community, state, and territory, whereas ethnic nationalism is based on a perception of blood relation and common descent. The civic nation has been identified with a benign Western European liberal model epitomized by Britain and France, whereas

xenophobic ethnic nationalism supposedly characterized Central and Eastern Europe.... This picture is largely misleading.[79]

Multilingualism camouflaged a hierarchy of languages in which the high language of the state – and of power – overshadowed the languages of disadvantaged or marginalised minorities.

The nation dates back to the sixteenth and seventeenth centuries in Europe, when the beginnings of secularisation, the end of religious domination and the birth of a scientific revolution took place. England is sometimes identified as 'God's first-born', whereas as late as the nineteenth century, Germany, Italy, Russia and other European colossi were still in the throes of birth pangs.[80]

But this understanding of the formation of nations has been challenged. Recent scholarship has emphasised an old truth: very few nations are unconnected to ethnicity and culture. Gat in particular is a leading proponent of la longue durée of nations. He contends that nationalism antedated modernity, nations are hardly recent formations, and they are not superficial or contrived, as modernist experts on nationalism believe. He takes issue with instrumentalist approaches that claim that 'leaders use the nation for their own purposes', or the social constructivist argument that 'we imagine that there are such things as nations'.[81]

Ethnic and national sentiments are engraved in human nature and are as ancient as human civilisations, Gat contends. Thus, 'ethnic and national identities, though they are always in flux, are also among the most durable, and most potent, of human cultural forms. They often span centuries and even millennia.' National sentiments of common identity, affinity and solidarity long precede the modern era. Indeed, 'Ethnicity made the state and the state made ethnicity, in a reciprocal and dialectical process.'[82]

Crucial for Gat is that what he defines as nationhood signifies statehood for a people shaped by culture and kin: in other words, a shared cultural matrix and sense of kinship (Box 1.3). Kinship, not descent, is constitutive of ethnicity:

> The key to the fusion of a shared ethnic identity, even in the absence of a belief in common descent, is extensive intermarriage among the founding groups and the adoption of a common culture. Over time these processes both turn the populations in question into self-perceived kin or a 'community of blood'.[83]

The propensity to bond with genetic fellow travellers seems to have a deterministic function: 'people tend to prefer closer kin, who share more genes with them, to more remote kin or "strangers"'.[84] Gat comes even closer to my understanding of nationhood when he proposes the following dynamic: 'civic nationalism *in particular* generates assimilation into the ethnonational

---

Box 1.3 Tenacity of ethnic and national identities

Ethnic and national affinities are not merely a phase, a manipulative invention by cynical state authorities, or an inexplicable and insufferable atavistic relic in a liberal, cosmopolitan, and universalist age. While always subject to change, ethnic and national identities are not going away any more than are other deeply rooted and changing human associations and relations, such as the family. The news of their demise has been premature.

Source: Azar Gat, 'The Other N-Word', *Foreign Policy*, 21 April 2017, available at <https://foreignpolicy.com/2017/04/21/the-other-n-word-nationalism-trump-immigration/>.

---

community ... not only to old ethnicities and nations, but also to new ones'.[85] These are most clearly perceptible in immigration societies shaped by processes of integration, hybridisation and amalgamation. Of critical importance is the exogenous marriage that blurs genetic lines and eventually becomes indistinguishable from endogenous marriage: 'The more ethnic and national collectives integrate through marriages over generations and centuries the more they feel them to be a kin community.'[86]

Shared common features are no guarantee of a sense of common nationhood. Yet

> In the vast majority of nations there are strong ties of common culture; and over time these ties also produce a perception of the nation as an extended family, if a sense of kinship did not exist from the outset.[87]

It follows that an immigrant, once naturalised, joins the host nation even if she may preserve different markers of cultural distinctiveness.

Gat claims that 'the perception of a common nationhood strongly correlates with shared kin-culture identity',[88] but he may be taking an overly dependent view since kin and culture seldom mix when societies are segregated by ethnicity, language and even a we-feeling.

MINORITIES INTO MAJORITIES

Hardly a nation exists, states Gat, that is based solely or even mainly on a national community's political allegiance to the state. This is a contentious assertion that raises questions as to whether the modern state is defined by the support it enjoys from its citizens, residents, denizens and sojourners. European election results, for example, show that few alliances of any kind can boast of having won even 40 per cent of the popular vote.

Some time ago, a dilettante British politician believed that cricket would ultimately reveal national allegiances to the state (significantly, cricket is the second most popular game in the world). In 1990 Norman Tebbit, long-serving Member of Parliament for Chingford and informal cheerleader for Margaret Thatcher, suggested that immigrants who supported their countries of origin rather than England were simply not integrated. He claimed that 'A large proportion of Britain's Asian population fail to pass the cricket test. Which side do they cheer for? Are you still harking back to where you came from or where you are?'[89] West Indians were also included in this allegiance test, although their fortunes on the pitch ebbed shortly after Tebbit had raised the stakes.

The rights of the majority, nativist population in a country have received more attention, at times in proportion to immigration numbers accepted by their country. A slippery argument is made that the assemblage of a minority group is less in need of protection of its rights than the majority. A useful illustration is Canada. The updated 2011 census found that over 20 per cent were foreign-born, highest in the G8 group of rich nations. In its largest city, Toronto, 49 per cent comprised visible minorities. Of these 1.26 million non-Whites, about 70 per cent were of Asian ancestry.[90]

In *The Cultural Defense of Nations*, Liav Orgad, also an Israeli-educated migration specialist, contested what the rights of a political majority are:

> For the past half-century, the preservation, protection, and, indeed, active promotion of the cultures of minority groups have been widely championed, as part of an effort to defend the rights of the weak against the crushing dominance of the majority. But with the swing of the pendulum, are majority national cultures entitled to equivalent rights?[91]

He agreed that liberal thinking and human rights law recognise the rights of minority groups to hold on to their cultural identity but, thus far, majority groups have not been granted a similar right because, it is assumed, their culture has not been at risk. Yet the scale and proportions of immigration, the character – Western and other – and the intensity – its pace and urban growth – have been massive.[92]

Orgad's book proposes a novel approach that allows liberal democracies to welcome immigrants without changing their cultural heritage, surrendering their liberal traditions or slipping into extreme nationalism. 'Contemporary immigration yields demographic shifts of historical significance between dominant majorities and immigrant communities.... Trans-cultural diffusion is greater today than in any other period in human history.' He is concerned about three demographic changes: 'the effect of massive population movements on the cultural composition and self-image of Western democracies – their national identities; the backlash against multiculturalism in immigration policy; and the rise of majority nationalism, or "cultural defense policies"'.[93]

Immigration encourages nation–states to define themselves without having to return to policies of forced cultural assimilation. What Orgad calls cultural defence policies include such features of integration as citizenship tests, loyalty oaths, integration contracts and language expectations. Integration into majority cultures can remove public hysteria – in Europe, for example – on relations with Muslims over handshaking, swimming lessons and minarets. But cultural defence policies reveal even more about integration processes:

> Liberal democracies are citizen makers. They have a long tradition of attempts to 'Protestantize' Catholic immigrants and 'Westernize' non-Western immigrants. In contemporary liberal democracies, the ultimate goal of the naturalization process is to 'liberate' the illiberal and channel immigrants into the dominant customs, beliefs, and values of the dominant majority.[94]

Orgad stipulates the conditions under which 'it is justified, from a liberal perspective, to defend the majority culture by means of immigration law and, if so, what can be the legitimate ways to achieve it'.[95] Cultural defence policies can preserve the cultural hegemony of the majority, whose members have an interest in adhering to their culture and sustaining it.

The most fundamental issue facing immigration societies is, then,

> whether it is legitimate for a people and nation to seek to preserve their core culture, most notably when they feel it is threatened by large masses of immigrants whose integration into their adopted country is slow and problematic and whose values are often illiberal.[96]

NATIONHOOD SUMMARISED

For it to exist, nationhood has to rest on three different pillars of authority. The first is the political system. Political institutions need to be open to various migrant communities and extend the voting franchise to them when they qualify. Sometimes a federal system is established to acknowledge the autonomy of particular groups. Political leadership should embrace platforms that support migrant inclusion, leading to shared objectives. In fostering nationhood, major political parties should stress the inclusion of ethnic groups and emphasise the importance of forging cross-ethnic ties.

Second, the role of legislation and rule making is crucial in forging nationhood. Prerequisites for citizenship, such as length of residence or marriage to a citizen, need to be reasonable. Linguistic assimilationist pressure should be realistic but indispensable for integration. The education system should allow for opening minority schools where needed but education should be conducted primarily in majority schools. There should not be any ethnic preferences or quotas, and school curricula should refrain from nationalist discourses that may offend minorities.

Cultural and religious autonomy should be provided to bond groups to the nationhood principle. Funding for ethnic minority programmes should be encouraged. Property ownership cannot impose restrictions on migrant groups.

Third, grassroots engagement is central to nationhood. Ethnic schisms reflecting cleavages in attitudes and values should be resolved. Ethnic stereotyping and scapegoating are unacceptable. The foci of identity may be ethnic, religious and cultural, but cross-ethnic bonding – bonding social capital – needs to be promoted.

These are desiderata that should form a part of majority culture. But the real world of immigrants often consists of fears and phobias, discrimination and bias. Nationhood is not possible where majority cultures display such pathologies, the subject of Chapter 2. Conversely in Chapter 3, I analyse the significance of carrying out integration of immigrants; growing electoral pressures in many parts of the world make this incumbent. Insisting on introducing majority rights regimes becomes incidental when compared to achieving all-important social cohesion in host societies.

NOTES

1. Gunderson, Lance H., and C. S. Holling, *Panarchy Synopsis: Understanding Transformations in Human and Natural Systems* (Washington, DC: Island Press, 2001), p. 2.
2. Ibid., p. 8.
3. Yacef, Amel, 'Foreword', *Racism and Discrimination in the Context of Migration in Europe: ENAR Shadow Report 2015–16*, European Network against Racism, 2 May 2017.
4. 'Migrant Crisis', *BBC News*, 4 March 2016, available at <http://www.bbc.com/news/world-europe-34131911>.
5. Bhabha, Homi K., *The Location of Culture* (London: Routledge, 1994).
6. Benhabib, Seyla, *The Claims of Culture: Equality and Diversity in the Global Era* (Princeton, NJ: Princeton University Press, 2002), pp. 148–9, 152.
7. Spivak, Gayatri Chakravorty, *Nationalism and the Imagination* (New York: Seagull Books, 2010), p. 79.
8. Spivak, Gayatri Chakravorty, *A Critique of Postcolonial Reason: Toward a History of the Vanishing Present* (Cambridge, MA: Harvard University Press, 1999), p. x.
9. Chakrabarty, Dipesh, *Provincializing Europe: Postcolonial Thought and Historical Difference* (Princeton, NJ: Princeton University Press, 2000), p. 3.

10. Ibid., p. 4.
11. Ibid., p. 8. 'Not yet' is taken from Martin Heidegger, *Being and Time* (New York: Harper Perennial, 2008), Division II.
12. Chatterjee, Partha, *Nationalist Thought and the Colonial World: A Derivative Discourse* (London: Zed Books, 1986), p. 2.
13. Chatterjee, Partha, *The Nation and its Fragments: Colonial and Postcolonial Histories* (Princeton, NJ: Princeton University Press, 1993), pp. 14, 11.
14. Frank, Andre Gunder, *ReOrient: Global Economy in the Asian Age* (Berkeley, CA: University of California Press, 1998), p. 340.
15. Ibid., p. 334.
16. See Brubaker, Rogers, *Citizenship and Nationhood in France and Germany* (Cambridge, MA: Harvard University Press, 1992).
17. Ibid., p. 1.
18. Brubaker, Rogers, 'In the Name of the Nation: Reflections on Nationalism and Patriotism', *Citizenship Studies*, 8, no. 2, June 2004, p. 116.
19. Ibid., p. 115.
20. For a three-page synopsis of how social cohesion has historically been used, see John Bruhn, *The Group Effect: Social Cohesion and Health Outcomes* (Dordrecht: Springer, 2009), pp. 32–4.
21. Applebaum, Diana Muir, 'Defining Nationhood', undated, available at <http://www.dianamuirappelbaum.com/?page_id=324#.WgNc_BNSzVo>.
22. Bendix, Reinhard, *Nation-Building and Citizenship* (Berkeley, CA: University of California Press, 1977).
23. Gat, Azar, *Nations: The Long History and Deep Roots of Political Ethnicity and Nationalism* (Cambridge: Cambridge University Press, 2013), p. 219.
24. Bauman, Zygmunt, *Retropia* (Cambridge: Polity Press, 2017), pp. 156–7.
25. Ibid., p. 159.
26. Trilling, Daniel, 'Should We Build a Wall around North Wales?', *London Review of Books*, 39, no. 14, 13 July 2017, p. 18.
27. Ibid., p. 17.
28. Skocpol, Theda, 'Bringing the State Back In: Strategies of Analysis in Current Research', in Peter B. Evans, Dietrich Rueschemeyer and Theda Skocpol (eds), *Bringing the State Back In* (New York: Cambridge University Press, 1985), pp. 3–38.
29. Akopov, Sergei, 'Aidar Sultanov: A "Russian European Intellectual Against the Formidable Sacrifice of Security to Security"', *Review of Central and East European Law*, 41, 2016, p. 11.
30. Chua, Amy, *World on Fire: How Exporting Free Market Democracy Breeds Ethnic Hatred and Global Instability* (New York: Anchor Books, 2004).
31. Aronczyk, Melissa, *Branding the Nation: The Global Business of National Identity* (New York: Oxford University Press, 2013), pp. 5, 9.
32. Ibid., p. 13.
33. Brubaker, Rogers, 'Populism's Perfect Storm', *Boston Review*, 11 July 2017, available at <http://bostonreview.net/politics/rogers-brubaker-populisms-perfect-storm#.WWeOMIkyuaU.facebook>.
34. Aronczyk, *Branding*, pp. 17, 22.
35. Ibid., p. 31.

36. Ibid., p. 168.
37. Betts, Alexander, 'International Relations and Forced Migration', in Elena Fiddian-Qasmiyeh, Gil Loescher, Katy Long and Nando Sigona (eds), *Oxford Handbook of Refugee and Forced Migration Studies* (Oxford: Oxford University Press, 2014), pp. 64–5.
38. Taylor, John, and Helen Lee (eds), *Mobilities of Return: Pacific Perspectives* (Canberra: Australian National University Press, 2018).
39. 'Migration and Home Affairs: Common European Asylum System', *European Commission*, available at <https://ec.europa.eu/home-affairs/what-we-do/policies/asylum_en>.
40. 'Collomb: distinguer "réfugiés" et "migrants" pour sauvegarder le droit d'asile', *France24.com*, 6 August 2017, available at <http://www.france24.com/fr/20170806-distinguer-refugies-migrants-economiques-gerard-collomb-terroriste-syrie-irak>.
41. Edwards, Alice, 'Human Rights, Refugees, and the Right "to Enjoy" Asylum', *International Journal of Refugee Law*, 17, no. 2, January 2005, pp. 293–330.
42. See O'Nions, Helen, *Asylum – A Right Denied? A Critical Analysis of European Asylum Policy* (London: Routledge, 2014).
43. Michta, Andrew A., 'Unchecked Migration Continues to Splinter Europe', *Carnegie Europe*, 27 July 2017, available at <http://carnegieeurope.eu/strategiceurope/72664?lang=en>.
44. Available at <http://www.un.org/sustainabledevelopment/blog/2016/01/244-million-international-migrants-living-abroad-worldwide-new-un-statistics-reveal/>.
45. Yacef, 'Foreword'.
46. Ibid.
47. Calhoun, Craig, 'The Class Consciousness of Frequent Travelers: Toward a Critique of Actually Existing Cosmopolitanism', *South Atlantic Quarterly*, 101, no. 4, 2002, pp. 872–3.
48. Laqueur, Walter, 'So Much for the New European Century', *The Chronicle of Higher Education*, 11 May 2007. Excerpted from his *The Last Days of Europe: Epitaph for an Old Continent* (New York: Thomas Dunne, 2007).
49. For an overview of how migration industries assist and constrain migration, see Sophie Cranston, Joris Schapendonk and Ernst Spaan, 'New Directions in Exploring the Migration Industries: Introduction to Special Issue', *Journal of Ethnic and Migration Studies*, 14 July 2017, pp. 1–15.
50. Renan, Ernest, 'Qu'est-ce qu'une nation?' (Calmann Lévy: 1882), pp. NP-30. English translations of the text often use nationhood as a synonym for nation, available at <https://fr.wikisource.org/wiki/Qu%E2%80%99est-ce_qu%E2%80%99une_nation_%3F>.
51. Joppke, Christian, *Is Multiculturalism Dead? Crisis and Persistence in the Constitutional State* (Cambridge: Polity, 2017), p. 3.
52. MacLennan, Hugh, *Two Solitudes* (Toronto, ON: New Canadian Library, 2008).
53. Lasswell, Harold D., *Politics: Who Gets What, When, How* (New York: Meridian Books, 1972).
54. Taras, Raymond, and Rajat Ganguly, *Understanding Ethnic Conflict*, 4th edn (New York: Longman, 2010), pp. 1–26.
55. Hobsbawm, Eric, *Nations and Nationalism Since 1780: Programme, Myth, Reality*, 2nd edn (Cambridge: Cambridge University Press, 1992), Chs 4–5.

56. Safran, William, 'Language, Ethnicity and Religion: A Complex and Persistent Linkage', in *Nations and Nationalism*, 14, no. 1, January 2008, p. 176.
57. Hayes, Carlton J. H., *The Historical Evolution of Modern Nationalism* (New York: R. R. Smith, 1931), pp. 10–11.
58. Kedourie, Elie, *Nationalism*, 3rd edn (London: Hutchinson, 1966), p. 196.
59. Seers, Dudley, *The Political Economy of Nationalism* (New York: Oxford University Press, 1983), p. 6.
60. Kohn, Hans, *Nationalism: Its Meaning and History* (Huntington, NY: Robert E. Krieger, 1982), p. 14.
61. Barker, Ernest, *National Character and the Factors in its Formation* (London: 1927), p. 17.
62. Smith, Anthony D., 'The Ethnic Sources of Nationalism', *Survival*, 35, no. 1, Spring 1993, pp. 50–1.
63. Lake, David, and Donald Rothchild, 'Spreading Fear: The Genesis of Transnational Ethnic Conflict', in Lake and Rothchild (eds), *The International Spread of Ethnic Conflict: Fear, Diffusion, and Escalation* (Princeton, NJ: Princeton University Press, 1998), p. 5.
64. Ibid., p. 6. See also Ted Robert Gurr, *Peoples Versus States: Minorities at Risk in the New Century* (Washington, DC: United States Institute of Peace Press, 2000), p. 4.
65. Brass, Paul R., *Ethnicity and Nationalism: Theory and Comparison* (Newbury Park, CA: Sage, 1991), p. 8.
66. Mandela, Nelson, *Long Walk to Freedom: The Autobiography of Nelson Mandela* (Boston, MA: Back Bay Books, 1995).
67. Stone, John, 'Race, Ethnicity, and the Weberian Legacy', *American Behavioral Scientist*, 38, no. 3, January 1995, p. 396.
68. Ibid.
69. Phillips, Anne, *Multiculturalism without Culture* (Princeton, NJ: Princeton University Press, 2007).
70. Taguieff, Pierre-André, 'Racisme, racialisme, ethnocentrisme, xénophobie, anti-sémitisme et néoracisme: réflexions sur des termes problematiques', in Commission Nationale Consultative des Droits de l'Homme (ed.), *La Lutte contre le racisme, l'antisémitisme, et la xénophobie: anneé 2007* (Paris: La Documentation française, 2008), p. 251.
71. Seton-Watson, Hugh, *Nations and States: An Enquiry into the Origins of Nations and the Politics of Nationalism* (Boulder, CO: Westview Press, 1977), p. 5.
72. Toynbee, Arnold J., *The New Europe: Some Essays in Reconstruction* (London: Dent, 1915), p. 13.
73. Quoted by Snyder, Louis, *The Meaning of Nationalism* (Westport, CT: Greenwood, 1954), p. 61.
74. Renan, 'Qu'est-ce.'
75. Safran, 'Language', p. 171.
76. Alter, Peter, *Nationalism* (London: Edward Arnold, 1989), p. 15.
77. Ibid., p. 14.
78. Gat, Azar, 'The Other N-Word', *Foreign Policy*, 21 April 2017, available at <https://foreignpolicy.com/2017/04/21/the-other-n-word-nationalism-trump-immigration/>.
79. Gat, *Nations*, p. 260.

80. Greenfeld, Liah, *Nationalism: Five Roads to Modernity* (Cambridge, MA: Harvard University Press, 1993).
81. Gat, 'The Other N-Word'.
82. Gat, *Nations*, p. 3.
83. Ibid., p. 20.
84. Ibid., p. 27.
85. Ibid., p. 7.
86. Ibid., p. 38.
87. Ibid., pp. 311, 349.
88. Ibid., p. 385.
89. 'Cricket Test', *Wikipedia*, available at <https://en.wikipedia.org/wiki/Cricket_test>.
90. 'Immigration and Ethnocultural Diversity in Canada', available at <http://www12.statcan.gc.ca/nhs-enm/2011/as-sa/99-010-x/99-010-x2011001-eng.cfm>.
91. Orgad, Liav, *The Cultural Defense of Nations: A Liberal Theory of Majority Rights* (Oxford: Oxford University Press, 2015), p. 7.
92. Ibid., p. 21. See also UN Department of Economic and Social Affairs, Population Division 'Trends', available at <http://www.un.org/en/development/desa/population/migration/data/estimates2/estimates15.shtml>.
93. Orgad, *The Cultural Defense*, p. 2.
94. Ibid., p. 1.
95. Ibid., p. 236.
96. Gat, 'The Other N-Word'.

Chapter Two

Prejudices and partialities

Confronting bias

When immigrants arrive in a receiving society, what must they do to adapt and integrate into it? From various surveys we know that most migrants wish to belong to a host society, fit in, be accepted. Few will not try to hone labour skills to gain meaningful employment, or to ensure their children go to a school with good achievement scores. Some, typically from well-networked groups in this society, may be unwilling to accept all the conditions for integration. They may refuse to learn a new language when a kin group is there to support them. A small minority, on principle, rejects outright the hegemony of the host society.

Which values are singled out as critical for immigrants to adopt? Even when they accept such values, is there discrimination against them on the basis of racial, religious or ethnic backgrounds? Can some groups be racialised nevertheless: in other words, be attributed a racial category that may not be theirs?

Questions that immigrants face have typically to do with their religious background or the language spoken at home. Are primordial factors, such as ethnicity and race, less malleable than instrumentalist or constructivist ones, such as we-feeling and identification with a new country? Do receiving societies position immigrants in a hierarchy that can affect the welcome they receive? Is there bias based on their racially, religiously or linguistically anchored identities? France and Sweden prohibit the differentiation of people on the basis of race, but are other criteria used to discriminate against them: for instance, their country of origin, socio-economic class, educational achievement and, increasingly, religious values?

Chapter 2 considers the discriminatory snake pit in which migrants may find themselves. It comprises a tangle of racial, religious and linguistic pressures, taboos and norms. No society does not discriminate or have favourites

– not even Sweden.[1] This chapter surveys the sources of discrimination, bias and partialities that new arrivals encounter. The following list is not exhaustive but it gives a sense of the varied repertoire that steers public attitudes today. While this typology charts mainly contemporary Europe's phobias, some which have more significance in particular countries than in others, it captures public fears expressed during elections in other parts of the world too:

- anti-establishment, anti-system, anti-grand coalition voting behaviour
- anti-European Union blowback
- anti-immigration policies
- anti-illegal immigration abuse
- anti-Muslim cultural and/or security threat
- anti-Eastern European free movement principle
- anti-human smuggling backlash
- anti-human trafficking ethic
- anti-social inequality measures, pro-poverty reduction
- anti-non-governmental organisation (NGO) influence.

Elections in the second decade of this century are frequently based on particular combinations of these outlooks, some which may be abhorrent but others which advance noble sentiments. But it is the secular-religious cleavage running through society that many scholars seem captivated by.

THE SECULAR CLASH WITH RELIGIOSITY

Two brutal forms of xenophobia, anti-Semitism and Islamophobia, show the darkest sides of religious intolerance. Equally, measures taken to suppress a language and, with it, to suffocate a culture are scattered across history. Hundreds of minority languages and dialects remain at risk as pressures for linguistic assimilation into a hegemonic language are ramped up. These, too, reflect the ethnocentrism and xenophobia of a dominant group.

An important cleavage is between today's secular and religious philosophies. William Safran accepted that religions and cults existed before the nation–state, but 'The coupling of religion and nationhood ... applied largely to the pre-democratic age, and applies today to many pre-democratic societies that have not yet modernized (such as Iran, Pakistan and Saudi Arabia).' Modern democratic states are ones we associate with a plurality of religions when not with secularism. Nevertheless, 'Some religions are the harbingers of democracy and progress, whereas others are not.'[2]

Distinguishing the sacred from the profane is a time-honoured preoccupation. Anthropologist Ruth Benedict noted that 'The striking fact about ...

[the] plain distinction between the religious and the non-religious in actual ethnographic recording is that it needs so little recasting in its transfer from one society to another.'[3]

The dichotomy between what is Caesar's and what is God's is, then, nearly universally applicable. Gat was convinced that 'religion *per se* rarely serves as a basis for nationhood, unless it is a national religion, that is, unique to a people and therefore far more defining of its identity'. He found that the greater salience religion has had in the culture of a people, the more it has played a defining role in this culture. On the other hand, the primacy of language for a territory is more critical: 'shared religion in and of itself rarely trumps linguistic differences to create a common ethnic or national identity'.[4]

It is sometimes said that 'the ethnonation is a secularized religion' and the secular–religious binary is a familiar cleavage in many societies.[5] Political pragmatism rather than principles or ideals explains why secularism finds a way to transcend squabbling between religions. Supposedly, it most efficiently embodies the neutrality of the state and its separation from all churches. Furthermore, secularism is seen as an antidote to religious bigotry, while religiosity is often regarded as a root cause of them.

European discrimination against Jews is centuries old. Today it is being transposed to Islam. Safran already observed in 1986 that 'the old Jew-hatred, based on phobias about the excessive Judaisation (*Verjudung*) of French or German society, is now often supplanted by a phobia and hatred of Muslims'.[6] Already in the eighteenth century, European societies came to regard Islam not as a spiritual competitor with Christianity – they were regarded as not on a level playing field – but rather as a religious threat to secular institutions.

In a seminal study of Muslim immigrants in France and Germany, Safran estimated that about half of all postwar immigrants to France and more than a third to the Federal Republic of Germany were Muslims. It cannot be said therefore that Islam is a late arrival on the continent. Indeed, 'The foreignness and the alien social patterns, the economic and housing conditions of the Maghrebis and Turks have long been matters of concern to governments, trade unions, employers' associations, and researchers.' But he added a crucial caveat:

> Yet the Islamic aspect of these immigrants has been widely ignored. The typical French study of immigrants devotes little if any attention to religion; similarly, studies and government policies in West Germany convey the impression that Islam is not particularly relevant to the Turkish immigrant problem.[7]

Safran charged policy makers in the two countries of taking a cavalier approach to recognising the Muslim presence. In France political leaders and intellectuals assumed that 'Islamic or any other religious consciousness is artificial, temporary, and in the long run irrelevant, and that the Arab identity of Maghrebi immigrants can somehow be politically and analytically divorced from their Islamic identity.' Germany was misled by 'the myth of return (*Heimkehrillusion*), which in turn has led to assumptions of the temporary nature of all Islamic institutions; and the difficulty of accepting Islam as a religion that can be properly fitted into the Germanic cultural climate'.[8] These were prescient observations.

The early failure to identify Muslim immigrants as Muslims in great measure explains increased friction today between host and migrant groups. Eurocentrism and secularism may blind supporters from recognising an immigrant religious community with its special needs, rights and obligations. It is not the road to enlarging nationhood.

Polemicist Christopher Caldwell probed in 2009: 'Can Europe be the same with different people in it?' His conclusion was that erosion of Christian values has weakened cultural identity to the point that they were no match for the sway of Islamic identity.[9] The contest had even become transformed into a clash between two radicalised groups: 'like fundamentalist Muslims, white nationalists idealize a pure, imagined past. Both extremist visions feed off one another, and they have the power to tear Europe apart.'[10]

Specialists on Islam have spoken out against conflating religion with culture, or contrasting Islam with secularism. Mahmood Mamdani identified the flaw in treating religion and culture as a foundation upon which political structures emerge: 'By assuming that every culture has a tangible essence that defines it and explaining politics as the consequence of that essence, a civilization like Islam is reduced to a uniform universal fundamentalist paradigm.'[11] Essentialist reductionism, then, may provoke nationalist blowback.

Olivier Roy, a leading French expert on Islam, proposed decoupling religion from culture and ethnicity altogether.[12] He contended that 'Religions are more and more disconnected from the cultures in which they have been embedded. Immigration and secularization have separated cultural and religious markers.' What is more, 'To identify a religion with an ethnic culture is to ascribe to each believer a culture and/or an ethnic identity that he or she does not necessarily feel comfortable with.'[13] Roy's prerequisite for the existence of Islamophobia is, then, discrimination against Muslims *qua* religious community, not as a migrant group, as non-European or as foreign speakers.

Today one religion, Islam, is held accountable for aggravating religious differences and bigotry, whether in Europe, the US, India, Bangladesh, Australia or somewhere else. Safran's finding has proved prescient: 'hostility to Islam reflects a dislike for all organized religion'.[14]

The relationship between religion and nationalism *qua* nationalism is a source of much debate. Brubaker in 2012 identified four different approaches:

1. to treat religion and nationalism, together with ethnicity and race, as analogous phenomena
2. to specify ways in which religion explains the sources of nationalism, such as its origins, power and distinctive qualities
3. to conflate religion with nationalism and explain modes of interpenetration
4. to advance a distinctly religious form of nationalism.[15]

The religious–secular dynamic remains *du jour*.

ATTRIBUTING RACISM

Christian theologians made use of biblical justifications for religious hierarchies that were based on Whiteness and Blackness. In the Book of Genesis (9: 18–27), they referred to how Canaan, son of Ham, was punished by being subjected to servitude and Blackness. Racism is even older than the Bible.

The origins of the term race date back to the late fourteenth century, then became widely used in the sixteenth, but they did not have negative connotations at that time. An older word, *natio*, was employed in the Middle Ages to refer pejoratively to foreigners.[16] Back then barbarian was less a racial than a political and cultural concept.

Simply put, for W. E. B. Du Bois, a US sociologist and civil rights activist, 'no scientific definition of race is possible' since 'Race would seem to be a dynamic and not a static conception.'[17] The erasure of race makes logical sense since it is a socially constructed category based upon a problematic idea. But there are problems with the erasure of race.

French scholar Frantz Fanon from Martinique took a different perspective. Blackness and Whiteness not only are characteristics of the body, but also they are internalised in the psyche. Signs of Blackness are intuited as profoundly psychological processes. As an illustration, in *Black Skin, White Masks* he described how 'The Antilles Negro who wants to be white will be the whiter as he gains greater mastery of the tool that language is.'[18] Stuart Hall, a prolific English Caribbean writer who pioneered the field of cultural studies, offered yet another interpretation. He viewed Black identity as an on-going unfinished conversation since identities are forged in dialogue with others.[19]

Postmodern writers underscore the postracial character of Blackness. Its historical grounding was connected with the attention given after World War II to racelessness. Non-racialism of the anti-apartheid movement in South Africa became enshrined in the 1955 Freedom Charter, which stated: 'South Africa belongs to all who live in it, black and white.' Its founding principles are these: the people shall govern; all national groups shall have equal rights; the people shall share in the country's wealth.[20]

Further momentum was created by the colour-blindedness of the 1960s US civil rights movement. To be sure, Blackness, not postracialism, was emphasised, such as in the Black Power movements emerging from the early 1960s. It challenged the prevailing system of ingrained White domination of African American life.

In Africa, Aimé Césaire and Léopold Sédar Senghor launched the idea of *négritude*, an essentialist affirmation of Black identity linked to culture. The two authors disagreed, however, over the back-to-Africa consensus and the state sovereignty ideal fought for by national liberation movements. For his part, Césaire believed that the need to reject poverty required that the colonised take advantage of the labour and other resources available in Africa. For a time he supported the USSR: 'I make no secret of my opinion that at the present time the barbarism of Western Europe has reached an incredibly high level, being only surpassed, far surpassed, it is true, by the barbarism of the United States.' He went further: 'It is a fact: the nation is a bourgeois phenomenon.'[21]

Paradoxically, Césaire gave a backhanded compliment to the colonialists:

Western Europe undertakes on its own initiative a policy of nationalities, a new policy founded on respect for peoples and cultures – nay, more – unless Europe galvanizes the dying cultures or raises up new ones, unless it becomes the awakener of countries and civilizations.[22]

He even supported legislation that would integrate France's Caribbean and Indian Ocean colonies – Martinique, Guadeloupe, Guyana and Réunion – as full departments of the French state.

Senghor, long-time Senegalese political leader and, like Césaire, a poet, regarded federation with France – not state sovereignty or political independence – as vital for French-speaking West Africa. He 'disparaged independence as an "iron collar" and argued that federalism would herald a new era in which both Africans and Europeans would become full human beings, dispensing with the hierarchies that had divided them'.[23] It succinctly conveyed Jean-Paul Sartre's concept of anti-racist racism.[24]

Similar to Césaire, Senghor anticipated a French constitution that would transform the unitary French republic into a post-imperial, postnational federation. It would include former colonies and the former metropole as freely associated members. He envisaged it as a transcontinental, democratic, socialist union.

These idealistic visions of a revitalised anti-racist France were undone by unalloyed colonial French power, symbolised by the neocolonial term *Françafrique*. It emerged as a financial and military cordon on Africa's francophone leadership, hinting at a networked mafia-style organisation. It also discriminated against Africans from the colonies who made it to the Hexagon.

While some argue that there has been less overt racism in France than, for example, the US,[25] little comfort comes from this comparison.

Sri Lankan writer and theorist of race Ambalavaner Sivanandan has deemed the new xenophobia emerging in Europe as bearing all the marks of old racism, without its genetic underpinnings. It is 'xeno' in so far as 'It is a racism that is meted out to impoverished strangers even if they are white. It is xeno-racism.'[26] It can be colour-blind in paradoxical ways: 'Racism never stands still. It changes shape, size, contours, purpose, function, with changes in the economy, the social structure, the system and, above all, the challenges, the resistances, to that system.'[27]

An example of xeno-racism is British xenophobic attitudes towards migrants from other EU states; Poland may have sent 1 million EU citizens to live in the UK since enlargement. East Europeans are treated as a xeno-racist community even though they are White, physically indistinguishable from their hosts and overwhelmingly Christian.

For French writer Étienne Balibar, likening Blackness with Whiteness is regarded as 'racism typical of the era of "decolonisation"'. Its defining characteristic

> is a racism whose dominant theme is not biological heredity but the insurmountability of cultural differences, a racism which, at first sight, does not postulate the superiority of certain groups or people in relation to others but 'only' the harmfulness of abolishing frontiers, the incompatibility of life-styles and traditions.[28]

Comparative research on racism sifts through evidence of discrimination that is based on the categories of race and racialisation, and it applies these to such factors as religion, ethnicity, national origins and language.[29] Let me look more closely at cases of the erasure of Blackness.

France

Writing of the French experience, Pierre-André Taguieff believed that xenophobia subsumes racism. As a modern phenomenon, it has produced two far-reaching ideological constructs: anti-Negritude and anti-Semitism, both of which reflect White supremacy.[30] In this century these two racist ideologies have been conjoined by Islamophobia, also a racist or cultural racist construct.[31]

These ideological constructs share three cognitive processes. First, they advance an essentialist categorisation of individuals and groups in which people's identity is reduced to their community of origin. Second, they insist on symbolic exclusion of particular groups, stigmatising them and turning their exclusion into an imperative. Third, such racist constructs require the barbarisation of others judged inferior and incapable of becoming civilised, educated, assimilable.[32] Bauman added that racism is a strategy of estrangement requiring that the offender be removed from the territory occupied by the group that is offended.[33]

Taguieff elaborated a typology of racism that functioned on three levels. Primary racism is the most natural reaction to the presence of strangers and it can extend from antipathy to aggression. Secondary racism entails reactions to the presence of a stranger through a rationalised racism. Both xenophobia and ethnocentrism are such rationalised dispositions. Tertiary racism is mystificatory, presuming the existence of the two other racisms and building on them by invoking quasi-biological arguments for their exclusion.[34] This last type of racism produced the social engineering that led to the Holocaust.

Since the 1789 Revolution, France has regarded its political ideals as a model for whole civilisations. French empire builders were charged with applying the colour-blind Republican model wherever they ventured. Ariane Chebel d'Appolonia enquired, therefore: 'Does the denial of the category of "race" undermine the fight against racism?'[35] She hypothesised that the concept of indifferentiation now trumped that of differential racism.

The National Consultative Commission for Human Rights (Commission Nationale Consultative des Droits de l'Homme, CNCDH), set up by the French legislature in 1990, has provided empirical findings to answer this question. Its 2004 report claimed that only 15 per cent of the French population believed 'there is a hierarchy between races'. A seemingly contradictory result was that a higher percentage (24 per cent) alleged that 'some races are less capable than others'.[36] The 2010 report warned how 84 per cent of respondents identified racism as a growing phenomenon; this was confirmed by higher figures on the number of racist acts committed in recent years.[37]

In its 2011 study (the twentieth such annual report), the CNDCH discovered an increase in most indicators of anti-immigrant and racist attitudes, though fewer violent incidents of racism, Islamophobia and anti-Semitism were recorded. This led to the captivating conclusion that most citizens rejected violence – but not racist mindsets.[38]

This survey asked respondents to evaluate racism based on the insults thrown at targeted groups. While 82 per cent agreed that the insult 'dirty Black' should be condemned by the courts, fewer said that about 'dirty Jew' (78 per cent) and 'dirty Arab' (69 per cent).[39] In a convoluted way, French respondents were more sensitive to Black feelings.

French public opinion turned on Muslims compared to other racialised groups as the second decade of the twenty-first century progressed. This was even before the attacks launched by jihadists on *Charlie Hebdo* and *Bataclan* in Paris, the Nice killings of pedestrians, and others. Arousing French public opinion, in 2010 sociologist Hugues Lagrange provoked a national debate with the publication of his book *Le Déni des cultures* ('The Denial of Cultures'). In his view, cultures did matter when explaining differences in French rates of delinquency, defined as 'encounters with the law'. His diagnosis of security threat focused on culture and, by extension, people's ethno-religious and racial attributes. He singled out immigrants from the Sahel, a sliver of countries south of the Sahara, as habitual recidivists. The implication was that such groups who violated French norms do not belong to France.

Sweden

Rather than racism, White Melancholia is a coded critique of Sweden's efforts to consolidate nationhood without race-based classifications. Two Whiteness Studies scholars attacked what they viewed as the double crisis of Swedish Whiteness:

> 'old Sweden', that is, Sweden as a homogeneous society, and 'good Sweden', that is, Sweden as a progressive society, are both perceived to be threatened by the presence of non-white migrants and their descendants. Both the reactionary and racist camp and the progressive and antiracist camp are mourning the loss of this double-edged Swedish whiteness.[40]

The sameness of Swedishness and Whiteness was experienced not only by non-White migrants and their descendants, but also by adopted and mixed Swedes of colour, such as those with South American, African or Asian parentage. In spite of being attributed Swedishness in terms of ethnic, linguistic, religious and cultural experiences, these individuals faced racialising practices as a result of their 'non-Swedish' bodies.[41]

Sweden's predicament is that it is often regarded as the embodiment of liberal internationalism.

> The fact of having held the title of the world's most progressive and left-liberal country, combined with Sweden's perception of itself as the most racially homogenous and pure of all white nations, forms a double bind that makes it almost impossible to transform Swedishness into something that will also accept people of colour.[42]

As a result, White Melancholia 'is as much about the humiliating decline of Sweden as frontrunner of egalitarianism, humanitarianism and antiracism as about the mourning of the passing of the Swedish population as the whitest of all white peoples.'[43] Adhering to moralistic practices may transform Swedish society into intolerance towards anybody who deviates from these norms. Repressive tolerance – a tolerance for all viewpoints, which in fact contributes to social oppression – suggests we face a double bind. A preferable term may be tolerant-anchored intolerance.

Whatever its construct, racism takes multiple forms – hostile attitudes, insults, threats, hate speech, stereotypes – that lead to stigmatisation. It includes behavioural and societal practices that racialise relations between groups. Racism employs institutions to carry out discriminatory actions. Finally, it comprises ideological discourses that pit one group against another: for example, Aryans and Semites.[44]

In 1994, as South Africa was doing away with the apartheid regime and holding its first democratic elections (discussed in Chapter 8), Nelson Mandela invoked key passages from the 1955 Freedom Charter: 'We enter into a covenant that we shall build the society in which all South Africans, both black and white, will be able to walk tall. A Rainbow Nation at peace with itself and the world.' Yet fourteen years later, in 2008, he was forced to speak out against the new wave of xenophobic violence: 'Remember the horror from which we come. Never forget the greatness of a nation that has overcome its divisions. Let us never descend into destructive divisiveness.'[45]

At about the same time in Europe, the European Commission against Racism and Intolerance warned that xenophobia as a 'type of argument is no longer confined to the sphere of extremist political parties, but is increasingly contaminating mainstream political parties'.[46] Race may have disappeared as a category from some countries' law books but racialisation has not vanished with it.

RELIGIOUS INTOLERANCE

What is true of racism and racialisation is true today for religious intolerance. Surveys conducted in 2016–17 suggest that religious beliefs may bias attitudes to welcoming migrants.

Surveys present static views, not time-series analyses that change over time, so they are not hard-and-fast beliefs by a particular group regarding another. In the case study selected, the focus is attitudes towards Muslim immigrants.

The Chatham House survey of more than 10,000 people from ten European states reported that public opposition to further migration from predominantly Muslim states had become widespread across Europe.[47] The survey asked the extent to which respondents agreed or disagreed with the statement 'All further migration from mainly Muslim countries should be stopped.' An average of 55 per cent in the ten European states stated that all further migration from mainly Muslim countries should be stopped; 25 per cent neither agreed nor disagreed, and only 20 per cent disagreed. Majorities supporting an outright ban ranged from 71 per cent in Poland, 65 per cent in Austria, 53 per cent in Germany, and 51 per cent in Italy, to pluralities favouring the ban in the UK (47 per cent) and Spain (41 per cent).

Poland and Hungary, with relatively few Muslims, shared high rates of antipathy with Austria, Germany, France and Belgium, which had many. With the exception of Poland, these countries were either at the centre of the refugee crisis that began in 2015 or had experienced terrorism recently. Moreover, most of these states had significant anti-immigrant parties seeking to convert fear of Islam at the ballot box.

Once the data are disaggregated, opposition to Muslim immigration was especially intense among retired, older age cohorts; those under 30 were less opposed. A clear educational divide was also present: 59 per cent of those with secondary-level qualifications opposed further Muslim immigration while under 50 per cent of all degree holders supported further migration curbs. Opposition was also strong among 'left-behind' voters: nearly two-thirds of those who felt they did not have control over their own lives supported the statement.

The Chatham House research was consistent with other findings examining attitudes to Islam in Europe. In a Pew survey of ten European countries in 2016, majorities in five countries had an unfavourable view of Muslims living in their country: Hungary (72 per cent), Italy (69 per cent), Poland (66 per cent), Greece (65 per cent) and Spain (50 per cent). However, countries receiving significant recent inward migration of Muslims appeared to be less xenophobic: the UK (28 per cent), Germany (29 per cent) and France (29 per cent).

A 2017 Gallup World Poll survey examined EU attitudes towards Syrian refugees, in this way highlighting their asylum seeking rather than religious character. This survey was just as negative about granting Syrians refuge. In 9 out of 15 Eastern European countries examined in 2016, at least half the population believed their country should not accept any Syrian refugees (Table 2.1).[48]

The Gallup survey in Eastern Europe followed an agreement concluded with Turkey in 2016 that it would send migrants back to Syria if they had not applied for asylum or if their claim had been rejected. Many of the countries voicing the strongest opposition to granting refugee status to Syrians were located along the Balkan route, which was shut down in March 2016 but had previously directed asylum seekers from Greece to Germany. Anti-refugee sentiment was highest in Hungary, which erected border fences to keep migrants out and in 2017 passed legislation confining asylum seekers to camps made out of shipping containers. By contrast, residents of countries with sizeable Muslim populations, such as Bosnia–Herzegovina, Albania and Kosovo, were most open to allowing refugees from majority-Muslim Syria to stay, even though they did not have the resources to provide asylum.

Religious affiliation was the strongest predictor of public attitudes toward Syrian refugees. Those identifying as Muslim were least likely to say

Table 2.1 Accepting Syrian refugees (Gallup World Poll, 2016)

Which opinion is closest to yours? 'Our country ...'

	% Should accept ALL Syrian refugees	% Should accept ONLY a limited number	% Should NOT accept any
Hungary	3	22	70
Macedonia	2	16	66
Montenegro	2	27	65
Slovakia	1	32	61
Latvia	2	33	57
Bulgaria	1	33	56
Czech Republic	2	34	56
Romania	2	35	56
Poland	2	42	50
Serbia	3	39	49
Greece	4	47	47
Albania	7	45	44
Bosnia and Herzegovina	8	35	42
Croatia	5	39	40
Kosovo	6	49	38

Source: Neli Esipova and Julie Ray, 'Syrian Refugees Not Welcome in Eastern Europe', *Gallup*, 5 May 2017, available at <http://www.gallup.com/poll/209828/syrian-refugees-not-welcome-eastern-europe.aspx>.

that their countries should not accept any Syrian refugees (36 per cent). Among Christians, roughly similar proportions of Protestants (57 per cent), Orthodox (54 per cent) and Catholics (53 per cent) said their countries should not accept any Syrian refugees (Table 2.2). Admittedly, selecting religious affiliation skews results since alternative explanations are unavailable.

A final survey conducted in Germany found that Muslims were more often the victims of housing discrimination than other people. Despite being of similar age and employment status, apartment seekers with Turkish or Arabic names in ten German cities were significantly less likely to be contacted by landlords to view a flat than applicants with German names. The report concluded: 'The tighter the housing market, the greater the discrimination. We also see a trend of groups, nationalities or asylum seekers being excluded from the outset in residency listings.' This is in spite of the fact that no one in Germany can deny apartment viewing or drawing up a lease because of ethnic background or racial reasons.[49]

Recognition that religious affiliation counts is reflected in these surveys.

Table 2.2 Religious denomination and Syrian refugees (Gallup World Poll, 2016)

Attitudes toward Syrian refugees by religious affiliation: Eastern Europe overall

	% Should accept ALL Syrian refugees	% Should accept ONLY a limited number	% Should NOT accept any Syrian refugees
Christian	2	38	54
Islam/Muslim	8	44	36
Atheist	1	32	63

Source: Neli Esipova and Julie Ray, 'Syrian Refugees Not Welcome in Eastern Europe', *Gallup*, 5 May 2017, available at <http://www.gallup.com/poll/209828/syrian-refugees-not-welcome-eastern-europe.aspx>.

Practising religion in private rather than public is not so neat a formula that it can solve religious discrimination.

LANGUAGE PREJUDICE

When scholars study the emergence of nations, they are inclined to search for breakthroughs in the creation of a centrally administered state, the flourishing of a national culture, the crystallisation of a national character and the adoption of a vernacular national language. They assume that a relationship exists among the state, its culture, the language and nationhood. Hans Kohn articulated this perspective when he maintained that a feeling of nationality was prevalent among peoples before the birth of modern nationalism.[50]

A causal connection between the birth of a nation and the emergence of a national language is tenuous, although the two phenomena are intricately linked. Safran underscored the centrality of language as a marker of national identity: 'a vehicle for expressing a distinct culture; a source of national cohesion; and an instrument for building political community'.[51] Gat emphasised how 'A shared language has been documented to be by far a nation's most common unifying bond.'[52]

The status and fate of languages are often attributed to decisions taken by the state and its leaders. Ill-considered state intervention in the linguistic sphere could trigger vehement reactions shaking an entire polity, so 'Languages are not only tools of nation-building but also means of political control.'[53] Nearly all states officially recognise one or more official languages. By contrast, the number of states that embraces a state religion has declined or diminished in importance, other than for Muslim-majority states.

State *dirigisme* seems, then, to prioritise language over religion, but 'the triumph of language over religion remains incomplete'.[54] The state's inability to tame organised religions, together with the revival of religious values in the twenty-first century, account for this unfinished victory.

Language and the body politic were not always so intertwined. During the Middle Ages, language was accepted as a natural fact and not treated as a political or cultural determinant of nation or nationhood. Its perceived insignificance was evident when Arab forces sweeping across the Mediterranean world at the end of the first millennium decided not to impose their language on conquered peoples. To be sure, like English in much of the contemporary world, the use of Arabic spread quickly, among Greeks, Visigoths, Persians and Berbers.

The emergence of national languages took place in the fourteenth and fifteenth centuries. This coincided with, and was a product of, the spread of anti-ecclesiastical national movements. The ascendancy of the vernacular had little political significance at first; some authors writing in the vernacular, like Christine de Pizan in French and Petrarch in Italian, drew humorous stereotypes of their own nations and that of others.

The primary cleavage before the Enlightenment continued to be religious:

> The main conflict of the Middle Ages was not between universalism and the desire of separation of individual groups, but between two forms of universalism, *Sacerdotium* and *Imperium*, a struggle unknown in the Eastern Church and unknown in Islam, where universalism remained a reality much longer than in Western Christianity.[55]

People thought of each other not in terms of nationality, language or race but confessionalism.

The significance of language was heralded in the eighteenth century. German writers Johann Gottlieb Fichte and Johann Gottfried Herder conjectured about the existence of natural cultural and linguistic communities. Herder considered that the mythical language of the *Volk* embodied its own special genius and made a unique contribution to world civilisation.

The process of linguistic unification in particular European countries was far from complete. As late as 1789, more than half of all people who lived in France could not speak French. Identifying the nation with a particular language entailed substantial myth-making. But the myth helped shape a self-fulfilling policy: 'By the early twentieth century, the use of the French language had become a mark of republican patriotism and had become so generalized that ethnic minority languages – and ethnic minorities as such – had become juridically nonexistent.'[56]

Before the expansion of general primary education, it was not easy to distinguish spoken national languages. Familiarity with their literary variants was limited to a narrow elite. As Benedict Anderson observed, 'a particular script-language offered privileged access to ontological truth'. Administrative vernaculars had been in use before the sixteenth century but 'nothing suggests that any deep-seated ideological, let alone proto-national, impulses underlay this vernacularization where it occurred'.[57] It was print capitalism that created 'languages-of-power' and 'unified fields of exchange and communication'.[58]

Language played a substantial part in Anderson's account of an imagined community: 'the convergence of capitalism and print technology on the fatal diversity of human language created the possibility of a new form of imagined community, which in its basic morphology set the stage for the modern nation'.[59]

It is easier to trace the development of national languages than it is to identify the emergence of a sense of nationhood. The two are related, but sharing a language has never by itself guaranteed that the combination of ethnic and ethnicised nationhood might emerge. It is when a language is put to political purposes that the struggle for nationhood begins. It can both unify – shared language is important for all, including those concerned about socio-occupational mobility – and it can fragment – refusing to accept a lingua franca is to be a dissenter.

Developing a national language where minority ones exist can be polarising. Affirming a need for linguistic unity can mask the need for deeper structural conditions of diversity management. The charge of xenophobia is frequently levelled at states that undertake unilingual policy change. Quebec's language laws are said to discriminate against English speakers, Estonia and Latvia's against Russian minorities, Xhosa against other South Africans, and Castile against Quechua and Aymara speakers in Peru.

The loss of minority languages is an overlooked by-product of the rise of nationalism and ethnocentrism. A linguistic group may compensate for this loss by emphasising other markers of identity to maintain cohesion: for instance, religious practices, folk customs, food, music, endogenous marriages. But the erosion of a community's language can start the process of reducing its culture to little more than folklore.

Few states, or international organisations, wish to appear to be opposed to linguistic flourishing. The Council of Europe's 1992 Charter for Regional or Minority Languages provided guarantees for the use of such languages in six areas: education, cultural activities, the media, economic and social life, justice and administration, and international exchanges. Signatories had to comply with at least three of the Charter's paragraphs. Greece and France deny the existence of minorities in their countries, and it has been joined by Spain in its treatment of Catalonia as little more than a region. But these countries too wish to be linguistically correct and have espoused norms for the protection of minorities.

State-directed language policy can, deliberately or unintentionally, produce diglossia – a high language of the state and of its power that over-whelms minority languages and dialects. Even so, 'The abandonment by an ethnic minority of its language in favor of the language of the majority does not guarantee the minority's full acceptance in the political community.'[60] Getting language policy wrong exacerbates mutual xenophobia and communal unrest.

Language is a tangible, concrete phenomenon in a way that nationhood is not. Nationhood can be built regardless of whether a state is polyglot or unilingual. Swiss-based academic André Liebich envisaged many different understandings of language: 'Under the rubric "language" censuses can understand maternal language, most frequently used language (*Umgangssprache*), or the language of work. In the latter case the dominant language of a region or country will be preferred.'[61] He even remarked how Ernest Gellner, a specialist on nation building, believed that the language employed in preschool would determine which one the individual would prefer most.

Canadian political scientist Jean Laponce posed a series of questions some thirty years ago about the far-reaching character of language:

> Should a state that is multilingual regret that fact or congratulate itself? Can a unilingual state better integrate its economy, mobilize its political system, develop and diffuse its culture? Conversely, is it better for a language to be concentrated in one single state, to express one single political ideology, to have only one type of economic system? Or should it, for survival and diffusion, diversify its options?[62]

Laponce described the agonising choices that many new states have had to make: 'Is it better to protect one's language or one's economic interests, one's religion or the political ideology of one's preference?'[63] In order to avoid zero-sum games, he allowed that each state should be able to choose freely:

> since we are dealing with linguistic rights, it will simplify the argument if we assume – as did Aristotle – that language is a value in its own right, not a simple interchangeable instrument of communication, a value in which the *polis* finds its bonding and its soul.[64]

In other words, every language has value.

State language policies not only are important to philosophical questions of tolerance and inclusion, but also they have an impact on a practical and concrete matter. For example, linguistic flexibility can attract immigrants that will expand the nation. Assimilability highlights the critical role language plays. Some migrants thrive on linguistic diversity and many learn several languages in school. Others prefer to speak only their maternal language; Samuel Huntington's example (described in Chapter 6) of Mexican migration to the US over the last three decades resulting in English being superfluous is debatable.[65] We come full circle to diglossia, the language of power, which may prove to be inescapable.

Historical minorities, Indigenous and Aboriginal peoples claim to have special status. Others say that those who first set foot in unconquered lands centuries ago are no different from recent immigrants. The mantra is that we are all Canadians, Americans, Peruvians, and have no God-given privileges. But for Will Kymlicka, a Canadian multicultural expert, Aboriginal people merit special consideration.

Indigenous peoples are exempt, he considered, from the demands of multi-culturalism that immigrant groups confront.[66] He reasoned that 'multination states' are defined by 'a range of minority and indigenous rights that include regional autonomy and official language rights for national minorities'.[67] The crucial reason for exempting national minorities from these requirements is that *eo ipso* they are *national* communities whose laws and norms precede those who have arrived since. They are the lynchpins of nationhood, of what I describe as the first belongers to the nation. In addition, minority rights provisions have not suffered the setbacks that cultural majorities have, so that Kymlicka's views combine political realism with natural law: certain rights are inherent by virtue of human nature. Chapter 3 returns to this issue.

It may be surprising that Kymlicka, who developed the Migrant Integration Policy Index (MIPEX) measuring integration, contended that in Europe 'multiculturalism "went too far" in the context of predominantly Muslim immigrants'.[68] It is a controversial subject, raised by Austria's leader elected to office in 2017. Sebastian Kurz believed that all-Muslim kindergartens had to be closed since no German was spoken there. Language issues remain pivotal in the integration of immigrants.

Comparing biases

The vast majority of scholars engaged with nationalism and nationhood have identified religious and linguistic affiliations as critical. Religious identities are sometimes thought of as fluid and malleable. But Muslims, for example, may come under pressure to abandon their religious beliefs; Christianity or, especially, secularism will open doors for them. Conversion to different forms of Christianity is a tried-and-true practice. Many Turks living in the Balkans 400 years ago were offered conversion to Christianity as incentives to pursue socio-economic mobility.

Religion is more often cited as a factor that promotes xenophobia in con-trast to language. Stereotyping on the basis of religious affiliation appears more commonplace than raising linguistic differences. Over recent decades, the clash of religions has been given more weight in scholarly analysis than clashes of languages, and this line of research appears justifiable. This is not to disregard the weight of linguistic stereotyping, which can include frowned-upon use of dialects and *patois* in contact regions where two languages compete. Rigorous state language policies are a relatively painless way to control membership in a linguistic group.

Language, in turn, may be more relevant to promoting an ethnocentric view of the world than religion. That is because language divides are tangible and not as easily breachable as those based on faith and values. Nevertheless, my finding is that both are implicated deeply in the process of othering communities different from our own.

Neither language nor religion is *sensu stricto* an essentialist or primordial feature of our existence. They are not innate genetic characteristics that originate from birth. At the same time, language has a tangible existence and we cannot aspirationally acquire a linguistic identity without hard work.

Religion belongs squarely in the instrumentalist or constructivist camp. Karl Marx's hyperbole captured the spirit of the instrumentalist or constructivist approach: 'Religion is the sigh of the oppressed creature, the heart of a heartless world, and the soul of soulless conditions. It is the opium of the people.' That cannot be said of language. Religiously anchored identities can be made liberal or illiberal depending on how they are constructed and to which purposes they are employed. But language is value-neutral, not reducible to mere social construction.

Let me conclude with a thought experiment. Many scenarios can be imagined in which a state becomes unstable, but below are two sets of dyads, each of which can lead to the same outcome:

1a. Political authorities are indifferent to integrating religious and linguistic communities, thereby creating unequal parallel societies, ghettoisation and marginalised communities.
1b. Political authorities pursue forced assimilation of religious and linguistic communities, thereby triggering a backlash against the state.
2a. Religion and/or language are key markers of identity but can be dangerously divisive when revived.
2b. Religious and/or linguistic identities are irrelevant and can be ignored, thereby undermining a country's diversity and fostering chaos.

Steering between dyads is critical. Otherwise policies that are either too religious or overly secular, too unilingual or excessively multilingual, too strongly assimilationist or one-sidedly multicultural, can produce dysfunctional outcomes and trigger disintegrative tendencies. Enlarging the nation beyond its core constituency may therefore produce the right equilibrium.

NOTES

1. Pred, Allan, *Even in Sweden: Racisms, Racialized Spaces, and the Popular Geographical Imagination* (Berkeley, CA: University of California Press, 2000).
2. Safran, William, 'Introduction', in Safran (ed.), *The Secular and the Sacred: Nation, Religion and Politics* (London: Frank Cass, 2003), pp. 1–2.
3. Benedict, Ruth, 'Religion', in Franz Boas (ed.), *General Anthropology* (New York: D. C. Heath, 1938), pp. 628–9.
4. Gat, Azar, *Nations: The Long History and Deep Roots of Political Ethnicity and Nationalism* (Cambridge: Cambridge University Press, 2012), pp. 311, 25.
5. Safran, William, 'Language, Ethnicity, and Religion: A Complex and Persistent Linkage', *Nations and Nationalism*, 14, no. 1, 2008, p. 173.
6. Safran, William, 'Islamization in Western Europe: Political Consequences and Historical Parallels', *Annals of the American Academy of Political and Social Science*, 485, May 1986, p. 109.
7. Ibid., p. 100.
8. Ibid., p. 101.
9. Caldwell, Christopher, *Reflections on the Revolution in Europe: Immigration, Islam and the West* (New York: Anchor, 2010).
10. Polakow-Suransky, Sasha, 'Is Democracy in Europe Doomed?', *New York Review of Books*, 16 October 2017, abridged from his *Go Back to Where You Came From: The Backlash Against Immigration and the Fate of Western Democracy* (New York: Nation Books, 2017), available at <http://www.nybooks.com/daily/2017/10/16/is-democracy-in-europe-doomed/>.
11. Mamdani, Mahmood, *Good Muslim, Bad Muslim* (New York: Doubleday, 2004), p. 22.
12. Roy, Olivier, *Holy Ignorance: When Religion and Culture Part Ways* (New York: Columbia University Press, 2009).
13. Roy, Olivier, *The Mediterranean and its Metaphors* (Montecatini Terme: European University Institute, Robert Schuman Center for Advanced Studies), Distinguished Lecture 2009/02, pp. 8–9.
14. Safran, 'Islamization', p. 103.
15. Brubaker, Rogers, 'Religion and Nationalism: Four Approaches', *Nations and Nationalism*, 18, no. 1, 2012, pp. 2–20.
16. Taras, Ray, *Liberal and Illiberal Nationalisms* (Basingstoke: Palgrave, 2002), Ch. 1.
17. Cited in Appiah, Anthony, 'The Uncompleted Argument: Du Bois and the Illusion of Race', *Critical Inquiry*, 12, no. 1, Autumn 1985, p. 23.
18. Fanon, Frantz, *Black Skin, White Masks* (New York: Grove Press, 1994), p. 29.
19. 'The Unfinished Conversation: Stuart Hall in Dialogue with History', *Museum of Modern Art*, Exhibition on view 19 March to 30 July 2017, available at <https://stories.moma.org/the-unfinished-conversation-stuart-hall-in-dialogue-with-history-aad38e9b40b2>.
20. 'The Freedom Charter', 25–6 June 1955, available at <http://www.historicalpapers.wits.ac.za/inventories/inv_pdfo/AD1137/AD1137-Ea6-1-001-jpeg.pdf>.
21. Césaire, Aimé, 'Discourse on Colonialism', p. 8, available at <http://abahlali.org/files/_Discourse_on_Colonialism.pdf>.
22. Ibid., pp. 22–3.
23. Younis, Musab, 'Against Independence', *London Review of Books*, 39, no. 13, 29 June

2017, p. 27. See Léopold Sédar Senghor, *Négritude et civilisation de l'universel* (Paris: Seuil, 1977).

24. Jeanpierre, W. A., 'Sartre's Theory of "Anti-Racist Racism" in his Study of Negritude', *The Massachusetts Review*, 6, no. 4, Autumn 1965, pp. 870–2.

25. Lamont, Michèle, *The Dignity of Working Men: Morality and the Boundaries of Race, Class, and Immigration* (Cambridge, MA: Harvard University Press, 2002).

26. Sivanandan, Ambalavaner, 'UK Commentary: Racism 1992', *Race and Class*, 30, no. 3, 1989, pp. 85–90.

27. Sivanandan, Ambalavaner, 'The Contours of Global Racism', IRR News website, 26 November 2002, available at <http://www.irr.org.uk/2002/november/ak000007.html>.

28. Balibar, Étienne, and Immanuel Wallerstein, *Race, Nation, Class: Ambiguous Identities* (London: Verso, 1991), pp. 34, 21.

29. Meer, Nasar, *Key Concepts in Race and Ethnicity* (Thousand Oaks, CA: Sage, 2014).

30. Taguieff, Pierre-André, 'Racisme, racialisme, ethnocentrisme, xénophobie, anti-sémitisme et néoracisme: réflexions sur des termes problématiques', in Commission nationale consultative des droits de l'homme, *La Lutte contre le racisme, l'antisémitisme, et la xénophobie: année 2007* (Paris: La Documentation française, 2008), p. 243.

31. Goldberg, David Theo, 'Racial Comparisons, Relational Racisms: Some Thoughts on Method', *Ethnic and Racial Studies*, 32, no. 7, 2009, pp. 1271–82.

32. Taguieff, 'Racisme', p. 261.

33. Bauman, Zygmunt, *Modernity and the Holocaust* (Ithaca, NY: Cornell University Press, 1993), p. 65.

34. Taguieff, Pierre-André, *La Force du préjugé: essai sur le racisme et ses doubles* (Paris: La Découverte, 1988).

35. Chebel d'Appolonia, Ariane, 'Race, Racism and Anti-discrimination in France', in Sylvain Brouard, A. Mazur and Andrew M. Appleton (eds), *The French Fifth Republic at Fifty: Beyond Stereotypes* (London: Palgrave Macmillan, 2008), p. 268.

36. Reported by Chebel d'Appolonia, 'Race', p. 275.

37. 'Racisme: Les Français sont dans l'acceptation tant qu'on ne touche pas à leur petit jardin', *Libération*, 19 July 2010.

38. 'Racisme: Un verrou a sauté dans le discours politique admis ou admissible', *Le Monde*, 12 April 2011.

39. *La Lutte contre le racisme*, Annexe, pp. 316–18.

40. Hübinette, Tobias, and Catrin Lundström, 'White Melancholia: Mourning the Loss of "Good Old Sweden"', *Eurozine*, 18 October 2011, available at <http://www.eurozine.com/white-melancholia/>.

41. Ibid.

42. Brysk, Alison, *Global Good Samaritans: Human Rights as Foreign Policy* (Oxford: Oxford University Press, 2009), p. 2.

43. Hübinette and Lundström, 'White Melancholia'.

44. Taguieff, 'Racisme', pp. 244–5.

45. Brown, Audrey, 'Rainbow Nation – Dream or Reality?', *BBC News*, 18 July 2008.

46. European Commission Against Racism and Intolerance, 'Annual Report on ECRI's Activities Covering the Period from 1 January to 31 December 2005', Strasbourg, May 2006, available at <https://www.coe.int/t/dghl/monitoring/ecri/activities/Annual_Reports/Annual%20report%202005.pdf>.

47. Goodwin, Matthew, Thomas Raines and David Cutts, 'What Do Europeans Think About Muslim Immigration?', 7 February 2017, available at <https://www.chathamhouse.org/expert/comment/what-do-europeans-think-about-muslim-immigration#sthash>.

48. Esipova, Neli, and Julie Ray, 'Syrian Refugees Not Welcome in Eastern Europe', *Gallup*, 5 May 2017, available at <http://www.gallup.com/poll/209828/syrian-refugees-not-welcome-eastern-europe.aspx>.

49. 'Foreigners Discriminated Against in German Renting Market', *Deutsche Welle*, 22 June 2017, available at <http://www.dw.com/en/foreigners-discriminated-against-in-german-renting-market-report-finds/a-39359215>.

50. Kohn, Hans, *The Idea of Nationalism: A Study in Its Origins and Background* (New York: Macmillan, 1969), p. 6.

51. Safran, William, and J. A. Laponce (eds), *Language, Ethnic Identity and the State* (London: Routledge, 2005), p. 1.

52. Gat, *Nations*, p. 310.

53. Safran and Laponce, *Language*, p. 4.

54. Safran, 'Language, Ethnicity, and Religion', p. 188.

55. Kohn, *The Idea of Nationalism*, p. 79.

56. Safran, William, 'Language, Ideology, and State-Building: A Comparison of Policies in France, Israel, and the Soviet Union', *International Political Science Review*, 13, no. 4, October 1992, p. 400.

57. Anderson, Benedict, *Imagined Communities: Reflections on the Origin and Spread of Nationalism* (London: Verso, 1983), pp. 36, 41.

58. Ibid., pp. 44–5.

59. Ibid., p. 46.

60. Safran, 'Language, Ideology, and State-Building', p. 408.

61. Liebich, André, *Les Minorités nationales en Europe centrale et orientale* (Geneva: Georg Editeur 1997), p. 36.

62. Laponce, Jean, *Languages and Their Territories* (Toronto, ON: University of Toronto Press, 1987), p. 94.

63. Ibid., p. 94.

64. Ibid., p. 152.

65. Huntington, Samuel P., *Who Are We? The Challenges to America's National Identity* (New York: Simon and Schuster, 2005).

66. Kymlicka, Will, *Multicultural Odysseys: Navigating the New International Politics of Diversity* (Oxford: Oxford University Press, 2007), pp. 66–7.

67. Ibid., p. 80.

68. Ibid., p. 52.

CHAPTER THREE

Who belongs

MIGRATION RISING

This chapter connects nationhood to the processes of social integration and social cohesion. If homogeneous nations are disappearing and migrants with their often far-flung networks are replacing them, how does nationhood take on the bounded form that it does? How is it able to incorporate millions of migrants over the decades, successfully integrate them, convince them they belong, and create socially cohesive communities that constitute nationhood?

In 2017 there were 258 million international migrants making up 3.4 per cent of the world's population. Since 2000 migrants have increased by 85 million, or 49 per cent. Women account for nearly half of the total, giving short shrift to the impression that they are the ones invariably left behind.[1] Approximately one-third of migrants were under the age of 30. More than 150 million were workers. Asylum seekers represented just a small proportion, 15 per cent in Europe and 10 per cent globally. In 2017, Asia hosted the largest number of migrants (80 million), edging out Europe (78 million) and well ahead of North America (58 million).[2]

Integration has been watered down in the twenty-first century. Zygmunt Bauman noted that 'unlike the now abandoned postulate of "assimilation", the policy of integration does not require of the newcomers the renunciation of what they are'.[3] Integration means that migrants do not need to sell their souls when moving to another country, but expectations are that they will adapt and adjust to changes in their social lives. They need to take steps to learn a foreign language, if not because of its intrinsic value then for its practicality.

This chapter examines processes of integration that are sometimes successes and other times failures. Here is a general definition. According to the Migration Policy Institute, immigrant integration is the process of economic mobility and social inclusion for newcomers and their children. As such, integration touches upon the institutions and mechanisms that promote development and growth within society, including early childhood care; elementary, postsecondary, and adult education systems; workforce development; health care; provision of government services to communities with linguistic diversity; and more. Successful integration builds communities that are stronger economically and more inclusive socially and culturally.[4]

As discussed already, immigration gives a country the opportunity to broaden the nation and make it post-ethnic. The first step involves making immigrants feel they belong to the receiving society and affirming that nationhood encompasses immigrants. This is a departure from the narrower understanding of nationhood as comprising on the one hand a group of nativists and assimilated immigrants, and on the other a peripheral 'waiting room' accommodating peoples viewed as not yet belonging, even being excluded.

When we introduce the term super-diversity to apply to contemporary nations with complex demographic makeups, the situation becomes even more complicated: 'The concept of super-diversity to some extent complements the notion of transnationalism which highlights that migrants often maintain relations with two or more countries and live in transnational social spaces.'[5] Rethinking immigrant integration in terms of the multidimensionality of the migrant experience can become unmanageable, inadequate and often flawed. It can be a cosmopolitan experience that transcends a number of countries. I limit this discussion to migrants from a sending society seeking to integrate into one receiving society.

BELONGING: ELUSIVE OR ILLUSIONARY?

When we speak of a German nation, it may be more accurate to talk of different peoples in Germany that make up its nationhood. More politically contentious is identifying other states in which, for example, 'Turkish Kurds' would more precisely be called Kurds in Turkey – an important component of Turkey's nationhood. The same may apply to Catalan speakers in Spain in spite of the Madrid government insisting that there is but one Spain.

In 2017 German Foreign Minister Sigmar Gabriel spoke out about Turks in Germany: 'one thing is clear: you, people of Turkish roots in Germany, belong here with us, whether you have a German passport or not'. Germany acknowledges that the 3 million individuals of Turkish descent belong to the country, form 'part of the fabric of the nation' and represent 'a great treasure'.[6] This is the definition of nationhood.

It is futile to determine where people naturally belong. In the first instance, belonging may occur in the place where people are born. But others claim they belong where they have chosen to settle. In order to contrast aspects of belonging, let me examine an intriguing, perhaps unwitting, debate that took place between two Jesuit intellectuals who head the Catholic Church.

Chosen by Pope Francis to be new Undersecretary of the Section for Migrants and Refugees in the Vatican department for the Promotion of Integral Human Development, Father Michael Czerny stressed that 'no one should ever be forced to leave his or her home due to lack of development or peace'. Rather than view that person as a prospective emigrant to a safer country, he underscored that

> The right to remain helps to focus the international community's efforts on its prior obligation to ensure the sustainable and integral human development of all people in their *place of origin* and to enable them to become active agents of their own development.[7]

Speaking to a UN symposium studying the linkage between migration and development, Czerny expressed concern that migrants might be pressured to leave their country of origin rather than remain, in this way raising the social, economic and cultural costs to the country being abandoned: 'It is by ensuring the conditions for the exercise of the right to remain, then, that makes migration a *choice*, not a necessity.' This logic is more than Jesuitry.

For his part, Pope Francis, a powerful advocate for migrant rights, underlined other priorities for migrants. The Migrants and Refugees' Action Plan published in 2017, titled *Responding to Refugees and Migrants: Twenty Action Points*, emphasised respect for migrants' dignity and rights. The task of governments was to 'welcome, protect, promote, and integrate' them so that the 'ultimate goal is the building of an inclusive and sustainable common home for all'. Welcoming 'the rejected strangers of every age' was an obligation.

Pope Francis went further, convinced that personal safety was a greater priority than national security. Border guards should be trained to protect migrants. Unaccompanied minors needed special protection. Family reunification should be accompanied by accelerated procedures for citizenship. Questioning the realism of the Pope's approach, however, an official in the Italian anti-immigrant *Lega* party responded: 'If you want to do it in the Vatican go ahead. But as a Catholic I don't think Italy can welcome and support the whole world.'[8] In early 2018 Italian voters offered resounding support for immigration-sceptic parties of all types – *Lega*, the Five-Star Movement and the right-wing party.

There is nothing natural about belonging to a state because a citizen was born in it: that is, unless the doctrine of *jus soli* – the right of anyone born on the territory of a state to its nationality – is applied. The most clear-cut case we have of the firmness of the *jus soli* principle concerns Indigenous people born in a state but often made to feel they do not belong to it. Indigenous peoples are a gateway to the nature of nationhood.

First Nations

Indigenous peoples occupied lands in what is today North America, had well-developed cultures and established their own languages. One pioneering group were the Skraeling, a people later called Thule, who were the ancestors of the Inuit in Greenland and Canada, and the Iñupiat in Alaska. Their continuity on the inhospitable continent is extraordinary: 'The indigenous people hadn't always been there, nor had they originated there, as some of their traditions state, but they had occupied these American lands for at least 20,000 years.'[9]

Aboriginal or Indigenous peoples do not need to integrate into societies that they have been an integral part of for centuries. In their different spiritualities, they believe that the land, lakes, rivers, rocks, forests, fauna and flora belong to them. Many of these objects are thought to have a soul. But these peoples came under increasing domination by outsider settler populations who tried to change their beliefs, whether through conversion to Christianity, secularism or something else. Woody Guthrie's anthemic 'This land is my land, this land is your land' is an inspiring elegy to shared resources. But over the centuries Indigenous peoples became the largest losers as their resources were turned into public property or were privatised.

Indigenous peoples are descendants of those who were there before others arrived and redefined their societies. The early inhabitants are identifiable partly by descent and partly by distinctive features: language, way of life, hunting-and-gathering skills, animism. Indigenous peoples were those who controlled their lands until stripped of them by later arrivals, succumbed to their domination, suffered their neglect. They are more than first settlers, since their way of life and economic principles were totally upended.

Canada's First Nations are a case in point. On the 150th anniversary of Canadian Confederation in 2017, First Nations political activist Arthur Manuel, in the last article he ever wrote, asserted: 'I do not wish to celebrate Canada stealing our land. That is what Canadians will be celebrating on July 1, the theft of 99.8 percent of our land, leaving us on reserves that make up only 0.2 percent of the territories given to us by the Creator.'[10]

From ownership of all land, founding nations were reduced to living on 0.2 per cent of land. Territory and, with it, natural resources were stripped from them, causing chronic Indigenous poverty. By contrast, settler Canadians, including recent immigrant communities, enjoy and benefit from 99.8 per cent of Indigenous lands held by federal and provincial governments.

The first Canadian Constitution, under the British North America Act

54

Box 3.1 Indigenous fightback

Our Indian reserves are only .02 percent of Canada's land and yet Indigenous peoples are expected to survive on them. This has led to the systematic impoverishment of Indigenous people and the crippling oppression that Indigenous peoples suffer under the current colonial system. The .02 land based is used to keep us too poor and too weak to fight back. It is used to bribe and co-opt the Indigenous leadership into becoming neocolonial partners to treat the symptom of poverty on Indian reserves without addressing the root cause of the problem, which is the dispossession of all of the Indigenous territory by Canada and the provinces.

Source: Arthur Manuel, 'Are You a Canadian?', *First Nations Strategic Bulletin*, August–December 2016, pp. 1-2. See also Arthur Manuel, *Unsettling Canada: A National Wake-Up Call* (Toronto: Between the Lines, 2015).

---

of 1867, placed Indigenous lands under the Crown. Manuel, who had served as long-time co-chair of the North American Indigenous Peoples Caucus of the UN Permanent Forum on Indigenous Issues, was among those who condemned the 'doctrine of discovery', long used to justify colonialism across the world. According to this notion, Europeans claimed that they discovered lands where no one had lived, believing that the Indigenous people who greeted them when they arrived were not human (Box 3.1).

Thomas King, author of *The Inconvenient Indian*, which recounted the sorry experience of the offspring of Indigenous communities, explained the difference between Indigenous peoples and settlers in this pitiless way:

> The Lakota didn't want Europeans in the Black Hills, but Whites wanted the gold that was there. The Cherokee didn't want to move from Georgia to Indian Territory (Oklahoma), but Whites wanted the land. The Cree of Quebec weren't at all keen on vacating their homes to make way for the Great Whale project, but there's excellent money in hydroelectric power. The California Indians did not ask to be enslaved by the Franciscans and forced to build that order's missions.[11]

With a nod to Indigenous peoples, in 2017 Prime Minister Justin Trudeau recognised that 'Today isn't really our 150th birthday, we're much older than that.' The Fathers of Confederation had wished to create a strong country as the US Civil War was ended and the threat of an American takeover was tangible. But even then, First Nations in Canada remained among the poorest of all Canadians.

Canada boasts that it has become the most educated society on earth.

That is because immigrant communities add to its composite added value and invigorate a sense of shared nationhood. Few claim they face discrimination. It is branded as the land of opportunity that has replaced the US. But even as well-educated Canadians and immigrant communities prosper, First Nations suffer poverty and indignities, and lag far behind. It is as if, paradoxically, First Nations had no stake in nationhood.

As Canada admits more immigrants – the Immigration Office announced that under 'the new normal' 1 million will arrive between 2018 and 2020 – Idle No More, a First Nations activist group, reports that little has changed: 'We're still seeing children dying, still seeing women going missing.... Everything is crisis and poverty. Water crises, suicide crises, missing women crisis, drug overdoses, rampant alcoholism, unemployment rates. These things are not changing.'[12] The incongruity of a $500-million party to celebrate Canada Day 2017 when Indigenous communities struggle with meeting basic needs hits home.

Aboriginal peoples lost the right to hold lands through a series of unequal treaties. While these are sometimes labelled outright land grabs, Elders recall that they never formally ceded their territories to newcomers. In 2017 the Indian Act was 140 years old but its nefarious provisions were never reversed.

But some nativists remain patronising. A well-known writer reported on the 'burden' Canadian bureaucrats bear in administering Indian lands:

> most first nations do not own their lands; the federal Crown has legislative jurisdiction over Indian reserves and manages them for the use and benefit of their residents. In practice, this means many transactions involving reserve land have to be reviewed by the Department of Indian Affairs, adding layers of legal work and delay to an already cumbersome approval process.[13]

It is as if First Nations cause problems by their very existence.

First Nations have sought to reacquire lands but, for Tom Flanagan, Canada's leaders assume a posture of *laisse oblige*: 'those first nations wishing to take over the responsibility of ownership should be able to acquire the title to their reserves from the Crown, thus emancipating themselves from the stifling paternalism of the Indian Act'. Struggling to get their original lands back could help make Indigenous peoples rich: 'Canada's first nations are potentially wealthy landlords, with land reserves totaling nearly three million hectares.' Many reserves are situated near major cities such as Vancouver, Edmonton, Calgary and Montreal, so 'This land base represents an economic asset that could make a major contribution to raising first nations' standard of living.'[14] After 150 years Indigenous peoples are, for some analysts, being given the opportunity to enrich themselves.

A more sympathetic understanding of the precarious land question in Indigenous–settler relations has been offered:

The issue that came ashore with the French and the English and the Spanish, the issue that was the *raison d'être* for each of the colonies, the issue that has made its way from coast to coast to coast and is with us today, the issue that has never changed, never varied, never faltered in its resolve, is the issue of land. The issue has always been land. It will always be land, until there isn't a square foot of land left in North America that is controlled by Native people.[15]

The narrative of North American settler peoples distorts the Indigenous story: 'Despite the clamoring of history to pull us into the full sweep of accepted history – the one that starts with "discovery", segues into brave "explorers" and into the notion of "two founding nations" – the real history of Canada begins with native people.' The bottom line is that 'Ever since that moment, the history of the continent has been interpreted and articulated through settler eyes.'[16]

What are the minimal demands of Indigenous peoples reclaiming nationhood? They expect state recognition of their distinct ethnocultural nationality and, on its basis, collective cultural and political rights. Honouring original treaty agreements between the Crown and the Indigenous peoples of Canada would be a start. But the Canadian government has recognised that Indigenous people are distinct through the lens of the Indian Act, which defines how Indian reserves must be managed and decides who is and who is not an 'Indian'. This strips Indigenous peoples of self-determination.

The struggle for Indigenous rights covers the globe. First Nations and Inuit lead the charge in Canada together with Métis – Indigenous peoples of mixed blood. They account for 1.2 million of the Canadian population, made up of over 600 First Nations and bands.

In the US, one of the book's case studies, Native Americans comprise over 500 scheduled tribes. They originate with pre-Columbian Indigenous peoples now divided into several hundred ethno-linguistic groups. Native Americans were in conflict with immigrant Europeans over land rights, which exacerbated political tension, ethnic schism, violence and social disruption.

Indigenous peoples also suffered high casualties from their contact with diseases brought over from Europe, at times decimating them. While estimates vary widely about how many lived in the Americas in pre-Columbian times, a low figure is 8 million, while the upper range is 112 million. Using a rough estimate that approximately 50 million Indigenous people lived in all the Americas in 1492 (including 25 million in the Aztec Empire and 12 million in the Inca Empire), one estimate is that the death rate was 80 per cent. It brought down the overall population to 8 million in 1650. Some Native Americans such as Ward Churchill described this as the first ever genocide.[17]

About 6 million Mexicans are *indígenas*, who live largely in the south of the country. The Plurinational State of Bolivia consists of 56–70 per cent

Indigenous. In Peru, another of our case studies, about half of all Andean and Amazonian peoples is Indigenous. In Guatemala, too, they approach half the population. Brazil, with about 0.5 per cent Indigenous, is noteworthy for having 67 uncontacted tribes in existence in 2007.

Europe's population is rarely described as Indigenous. To be sure, in Britain, another of my case studies, when the Romans departed, Anglo-Saxons settled much of the east, Celtic groups parts of the west, and Viking groups lived on the fringes. Nevertheless, according to Nobel literature laureate Kazuo Ishiguro, an optimistic history of England after the Romans left would view the interbreeding of peoples 'native' to England. The reality may have been that, as described in *The Buried Giant*, arriving Anglo-Saxons slaughtered Britons.[18] Romano-Celtic peoples also disappeared with little trace, and when they fled an early genocide it was to take refuge in western parts of the country like Wales. Indigeneity was wiped out early on in England.

There are about 100,000 Saami peoples in the Nordic states and 25,000 Samoyedic peoples, a Uralic group, in northern Russia. Also serving as a case study, Russia recognises forty-one ethnic groups as small-numbered Indigenous peoples of the North, Siberia and the Far East. They are the only ones protected as Indigenous peoples. Many are nomadic, practise Shamanism and comprise hunter–gatherer communities.

Identifying as Indigenous people is much less common on the African continent. Here the category 'first peoples in a land' does not assure recognition as Indigenous. But in South Africa, a further case study, of the total population of around 50 million, 1 per cent is listed as Indigenous groups, classified collectively as Khoisan.

Another case, considered in greater detail in Chapter 7, is India. Scheduled Tribes, referred to as Adivasis, make up about 68 million of the total Indian population of 1.3 billion. In Indonesia, over 300 ethnic groups consisting of 200 million people have native Indonesian ancestry. The largest Japanese Indigenous group is the Ainu, who settled in Hokkaidō as well as the Russian Far East (the Kuril Islands and parts of Sakhalin). Australia lists over 500 members of 'the Aboriginal race of Australia', making up 670,000 (or 3 per cent) of Australians. In New Zealand, Māori account for 15 per cent of its population.

Nationhood signifies that Indigenous peoples belong to a country by birthright. More often than not, their socio-economic status is lower than that of settlers. For long periods when settler societies governed, Indigenous peoples were marginalised from politics, economic development and cultural affirmation. Ironically, these peoples, regarded as not belonging or forming an integral component of nationhood, were there first. Predictably, the history of various Indigenous societies has often been dismissive of their status as 'first inhabitants'. It is predictable, then, that Aboriginal writers have returned to the nationhood principle.

As we have stressed, for Sylvia McAdam (Saysewahum), 'Nationhood is primarily about land, language, and culture.' But it goes further: 'The Indigenous people's elements of Nationhood are tied to sovereignty.' It follows that 'when these factors no longer exist then we become assimilated into the dominant culture therefore facing the possibility of losing the uniqueness and sovereignty of First Nations.'[19]

McAdam describes the cultural pathways of the *nêhiyaw* – identified as a human (that is, Cree) person: '*nêhiyaw* history is written in the lands and waters. It's in the pictographs, petroglyphs, rock markings, in the ghost dance bundles, sacred sites, and the final resting places of Indigenous peoples.' The practice of smudging – lighting up sweetgrass or sage – is critical: 'The smoke clears the mind and prayers are carried to the spirit keepers or to the Creator.'[20] The Cree of Canada have met the same sorry fate as other embattled First Nations: 'Forty years of citizenship and we're more assimilated now than ever before, and we're losing our languages and traditions at a heart-breaking rate.'[21]

An idyllic retrospective on Indigenous history is vital to understanding its cultural pathways. McAdam writes:

> In the time before European settlement, forests full of tamarack, birch and pine trees were abundant and so were the cougars, wolves and bears that lived there. Much of the boreal forest in Big River has been decimated now, and blockades have been placed on the road to her people's traditional hunting lands.

She insists how 'Indigenous people lived by sustainable, environmentally guided laws. We didn't drive lands into destruction.'[22]

Another Indigenous writer, Pamela Palmater, has also focused on the meaning of nationhood for First Nations. In *Indigenous Nationhood*, she contemplates vital social issues: the murdered and missing Indigenous women, residential school atrocities, extreme poverty, unrecognisable cultural identity. She pays particular attention to eastern Canada and the Mi'kmaq experience in northern New Brunswick. Like McAdam, she asserts that in ecological terms 'First Nations are Canadians' last best hope of saving the lands, waters, plants and animals for our future generations.'[23]

Arguably, a less crucial issue is how non-Indigenous peoples use cultural appropriation to exploit First Nations. Palmater adopts an inclusive view of who is subsumed under the nationhood principle:

> If we, as communities of Aboriginal peoples, assert our Nationhood and even our right to be self-determining or sovereign nations, don't we also require legal and political recognition as such? If we deny legal and political recognition to our own citizens because they do not fulfill blood quantum levels or they don't have status

cards, how can we expect Canada or any other country to see our people as the Nations? Not only does exclusion of our rightful citizens speed up our own legal extinction, we will be excluding the very citizenship base which has shown pride and loyalty in our Nations.[24]

These authors argue that Indigenous peoples are true to the values of inclusive nationhood. But belonging – psychological wiring to a community – is not that simple.

NATIVISM AND NATIONHOOD

Multicultural societies have sometimes stood aside in the face of marginalisation and ghettoisation of immigrant communities. Failed integration policy, fraying social cohesion and proliferating multiple identities can splinter nationhood. The result of partial or unachieved nationhood can metamorphose into a failing or failed state.

No greater form of hospitality towards outsiders may exist than imbuing them with a sense of belonging to it. The conditions of belonging have been debated by sociologists, political scientists, semioticians, philosophers, and others seeking to capture who becomes integrated in immigration-based diversity. Among recent works, Bauman was particularly scathing about lack of belonging.

In *Wasted Lives: Modernity and its Outcasts*, he described how, when a sense of belonging is absent, the 'images of economic migrants and asylum seekers stand for wasted humans – the waste of globalization'. Unfortunately, 'refugees and immigrants, coming from "far away" yet making a bid to settle in the neighborhood, are uniquely suitable for the role of the effigy to be burnt'.[25] Furthermore, 'Refugees, the human waste of the global frontier-land, are 'the outsiders incarnate', the absolute outsiders, outsiders everywhere and out of place everywhere except in places that are themselves out of place – the 'nowhere places' that appear on no maps used by ordinary humans on their travels' (Box 3.2).[26]

State borders in a liquid Europe are malleable, based primarily on economic factors. Those people regarded as suspect are the ones seeking relief but are excluded because they are penniless and will cost us, as opposed to the affluent who will not. In one of his last, most cutting books, Bauman wrote about the fabricated 'carnivalesque explosions of solidarity and care' in Western societies that accompanied 'images of successive spectacular tragedies in the migrants' unending saga'. In *Strangers at Our Door*, he caustically added how 'the EU offers Syrians the prospect of heaven (life in Germany), but only if they first pay a crook and risk their lives'. Spectacular tragedies encompass migrant deaths by drowning (as in the Mediterranean), by thirst (as in the Sahara) or by violence (as in smugglers' makeshift barracks). Total

---

Box 3.2 Globalisation and the horror of exclusion

[Globalisation processes] reshuffle people and play havoc with their social identities, They may transform us, from one day to another, into refugees or 'economic migrants' ... dump at our doorsteps those people who have already been rejected, forced to run for their lives or scramble away from home for the means to stay alive, robbed of their identities and self-esteem. We hate those people because we feel that what they are going through in front of our eyes may well prove to be, and soon, a dress rehearsal of our own fate. Trying hard to remove them from our sight – round them up, lock them in camps, deport them – we wish to exorcise them.

Source: Zygmunt Bauman, *Wasted Lives: Modernity and its Outcasts* (Cambridge: Polity, 2004), p. 128.

---

deaths between 2000 and September 2017 compiled by the International Organization for Migration surpass 50,000.[27]

An accompanying danger has been the rise of what are called populist parties in Europe who wish to exclude migrants from their shores. Brubaker traced the causal chain of populism back to economic structures:

> The opening of national economies to immigrant labor is part of a broader set of economic transformations that have created opportunities for populists to speak in the name of 'ordinary people' against 'those on top' and against outside forces seen as threatening 'our' jobs, 'our' prosperity, and 'our' economic security.[28]

Robert Skidelsky, member of the House of Lords, recognises that

> Sociology, anthropology, and history have been making large inroads into the debate on immigration. It seems that *Homo economicus*, who lives for bread alone, has given way to someone for whom a sense of belonging is at least as important as eating.

Departing from economistic analysis, he raises an all-important question: 'At issue is the oldest debate in the social sciences. Can communities be created by politics and markets, or do they presuppose a prior sense of belonging?' In his view, 'Values are grown from a specific history and geography. If the make-up of a community is changed too fast, it cuts people adrift from their own history, rendering them rootless.'[29]

Skidelsky agrees with Robert Rowthorn that immigrants may take jobs from local workers and drive down wages. Raising the retirement age, the two concur, is preferable to further continuous migration.[30] But Skidelsky concludes that hostility to mass immigration is more than a protest against job losses, depressed wages and growing inequality: 'Economic welfare is not the same as social wellbeing.' How, then, can we ensure migrant belonging alongside the activity proper to *homo economicus*?

Belonging is listed as one of five conditions set out by political scientist Jane Jenson to create social cohesion:

1. *belonging*: the sense of connectedness to and pride in the community or nation
2. *inclusion*: equal access to resources, including education, employment, health care and housing
3. *participation*: political/civic participation as well as social/community participation
4. *recognition*: the extent to which there is mutual respect and tolerance
5. *legitimacy*: institutionally grounded issues, such as policies promoting pluralism and public confidence in the political system and government.[31]

For Jenson, social cohesion becomes problematic in ethnically diverse societies where migrant communities have different values and priorities.

Differences between generations of immigrant background also have salience. For Nancy Foner and Patrick Simon, a crucial issue is whether newcomers and their second-generation children come to feel that they belong.

> Now that a second, and indeed third, generation has come or is coming of age it is more pressing than ever to understand whether others recognize them – and they see themselves – as truly belonging to the societies that have been their home since birth.[32]

In welcoming foreigners, belonging confronts nativism, which is reflected in the conviction that they are the nation's keepers of tradition. Nativists, and populists, share similar concerns. A nativist reaction is likely in most societies experiencing an inflow of immigrants whose ethnic, racial, cultural and religious loyalties are perceived as unlike those of established residents. Indeed, 'Views about "unmeltable" differences are fueled by the attachments of newcomers to traditions and identities often seen as at odds with national cohesion.'[33]

In her research on belonging, Montserrat Guibernau contends that 'belonging by choice' comprises a defining feature of modern society because choice is a symbol of freedom.[34] She underscores how belonging is the measure of social acceptance:

> the emotional appeal of belonging to the nation, as a political community, stands as the most powerful agent of political mobilization, one able to establish a sharp

distinction between those who belong and those who are regarded as enemies and aliens.[35]

Belonging to nationhood defines the circle of the included. Those seen as not belonging are, in contrast, perceived to be foreigners, unknown peoples, strangers, aliens, faraway locals, outcasts. Guibernau concludes:

> Ethnically distinct people living within a nation other than their own should be welcomed into the host society and allowed to maintain their own cultures and languages, but they should also be expected to engage in a collective project able to unite all the members of the nation. The political engagement of diverse people living within the same nation should be based not upon a shared origin, but on shared values and principles involving the construction of an open society.[36]

A sense of belonging is likely to increase with successive generations of immigrants. One survey found that majorities in the Netherlands (66 per cent), Germany (63 per cent), Britain (63 per cent) and the US (69 per cent) considered the second generation to be integrating successfully into their society. Belonging was therefore easier for them to experience – once the colour bar was overcome.[37]

Not belonging

If there was a period in which minority rights chiselled away at a majority culture, today receiving societies from the US and Canada to Germany and Sweden have upped the stakes and ratcheted up, at a minimum, reasonable accommodation. Refugees needing asylum, shelter and economic opportunity may face a *Zeitgeist* where rising hostility to immigrants is expressed both through the ballot box and in street violence. Attacks on immigrants have occurred in immigrant-receiving BRICS nations such as South Africa, India and Russia. Xenophobic social attitudes across Europe are well documented.[38]

Survey research has investigated the details of why immigrants may not belong. To begin with, a cross-national study discovered the importance of the reception first experienced by immigrants in a new country: 'the "warmth of the welcome" faced by newcomers, whether the general populace tends toward openness or restrictiveness, arguably influences the tone of inter-group relations and resultant incorporation trajectories, with long-reaching implications for the outcomes of generations to come.' When they face hostility instead of welcome, migrants become 'permanent outsiders, resentful, skeptical, and rebellious'.[39] Disapproval and hostility have longer-term consequences.

Social and political attitudes may be in flux for various reasons. They may result from individual beliefs; the social circumstances people are conditioned by; the racial, cultural and religious differences involved; and perceptions of competition or threat of an economic or cultural kind. Even in the US, where welcoming immigrants is a catchphrase, Americans have displayed a history of scepticism towards immigration and a drawbridge mentality (explained in Chapter 6).

In some Western countries, it is taboo even to associate terrorist attacks with immigrant behaviour; naturally a backlash against this taboo occurs. Terrorist attacks 'have on many occasions been plotted by immigrants, providing fuel for far-right, ethno-nationalist movements to further fan immigration skepticism'. Research therefore tested the hypothesis: 'Threats to public safety, such as recent experience of terrorist events within the country, are associated with higher levels of immigration skepticism.'[40]

Using World Values Survey data from 2011 analysing responses in sixty-seven countries around the world, this research project found that 'there is a statistically significant positive correlation (r=.34) between the number of recent terrorist events experienced in a country and the prevalence of restrictive immigration attitudes'. There was also support for the belief that threats to public safety are linked to high levels of immigration scepticism. Put differently, 'our study finds that recent terrorist events are among the most consistent macro-level predictors of immigration skepticism and the effect of terrorism on attitudes is consistent across countries.'[41]

The number of such events shapes attitude formation, therefore. They influence the sense of security that average residents experience, thereby affecting the extent to which they welcome or shun new immigrants. Especially since 9/11, the way that terrorism structures attitudes, collective behaviours and immigration scepticism merits careful elucidation rather than taboo research.

A critical subject is whether race, rather than terrorism, explains patterns of exclusion. Visible physical differences as well as ancestry have justified a hierarchy of nations along which people are judged as inferior or superior. In an overview, Foner and Simon point to

> countries where postcolonial immigration has led to the creation of a significant population of racialized groups: North and sub-Saharan Africans, Caribbeans, and South Asians. In France and the Netherlands, for example, Afro-Caribbeans and sub-Saharan Africans perceive discrimination against them as based in good part on color. Color-based discrimination has been a central concern in Britain since the huge inflow of Afro-Caribbeans in the 1950s and 1960s and a fundamental element in policies and public discourse, in which a race-relations framework has been prominent. In Canadian society, color-coded race is also key. Indeed, immigrants from Asia, Arab countries, Africa, and the Caribbean and their descendants are officially referred to as visible minorities.[42]

Populist movements receive much of the blame for race baiting. Brubaker writes how

> the accelerated development of new communications technologies have made politicians less dependent on parties and more inclined to appeal directly to 'the people'. They have also encouraged a populist style of communication, character-ized by dramatization, confrontation, negativity, emotionalization, personaliza-tion, visualization, and hyper-simplification.[43]

Terrorism can be both cause and effect of other factors conjoining to produce social exclusion of immigrants. Sometimes, however, it may only serve as a pretext. Let me examine this idea of 'not belonging' across receiv-ing societies not serving as the book's case studies in order to assess how belonging is contested.

Austria

The EU's criticism of countries refusing to accept refugees does not include Austria. Austria has nevertheless sought to control the influx of immigrants. Its previous Foreign Minister, and Chancellor since 2017, has acted as a bad cop in a hardening policy on migrants.

Sebastian Kurz went on record in 2016 saying that Islamic kindergartens in Austria, where children have little or no command of German, should be closed: 'we don't need them. There should be no Islamic kindergartens,' he said. An alternative approach is that, with proficiency in German serving as a gateway to Austrian society, immigrant children having little or no command of German would have to attend kindergarten for longer than their Austrian peers. Further, kindergartens with Arab or Chechen pupils would not meet requirements for obtaining state certification and benefits, and would have to close.[44]

The controversial backstory to Muslim kindergartens was a study com-pleted earlier by an Austrian–Turkish academic. Ednan Aslan, a professor of Islamic education at the University of Vienna, found that more than 10,000 children aged two to six attend about 150 Muslim preschools in Vienna. They learn the Koran, thereby assuring parents of receiving a Muslim education, but they also create parallel societies where life in a multicultural society is rejected. According to Aslan's figures, up to a quarter of Islamic kindergar-tens were sponsored or supported by ultra-conservative Salafist organisations. Combined with surveys showing about 40 per cent of Muslim refugees in Austria putting religious commandments above the country's laws, this was a concern to right-wing political leaders.[45]

On his path to becoming Europe's youngest political leader, Kurz issued another controversial statement on the rescue of refugees crossing the

Mediterranean. He charged that being rescued from a sinking boat, such as non-governmental organisations (NGOs) had tried to do, was 'no ticket to Europe'.

Belgium

Populism may perhaps have penetrated the European Court of Human Rights (ECHR). In 2017 it ruled that Belgium's ban on the wearing of the full-face veil did not violate rights standards. The court ruled that conditions of 'living together' and the 'protection of the rights and freedoms of others' were jeopardised. Therefore Belgium 'sought to respond to a practice that it considered incompatible, in Belgian society, with social communication and more generally the establishment of human relations, which were indispensible for life in society'. As the final salvo, the ECHR found the measure was 'necessary in a democratic society'.

Belgium and Austria, like France in 2011, implemented a ban on clothing totally or partially covering the face. Quebec too has used France as a model for banning the *burqa*. In most of these states, violators face fines and even imprisonment for repeat offences.

Germany

What are the results of not integrating migrants? Some claim they show up immediately in election results. In the US and Europe more and more voters have given their support to parties promising to reduce immigration numbers. This is without documenting some of the most sceptical of European countries: the *Visegrád* group, comprised of Poland, Czechia, Slovakia and Hungary.

The 2017 German elections are a caesura because the *Alternatif für Deutschland* became the third strongest party in the country. Academic Claus Offe accurately remarked that '"Catch-all" parties catch less and less. They pay the price for their centrist complacency, consensus politics, and their silencing of contentious issues.'[46]

Many different aspects of migration have come under attack. A leader of the Green Party was appalled by a Malthusian 'survival of the fittest' asylum-seeking reality where 'the physically strong – usually young men – have been able to make the long journey; families, children and the elderly are often left behind' (Box 3.3).[47] Then German Interior Minister Thomas de Maizière ruled out asylum for asylum seekers, who relied on people smugglers: they had 'no prospect of staying' in Germany.[48]

Asylum applicants claim that they usually have little knowledge of a country's labour market conditions or welfare benefits before they arrive, but

66

Box 3.3 Interrogating Angela Merkel

There's the question of how we can integrate all these new arrivals. How do we set up housing in such a short time? Where do we find the kindergarten teachers, the educators, the German teachers, the schools and job training centers? For that, you need human resources and time, both of which are limited quantities. And, of course, we won't be able to integrate everyone. Based on experience, with their levels of qualification, we should realistically expect unemployment levels among the refugees to be around 50 percent after 10 years.

Source: Interview with Boris Palmer, Green Party, 'Refugees in Germany: "We won't be able to integrate everyone"', *Deutsche Welle*, 24 August 2017, available at <http://www.dw.com/en/refugees-in-germany-we-wont-be-able-to-integrate-everyone/a-40139185>.

---

this notion assumes that no diasporas – or family members – exist to help migrants. An argument is also made that asylum seekers are guided by the circumstances of their journey and have no destination in mind: when they do choose a country, they look for places where their compatriots or relatives already live. That suggests that diasporas – and family members – do exist. Migrants also imply they may know the language that they may have picked up from the colonial heritage. Oddly, as a prime magnet for asylum seekers, Germany and Austria belong to one of very few Germanic-speaking areas anywhere in the world, other than southern Africa.[49]

Social integration processes run into further obstacles:

> People who have grown up in a completely different culture – where women have a different role in society, where religion has a different role, where gays and lesbians have a different role, where clothing has a different role – when those people come to Germany, they won't just leave all that at the border and suddenly adopt our culture. This just isn't likely.

Germans claim they were conditioned to tolerate *Gastarbeiters* in the 1960s. But 'Such a consciousness has not existed in Germany. We simply tolerated guest workers, and it's no wonder they feel as if they don't belong.'

Norway

Norway and Denmark are *not* immigration magnates; to the contrary, they publicise how rigorous the prospect of social integration will be. In Denmark a fiancée must be over twenty-four to join her partner living in the country.

Danish customs can seize property above a certain amount and hold it as bond for immigrants pursuing immigration procedures. Refugee housing tends to be in barracks rather than flats.

Norway's immigration policy may be less benign than Denmark's. Where Sweden accepted over 160,000 asylum seekers in 2015, Norwegians took in 30,000. In 2017 it took in only 2,000, representing the sharpest fall in all of Europe. According to Norway's Minister for Immigration and Integration, with 65 million on the move around the world accepting several thousand at home will only ever be a token. For Sylvi Listhaug, the priority is to help refugees in camps abroad; the calculus is that for the cost of helping 3,000 refugees at home, the government can look after 100,000 refugees overseas. One per cent of its budget, high by the standards of the Organisation for Economic Co-operation and Development (OECD), goes on foreign aid, which includes overseas refugees. Norway can also afford the cost: the Government Pension Plan of Norway has over US$1 trillion in assets, making it the world's largest sovereign wealth fund.

Excluding migrants is not just about keeping wealth to oneself. Listhaug put it simply: 'If you are an economic migrant, you are declined in Norway. We give protection for the ones that need that, that are in danger in their own country. But we also spend a lot of money to return people that are declined in Norway, also by force.' Unlike in Sweden, the police search for illegal immigrants in restaurants and elsewhere where black market labour is common. When caught they are deported: 'That has also decreased the crime in Norway.' Although it is expensive to deport people to Afghanistan or Somalia, if they are not in need of protection 'it's well worth it'.[50] The deterrence effect discouraging others from coming becomes all-important.

There are moral grounds behind Norway's harsh migration policy: 'people trafficking is a modern evil that is being fed by the system of accepting whoever turns up. If you smuggle an unaccompanied minor from Afghanistan to Europe, they say it costs between $3,000 and $20,000.' Young girls are sometimes sold to old men to finance the journey, and children are killed or raped on their way. Bringing smuggling under control is urgent, therefore, and Listhaug believed that Norway's model may become the new consensus.

Sweden

The definition of social integration varies according to the country in question. Is a person socially integrated if she has a home, works in a job, pays taxes, stays out of trouble? Is it about adopting the social norms and values of a society? Does this become a moving target where some societies demand greater integration and others do not? Sweden is held as an exemplary society where researchers are funded to produce integration standards. Not surprisingly, it has had the highest MIPEX integration score: in 2014 it was 78 out of 100.[51]

The chief factors determining the MIPEX score are labour market mobility, promotion of permanent residence, family reunification, educational opportunity, access to nationality, political participation and access to health. Sweden has made it relatively easy for integration requirements to match scores required for permanent residence and citizenship.

By all accounts Sweden works hard at integrating immigrants, often in innovative and individualistic ways. If someone has not integrated into its society, it was once believed, Sweden must try harder. The country remains a magnate for asylum seekers. Between 2014 and 2016 about 280,000 people submitted asylum applications – this in a country of 10 million.

For one integration specialist, a common policy assumption is that

> integration means people coming to Sweden being given the right conditions to establish themselves within and become a part of Swedish society. It's about having respect for basic Swedish values – you have both rights and duties here – and also having the right opportunities to establish yourself in Swedish society. The chance to learn the language, start working for example.[52]

Until recently Swedish language proficiency was a moot issue even if it affected labour market mobility.

An improbable right-wing party, the Sweden Democrats (*Sverige Demokraterna*), has challenged the overall consensus about integration and immigration (in a 2017 poll it ranked behind only the ruling Social Democratic party). Sweden Democrats has opposed an open-door policy on refugees, insists on control over the country's borders, and vows to police crime, especially in inner cities where no-go zones are said to operate. According to police reports, in 2017 some 2,000 violent Islamist extremists are said to live in Sweden.

Feeling it was outflanked by Sweden Democrats, the Moderate Party (*Moderaterna*) has also become more immigration-sceptic and has raised the bar for immigrant integration in a number of ways. For example, those applying for a Swedish passport need to live in the country for five years (three years if with a Swedish partner for at least two years). For the 2018 election year, it affirms three basic requirements for integration: 'In Sweden people work, in Sweden people speak Swedish, and in Sweden Swedish laws apply.' Populism today often refers to leaders who pander to public opinion, and they come from anti-establishment parties. But Moderate leader Ulf Kristersson's demanding integration policy revisions reflect mainstream values. Thus, 'you shouldn't be able to live on subsidies year after year without doing your utmost to learn Swedish so you can get a job'. He estimated that 'It takes nine years before even half of new arrivals have any kind of job. There are primary schools where the majority don't make it into high school. Gang crime is spreading: 279 shootings already this year, 124 injured and 38 dead.'[53] Swedishness has been transformed.

A trivial issue like the safeguarding of passports even needs to be prioritised. In 2016 stolen or lost passports totalled more than 60,000. Using a false passport to arrive in Sweden was therefore criminalised. People reporting lost or stolen passports had to be given passports with shorter validity.[54]

Effective social integration measures require funding, resources and opportunity structures. The goal is to reduce poverty and crime, ethnic schism and fragmentation, and ghettoisation. The Swedish maxim, 'ask not what migrants can do for Sweden but what Sweden can do for migrants', is gradually being reversed.

How does integration apply to adolescents being socialised into cultural and social norms? To begin with, refugee children, more than 37,500 of whom arrived between 2015 and 2017, supposedly need help understanding Swedish values. Some find it difficult to grasp ideas like freedom of expression and gender equality. These refugees, it is thought, have lived in unsettled societies and, when inserted into one where social norms and habits are different, they face integration hurdles. Some have also led gender-segregated lives; others request advice on issues ranging from sexuality to mental health. Resocialising adolescents, above all young men brought up with highly gendered stereotypes, may require time.[55]

A second question is whether refugee children really are children. At the end of 2017 Sweden's national forensic medicine agency examined 8,000 recent migrants lodging asylum claims as children. It found that three-quarters (6,600) were over the age of 18, the maximum age. In 2015 and 2016, at the height of the European migration crisis, more than 80,000 minors, of whom 37,000 arrived in the country without a parent or guardian, had applied for asylum. Then, too, the Migration Agency determined that 80 per cent of cases were adults posing as children. The Migration Agency penalty was simply to reconsider the applicant as an adult even though their asylum application provided false information.[56] As with passport scams, so 'refugee children' may be reasons why Swedes were turning to the immigrant-sceptic Moderate Party, if not Sweden Democrats.

Accusations of rape need to be taken very seriously, but in some countries they can be taboo subjects or are covered up. A third issue is the problem of rape in one of the world's foremost feminist societies. Writing in an Israeli journal, Juliana Geran Pilon noted that 'the lying had begun' in Sweden when 'the disparity between the numbers of anticipated and actual immigrants grew by leaps and bounds'. Tolerance was also questioned; Muslim immigrants admitted by the country 'were, as a rule, far less tolerant than the local populations in whose midst they settled'.[57]

Rape occurrences flew below radar, Geran Pilon claimed, and the comparative MIPEX seemed to have no method to capture levels of migrant criminality or rape. As befits gender-egalitarian Sweden, however, data collection has been far-reaching, and rape includes not just violence and assault committed against women. Under the category of rape, other forms of sexual misconduct are included that would not be recorded by police in other countries. New legislation has also been proposed to toughen existing anti-rape laws. Accordingly, the accusation that Swedish authorities have turned a blind eye to criminal behaviour by foreigners may constitute exhibit A of 'fake news' in Sweden.

Labour market progress is Sweden's best MIPEX result. In recent years, responsibility for integration shifted from its social security bureau, handling the provision of benefits to immigrants, to the employment ministry, which expects newcomers to improve their educational standing or gain access to skilled employment. In 2014 labour market integration was encouraging. More than 40 per cent of Syrians admitted into the country had at least upper secondary education compared to 20 per cent from Afghanistan and just 10 per cent from Eritrea.

But the labour pool was not as impressive after 2016. In March 2017 the unemployment rate among the foreign-born population was 22 per cent compared to 4 per cent among Swedish-born citizens. In 2017–18 8 out of 10 new jobs were intended for the better-educated foreign-born population, but calculations were it would raise their overall employment rate by just 2 per cent.

Yet political scientist Bo Rothstein found data that indicated how social integration assists economic development:

> There is something very strange going on in the current debate on refugee immigration. There is a lot of alarmist talk about youth gang criminality, problems related to labor market integration, falling results in school, honor-related violence and oppression, increased social tensions, housing segregation, recruitment to various terrorist groups, ethnic discrimination and lack of respect for liberal norms such as gender equality and secularization.[58]

Rothstein questioned whether large-scale immigration could fetter the Swedish economy. After all, it takes time for refugees to get a job in the high-wage, mainly unionised Swedish labour market. His answer was straightforwardly Keynesian. Immigration forces the government to invest in the public sector:

> We are talking about new pre-schools and schools, expansion of the public health care sector, education centers for learning Swedish, housing programs, immigration officers, vocational training and other 'active' labor market programs and so on. Much of this spending can be seen as investment in human capital.[59]

In 2015 Sweden took in 163,000 asylum seekers; the equivalent number for the US would be 5.5 million (it admitted only 70,000). In 2016 Swedish growth was twice the average of other rich industrialised countries. In this respect, the influx of immigrants *and* the costs of integration have produced a multiplier effect that adds up to a positive sum game.

Language does play a major role in determining how long it takes a newcomer to integrate into the labour market. Malmö University scholar Pieter Bevelander was less optimistic than Rothstein, admitting it could take a decade for the majority of 2015 migrants to be integrated: 'The available evidence in Sweden suggests between five and ten years to achieve up to a 60-70 percent employment level.'[60]

Australia

Like the US, Australia has been founded on the myth of the welcoming of immigrants. Because it is an island nation rather than a continental one, it is simpler to choose which immigrants belong to Australia and which do not. Research has found that

> most indicators suggest positive outcomes for refugees who settle in Australia. Nonetheless there are some individuals and/or communities that may be socially excluded, and there is discrimination against particular groups. Moreover, there appears to be growing concern that some refugee groups do not 'fit in'.[61]

Research findings on how refugees in Australia describe their intercultural contacts indicate that they primarily take place *within* migrant and refugee groups; this may be the case with refugees in most parts of the world. Far less contact took place between migrants and Anglo-Australians, perhaps because refugees lack familiarity with Australian history. An absence of bridging social capital results, in which connections are made to other ethnicities: through networking, searching for flats and looking for jobs.[62]

Migrant and refugee groups had a tendency to stay within their own group or speak in their own language even when other people who did not speak their own language were around. This could be the result of lack of self-confidence or inadequate English language skills. But refugees suggested that the media were responsible for creating negative racial stereotypes, especially of particular minority groups such as Muslims, African groups, or refugees.

Migrants were portrayed as receiving preferential treatment in terms of government housing, financial support from social services and other perks. Accordingly,

> the legitimacy of refugees to be in Australia and utilize 'our' resources was questioned. This detracted from refugees' sense of belonging and desire to participate

and was related to the discrimination and racism refugees experienced in other spheres such as housing and employment.[63]

A study found that 'refugees who were "visibly different" from the Australian norm were the most common victims of racism and discrimination. These included refugees of black African background and also Muslim women wearing a head scarf'. The consequence is that racism and discrimination negatively affect belonging and inclusion.[64]

In a different study comparing dominant and non-dominant groups in three Australian states, the authors found that divisiveness – too much 'sticking together' – was identified by majority groups as having a negative impact on social diversity. This 'staying together can also be interpreted as lack of acceptance of what is Australian, or isolating themselves from Australian society and culture, a lack of willingness to integrate'.[65]

Australians' preference hierarchy was loaded in favour of White people. New Zealanders and British people were most liked. Arabs, Muslims and Lebanese were least liked. Such attitudes were 'linked to the desire to maintain Anglo-Australian dominance (privilege) and the othering of non-Anglo citizens within the Australian context (feared loss of the "Australian identity")'.[66]

If Australia rejected outsiders,

It is difficult to argue that Australia's 'hard-line' tactics towards humanitarian arrivals arose from a position of desperation, as immigration into Australia over this time continued apace. This may reflect upon either the nature of the asylum seekers themselves or concerns about their source country and religion.[67]

Furthermore,

While Australia is a leading provider of humanitarian settlement, priding itself on dedicated resettlement programs to assist those legitimately channeled through United Nations programs, people arriving by boat (boat people) are often described as 'queue jumpers'. This controversial term has featured prominently in Australian political and public discourse, and whilst its legitimacy has been challenged, is now embedded in the popular lexicon. Hostility is directed at queue jumpers who abuse ideals of impartiality and fairness.[68]

Belonging or not belonging to a society are crucial factors determining the fluidity of integration and social cohesion. Anomalies exist, to be sure. Terrorist attacks may have more to do with radicalised groups seizing opportunity structures than with struggling against neocolonialism, discrimination and racism. But questions related to integration and social cohesion allow us to measure the slippery topic of welcoming.

Canada

The reasonable accommodation of differences is a straightforward request to make. In Quebec, itself a minority culture in English-speaking North America, discussion about the meaning of reasonable accommodation, particularly towards the religious practices of others, has been impassioned since the Bouchard-Taylor Commission was appointed by the Quebec government in 2007 to clarify the bases for an integration model premised on secularism and interculturalism. While other communities having immigrant background – Jews, Sikhs, Indians, Tamils – had their own stakes, it was Muslims who dominated the reasonable accommodation debate.

For over a year meetings were held across the province with different immigrant communities. But the small town of Hérouxville, outside Montreal, became the epicentre of debate. Its mayor and municipal council approved a code of behaviour for cultures in Quebec and, in a quasi self-parody, it enumerated how stoning women, burning them alive, female genital cutting, and refusing arrest by a woman police officer were prohibited. Healthcare professionals did not have to ask permission to perform blood transfusions. The wearing of *burqa* and veils, and using Muslim-only swimming pools were contested in this provincial town.

Perhaps it was not just the Muslim community that was the target of the Hérouxville code. Urban–rural divides figured in them as well:

> There is something else at work here, and it's the revolt against the big city, its ideas, its lifestyle, its influence. What happened in Hérouxville is the ultimate expression of the fracture between the metropolis and the regions.... Hérouxville was angered by the tolerance of Montrealers, by their passivity towards the changes brought out by immigration, by their multi-ethnic culture, their rejection of religion, their 'gay village' and their arrogant elites. For small towns such as Hérouxville, the real threat to their identity has little to do with veil-clad Muslim women, it is the urban world that is gradually drifting away from the traditional model.[69]

In other words, this may have been a case of a small backwoods town taking on the powerful city of Montreal. Or of Hérouxville tackling the Rest of Quebec (ROQ) – a jibe about Quebec taking on the Rest of Canada (ROC). Or we may find that Hérouxville since then has become a model of reasonable accommodation. In 2017 Montreal moved towards the Hérouxville code when *burqas* were banned when using public services. It was left to the bus conductor to decide whether a Muslim wearing the *burqa* had to remove it or not.

PROPOSITIONS

Evidence indicates that many countries now enforce more rigorous integration policies for immigrants. Policies that expand the nation so as to co-opt well-integrated migrants are welcome, but a narrow-minded variant of social cohesion leading to exclusionary politics is unjust and counterproductive.

If society is little more than a collection of individuals – the standpoint of many liberals – integration typically is a non-issue. If social order exists, however, bonds of solidarity and affective links can be damaged with ill-conceived integration. This may be the product of nativists not creating conditions for inclusion, or of strangers rejecting these out of hand.

In Table 3.1, I list a set of propositions focusing on international migration and apply these to each of the six case studies examined in individual chapters. The major patterns are that Russia's total out-migration of some 10 million since 2000 is slowing down but in-migration has not made up the slack. President Vladimir Putin is on record, however, as supporting increased immigration and, possibly with it, more robust nationhood. Britain seeks to reduce immigration levels – Brexit promises that – but immigration policy remains deadlocked with different parts of the British Isles supporting it against the Brexit bloc. There seems to be no respite to high immigration levels to the US, President Donald Trump's discouraging policies notwithstanding. India leads the world in out-migration and lacks interest in changing the in-migration status quo. South Africa struggles to cap in-migration since xenophobic violence does the construction of nationhood no good. Peru is a rare country, having little in-migration, though a twist of fate shows large-scale movement to the cities. I provide evidence to indicate how migrant-friendly each state is.

Table 3.2 gives data on migration trends since 2000, indicating what trends may affect future immigration patterns in these societies. They will be analysed in the chapters that follow.

A battle is being fought between the entrenched, far-reaching migration industry and hardnosed immigration-sceptic political leaders who have benefited from increasing electoral backing. David Goodhart, founder of Britain's *Prospect Magazine*, formulates the challenge this way: 'It is the task of realistic liberalism to strive for a definition of community that is wide enough to include people from many different backgrounds, without being so wide as to become meaningless.'[70] Unrealistic liberalism, as well as illiberalism, has no place at the table.

Table 3.1 Historical immigration and prospects for nationhood

	Historic homogeneity	Trends favouring homogeneity	Legal immigration	Irregular immigration	Expanding nationhood
Britain	Diverse	Decreasing	High	High	Deadlocked
India	Diverse	Stable	Low	Medium	Disengaged
Peru	Diverse	Stable	Very low	None	Unchanged
Russia	Diverse	Increasing	Stable	Low	Solidifying
South Africa	Diverse	Stable	Increasing	Medium	Weakening
US	Diverse	Decreasing	High	High	Contesting

Table 3.2 Net international migration, 2000–15 (in thousands)

	Net number of migrants 2000–5	Net number of migrants 2005–10	Net number of migrants 2010–15	International migrant population in country	International migrant population leaving country	Rank as destination country	Rank as sending country
Russia	1,735	2,157	1,118	11,643	10,577	3rd	3rd
Britain	968	1,524	900	8,543	4,917	5th	10th
US	5,149	5,070	5,008	46,627	3,024	1st	20th
India	−2,206	−2,829	−2,598	5,241	15,576	12th	1st
South Africa	1,072	1,403	600	3,143	841	17th	76th
Peru	−635	−490	−240	91	1,410	135th	44th

Note: Net international migration represents movement across borders of people who change their residence. This estimate includes both in- and out-flows of foreign and native-born populations.

Source: Migration Policy Institute tabulation of data from the United Nations, Department of Economic and Social Affairs, *Trends in International Migrant Stock: Migrants by Destination and Origin* (United Nations 2015 database, POP/DB/MIG/Stock/Rev.2015), available at <http://www.un.org/en/development/desa/population/migration/data/estimates2/estimates15.shtml>.

Notes

1. Migration Policy Institute, 'Immigrant and Emigrant Populations by Country of Origin and Destination', mid-2015 estimate, available at <https://www.migration-policy.org/programs/data-hub/international-migration-statistics>.
2. United Nations Department of Economics and Social Affairs, Population Division, 'World Population Prospects: The 2017 Revision', available at <https://www.un.org/development/desa/publications/world-population-prospects-the-2017-revision.html>.
3. Bauman, Zygmunt, A Chronicle of Crisis, 2011–2016 (London: Social Europe Edition, 2017), p. 13.
4. Migration Policy Institute, 'Immigrant Integration', available at <http://www.migrationpolicy.org/topics/immigrant-integration>.
5. Grzymala-Kazlowska, Aleksandra, and Jenny Phillimore, 'Introduction: Rethinking Integration – New Perspectives on Adaptation and Settlement in the Era of Super-diversity', Journal of Ethnic and Migration Studies, Special issue, 16 August 2017, pp. 1–18, available at <http://www.tandfonline.com/doi/full/10.1080/1369183X.2017.1341706>.
6. '"You Belong Here", Foreign Minister Sigmar Gabriel tells Germany's Turks', Deutsche Welle, 22 July 2017, available at <http://www.dw.com/en/you-belong-here-foreign-minister-sigmar-gabriel-tells-germanys-turks/a-39800501>.
7. 'Vatican Official to UN: Migrants must be Treated as Human Beings', Crux, 25 July 2017, available at <https://cruxnow.com/global-church/2017/07/25/vatican-official-un-migrants-must-treated-human-beings/>.
8. Sherwood, Harriet, 'Pope Francis: Prioritize Migrants' Dignity Over National Security', The Guardian, 21 August 2015, available at <https://www.theguardian.com/world/2017/aug/21/pope-francis-prioritise-migrants-dignity-over-national-security>.
9. Rutherford, Adam, 'A New History of the First Peoples in the Americas', The Atlantic, 3 October 2017, available at <https://www.theatlantic.com/science/archive/2017/10/a-brief-history-of-everyone-who-ever-lived/537942/?utm_source=nl-atlantic-weekly-100617&silverid=MzEwMTkxMTQ3NzY4S0>.
10. Manuel, Arthur, 'Are You a Canadian?', First Nations Strategic Bulletin, August–December 2016, pp. 1–2. See also Arthur Manuel, Unsettling Canada: A National Wake-Up Call (Toronto, ON: Between the Lines, 2015).
11. King, Thomas, Interview on Q. Interviewed by Brent Bambury, CBC Radio, 13 November 2012. Also King, 'Inside the Charles Taylor Prize Shortlist: Read an Excerpt from Thomas King's The Inconvenient Indian', The Globe and Mail, 7 March 2014, available at <https://www.theglobeandmail.com/arts/books-and-media/inside-the-charles-taylor-prize-shortlist-read-an-excerpt-from-thomas-kings-the-inconvenient-indian/article17382030/>.
12. 'Indigenous Protesters Confront Carolyn Bennett at Canada Day Picnic', CBC News, 1 July 2017, available at <http://www.cbc.ca/news/canada/toronto/indigenous-protests-ilde-no-more-canada-day-1.4187477>.
13. Flanagan, Tom, 'First Nations Property Rights: Going Beyond the Indian Act', Globe and Mail, 22 March 2010, available at <https://www.theglobeandmail.com/opinion/first-nations-property-rights-going-beyond-the-indian-act/article1209790/>.
14. Ibid.

15. King, Thomas, *The Inconvenient Indian: A Curious Account of Native People in North America* (Minneapolis, MN: University of Minnesota Press, 2013).
16. Wagamese, Richard, 'The Inconvenient Indian: The True Story of Native North Americans – 'Whites Want Land', *Globe & Mail*, 30 November 2012, available at <https://www.theglobeandmail.com/arts/books-and-media/book-reviews/the-inconvenient-indian-the-true-story-of-native-north-americans----whites-want-land/article5841075/>.
17. Churchill, Ward, *A Little Matter of Genocide: Holocaust and Denial in the Americas 1492 to the Present* (San Francisco, CA: City Lights Publishers, 2001).
18. Ishiguro, Kazuo, *The Buried Giant* (New York: Vintage, 2016).
19. McAdam, Sylvia (Saysewahum), *Nationhood Interrupted: Revitalizing* nêhiyaw *Legal Systems* (Saskatoon, SK: Purish Publishing, 2015), p. 25.
20. Ibid., p. 11.
21. Ibid., p. 34.
22. '"A horrible history": Four Indigenous Views on Canada 150', *Globe & Mail*, 1 July 2017, available at <https://www.theglobeandmail.com/news/national/canada-150/canada-day-indigenous-perspectives-on-canada-150/article35498737/>.
23. Palmater, Pam, *Indigenous Nationhood: Empowering Grassroots Citizens* (Halifax, NS: Fernwood Books, 2015).
24. Palmater, Pam, 'What is Aboriginal Identity?', Blog, 22 January 2010, available at <http://www.pampalmater.com/what-is-aboriginal-identity/>.
25. Bauman, Zygmunt, *Wasted Lives: Modernity and its Outcasts* (Cambridge: Polity, 2004), p. 66.
26. Ibid., p. 80.
27. International Organization for Migration, 'Migrant Fatalities Worldwide', September 2017, available at <https://missingmigrants.iom.int/latest-global-figures>.
28. Brubaker, Rogers, 'Populism's Perfect Storm', *Boston Review*, 11 July 2017, available at <http://bostonreview.net/politics/rogers-brubaker-populisms-perfect-storm#.WWeOMIkyuaU.facebook>.
29. Skidelsky, Robert, 'Inconvenient Truths about Migration', *Social Europe*, 29 November 2017, available at <https://www.socialeurope.eu/inconvenient-truths-migration>.
30. Rowthorn, Robert, *The Costs and Benefits of Large-scale Immigration* (London: Civitas, 2015), pp. 33–9.
31. Jenson, Jane, *Mapping Social Cohesion: The State of Canadian Research* (Ottawa, ON: Canadian Policy Research Networks, CPRN Study No. F/03, 1998). See also Jenson, *Defining and Measuring Social Cohesion* (London: Commonwealth Secretariat, 2010).
32. Foner, Nancy, and Patrick Simon, 'Fear, Anxiety, and National Identity: Immigration and Belonging in North America and Western Europe', in Nancy Foner and Patrick Simon (eds), *Fear, Anxiety, and National Identity* (New York: Russell Sage Foundation, 2015), p. 1.
33. Ibid., p. 4.
34. Guibernau, Montserrat, *Belonging: Solidarity and Division in Modern Societies* (Cambridge: Polity Press, 2013), p. 74.
35. Ibid., p. 180.
36. Guibernau, Montserrat, *Nations Without States: Political Communities in a Global Age* (Cambridge: Polity Press, 2000), p. 182.
37. Foner and Simon, 'Fear', p. 23.

38. Taras, Raymond, *Xenophobia and Islamophobia in Europe* (Edinburgh: Edinburgh University Press, 2012), chs 4–6.
39. 'A Cross-national Analysis of Immigration Policy Attitudes across Economic, Cultural and Human Security Contexts', *Social Science Research*, forthcoming, pp. 1–2.
40. Ibid., pp. 7, 10.
41. Ibid., pp. 14, 16, 18–19.
42. Foner and Simon, 'Fear', p. 12.
43. Brubaker, 'Populism's Perfect Storm'.
44. "We Don't Need Them": Austrian FM Wants to End Islamic Kindergartens to Boost Integration', *Russia Today*, 22 June 2017, available at <https://www.rt.com/news/393550-austria-closure-islamic-kindergartens/>.
45. Topcu, Canan, 'The Unwelcome Glare of Publicity', *Qantara.de, 13 July 2017*, available at <https://en.qantara.de/content/controversial-study-about-muslim-kindergartens-in-vienna-the-unwelcome-glare-of-publicity>.
46. Offe, Claus, 'Germany: What Happens Next?' *Social Europe*, 3 October 2017, available at <https://www.socialeurope.eu/germany-happens-next>.
47. Interview with Boris Palmer, 'Refugees in Germany: "We Won't Be Able to Integrate Everyone"', *Deutsche Welle*, 24 August 2017. See his *Wir können nicht allen helfen: Ein Grüner über Integration und die Grenzen der Belastbarkeit* ('We Can't Help Everyone: A Green Politician on Integration and the Limits of Resilience') (Munich: Siedler, 2017), available at <http://www.dw.com/en/refugees-in-germany-we-wont-be-able-to-integrate-everyone/a-40139185>.
48. Kroet, Cynthia, 'German Minister: Refugees Who Rely on Smugglers Have No Future in Europe', *Politico.eu*, 7 September 2017, available at <http://www.politico.eu/article/german-minister-refugees-who-rely-on-smugglers-have-no-future-in-europe/>.
49. Rowthorn, Robert, and David Růžička, 'Schrödinger's Immigrant', *Social Europe*, 14 September 2017, available at <https://www.socialeurope.eu/author/robert-rowthorn-and-david-ruzicka>.
50. Nelson, Fraser, 'The Norway Model: A New Approach to Immigration and Asylum', *The Spectator*, 25 November 2017, available at <https://blogs.spectator.co.uk/2017/11/the-norway-model-a-new-way-to-think-about-immigration-and-asylum-in-europe/>.
51. Migrant Integration Policy Index, 'Sweden', available at <http://www.mipex.eu/sweden>.
52. 'How Is Sweden Tackling Its Integration Challenge?', 2 May 2017, available at <https://www.thelocal.se/20170502/how-is-sweden-tackling-its-integration-challenge>.
53. 'Swedish Opposition Leader: "In Sweden, We Speak Swedish"', *The Local* (Sweden), 15 December 2017, available at <https://www.thelocal.se/20171215/swedish-opposition-leader-in-sweden-we-speak-swedish>.
54. 'Swedish Conservatives Propose Stricter Rules for Citizenship', *The Local* (Sweden), 7 September 2017, available at <https://www.thelocal.se/20170907/swedish-conservatives-propose-stricter-rules-for-citizenship>.
55. 'How Is Sweden Tackling?'
56. 'Sweden Child Migrant Tests "Reveal Many Adults"', *BBC News*, 5 December 2017, available at <http://www.bbc.com/news/world-europe-42234585>.
57. Pilon, Juliana Geran, 'The Strange Death of Europe: Immigration, Identity, Islam/ The End of Europe: Dictators, Demagogues, and the Coming Dark Age', *Israel Journal*

of Foreign Affairs, 19 September 2017, available at <http://www.tandfonline.com/doi/full/10.1080/23739770.2017.1375282>.

58. Rothstein, Bo, 'Immigration and Economic Growth: Is Keynes Back?', *The Local* (Sweden), 20 June 2017, available at <https://www.socialeurope.eu/2017/06/immigration-and-economic-growth-is-keynes-back/>.

59. Ibid.

60. 'How Is Sweden Tackling?'

61. Dandy, Justine, and Rogelia Pe-Pua, 'The Refugee Experience of Social Cohesion in Australia: Exploring the Roles of Racism, Intercultural Contact, and the Media', *Journal of Immigrant and Refugee Studies*, 13, no. 4, 2015, pp. 339–40.

62. Ibid., p. 355.

63. Ibid., p. 353.

64. Ibid., pp. 354–5.

65. Dandy, Justine, and Rogelia Pe-Pua, 'Attitudes to Multiculturalism, Immigration and Cultural Diversity: Comparison of Dominant and Non-dominant Groups in Three Australian States', *International Journal of Cultural Relations*, 34, no. 1, January 2010, p. 43.

66. Ibid., p. 44.

67. Sulaiman-Hill, Cheryl M. R., Sandra C. Thompson, Rita Afsar and Toshi L. Hodliffe, 'Changing Images of Refugees: A Comparative Analysis of Australian and New Zealand Print Media 1998–2008', *Journal of Immigrant and Refugee Studies*, 9, no. 4, 2011, pp. 362–3.

68. Ibid., p. 359.

69. Quoted in Lysiane Gagnon, 'Montreal Versus the ROQ', *Globe & Mail*, 26 February 2007, available at <https://www.theglobeandmail.com/news/national/montreal-versus-the-roq/article20393796/>.

70. Goodhart, David, 'Discomfort of Strangers', *Prospect Magazine*, 20 February 2004, available at <https://www.prospectmagazine.co.uk/magazine/too-diverse-david-goodhart-multiculturalism-britain-immigration-globalisation>.

CHAPTER FOUR

'Imperial' Russia

FEDERALISM AND ETHNICITY

Many countries in the Western world like to repeat the mantra that diversity is their greatest strength. Russia is not one of them, which suggests that it may not be a Western state but a Eurasian one, as many writers in the West, and some in Russia too, suggest. Furthermore, one of Russia's distinctive features is a claim to embrace an imperial identity, in the past if not also in the present. How has empire affected the (re)making of the country's identity? Can nationhood comfortably slot into it?

The 2010 census revealed that 81 per cent of citizens in the Russian Federation are ethnic Russians. In addition, some 25 million ethnic Russians in other post-Soviet states formed a 'beached diaspora'. Some have moved back to the Russian Federation or have benefited from passportisation policies of the Russian government giving them special status while living abroad.

Data on international migration to and from Russia (see Table 3.2) show how the country is both third largest sending country and third largest receiving country for migrants; normally states are one or the other, such as India, which sends millions of its countrymen and women abroad, or the US, which has taken in vast numbers of immigrants. A second distinctive feature of Russian migration is that over 10 million people have emigrated out of Russia – after India the largest diaspora (Table 3.2). They comprise business people, professionals, the mafia too, who travel to distant parts of the globe. By contrast, until recently, in-migration has consisted of Russian speakers beached in neighbouring independent states returning home. Rarely do they involve foreign celebrities like Gérard Depardieu or Steven Seagal being awarded citizenship. More than 11 million have moved into Russia since 2000.

A corollary is that Muslim minorities, such as Tatars and North Caucasian groups who live in autonomous provinces, form a constituent part of the Russian Federation. Uzbeks, Kazakhs and other Central Asians from new independent states also migrate to Russia, where there are more jobs. But they are usually not given a warm welcome and rarely apply for permanent residency or citizenship.

The wedding-cake structure of Russia's diverse nationality groups begins with twenty-one – and with the annexation of Crimea twenty-two – ethnically defined republics. Although supposedly consisting of non-Russian ethnic groups described as titular republics, many of these republics in the Russian Federation are made up of Russian majorities. For example, in the Republic of Karelia that abuts Finland, the 1926 census showed 57 per cent Russians compared to 37 per cent ethnic Karelians; by 2010 the ratio was 82 to 7 per cent.[1]

Russian nationhood is constructed on the basis of peoples who are *rossiiskii* (or *rossiianin*). The best translation may be the German *Russländer*, which subsumes both ethnic Russians but also other ethnicities living on Russian lands and colonised by them. *Rossiiskii* is juxtaposed with the narrower term *russkii*, which incorporates exclusively ethnic Russians.

Valery Tishkov, Director of the Institute of Ethnology and Anthropology of the Russian Academy of Sciences, believed that Russia should promote a strong *rossiianin* identity: that is, a citizen of multicultural Russia. When Russian citizenship is awarded as a result of naturalisation rather than *jus sanguinis* and ancestry, recipients are termed *rossiiane*, regardless of ethnicity and mother tongue. According to Tishkov, stress on a multicultural back-ground would best preserve the unity and diversity of contemporary Russia. He argued strongly against 'the race for regional identities' that in the 1990s produced secessionist movements. He believed that though *Russia* forms the English spelling of the country, *Rossia*, denoting a multinational Russia, would be more accurate.[2]

When Russians emphasise who it is that runs their country, they will bluntly say *russkii*, the core group. Helge Blakkisrud and Pål Kolstø make clear that 'the "R" in RSFSR (Russian Soviet Federative Socialist Republic) did not stand for "*russkii*" – the Russian word for "Russian" in the ethnic and cultural sense – but for "*rossiiskii*" – an adjective derived from the pre-revolutionary name of Russia, *Rossiiskaia imperiia*'.[3]

Russia prides itself on the existence of a Russian world, of 'global Russians' and 'transnational Russianness' wherever Russian speakers live. This notion rests on *sootechestvenniki*, or compatriots of Russians. It rings alarm bells when it is used about people in the former Soviet republics like Ukrainians.[4] When the USSR collapsed in 1991, 17 per cent of Russians lived outside the Russian Republic. By this calculation they form the second largest diaspora in the world after the Chinese.

Under Vladimir Putin, Russia is built on ethnic Russian nationalism even if references abound to *rossiiskii* multinationalism. Can nationhood, understood as core ethnic and ethnicised (assimilated) nation, plus immigrants who have integrated into Russia, support a statist nationalism? Are sentiments of love, loss, trauma, pride and strength sufficiently ingrained in Putin's speeches to recreate a Russian-based global empire?

Putin has argued that

> economic growth, prosperity, and geopolitical influence are all derived from soci-
> etal conditions. They depend on whether the citizens of a given country consider
> themselves a nation, to what extent they identify with their own history, values,
> and traditions, and whether they are united by common goals and responsibilities.[5]

Has this produced a socially cohesive Russia that exults in rediscovered pat-riotism, social solidarity and statism?

To be sure, social cohesion has little to do with political unity since social cohesion theory signifies positive migration outcomes: educated, produc-tive, vibrant communities. Cohesion's importance is also shown in what serves as its opposite: crime, lawlessness, xenophobia, marginalisation, poor health, low labour market integration, youth recidivism, low school results, violence, oppression, discrimination, increased social tensions, housing seg-regation, recruitment to criminal or terrorist groups, radicalisation, ethnic discrimination, and contempt for liberal norms such as gender equality and secularism.

Putin has enjoyed personal popularity, as high as 90 per cent after Crimea's annexation. The party he is associated with, United Russia, accounts for 76 per cent of all seats in the State Duma, but key is whether it brings together constituent parts of nationhood – nativists and immigrants, nationalists and oppositionists, rural and urban populations – in an imagined solidarity.

Most of the nation's economic and political elite is in United Russia's ranks, but the party pales in comparison to the former, mass-based Communist Party of the Soviet Union (CPSU). Whereas United Russia has up to 2 million members in all regions of the country (about 1 per cent of the total popula-tion), membership in the CPSU exceeded 19 million (nearly 10 per cent in 1987). Support for Putin and his party is not on a scale that results in positive outcomes for nativists or immigrants.

THE IMPERIAL IDEA

Russian identity has been problematic in a way experienced by few other peoples. From its beginnings in Kiev – the city that today is capital of inde-pendent Ukraine – the Rus' nation and the territories it inhabited were murky: 'The motifs of land, prince, and faith thus defined the essence and the boundaries of Rus' from early times. . . . the notion of the "Russian people" was absent, perhaps because of the tribal and ethnic diversity of Rus'.'[6]

An additional factor confounding Russian identity was the role of the West in defining it. In the late eighteenth century, much of the Russian nobility could not 'deny Europe's importance to the very sense of nationhood yet Russia's obvious cultural inferiority made the realization of equality a seemingly hopeless proposition'.[7] Throughout much of its history, Russia was invariably cast as a nation striving to become like the West: 'Russia's specificity as Europe's Other does thus not reside along the spatial, but along the temporal dimension, as the country which is perpetually seen as being in some stage of transition to Europeanization.' It was 'constantly depicted as a pupil, a learner, a truant, sometimes gifted, sometimes pig-headed. Russia was always a "not yet" or "just"'.[8] At some point, 'the idea of apprenticeship had to give way to the idea of partnership'.[9] But in the third millennium this has not yet happened, and US resistance to partnership has proven stubborn and unyielding.

In the nineteenth century, Slavophil philosophers contended with Westernisers over Russia's future. If the latter stressed Europeanness, Slavophils insisted that 'The Russian road entailed a mixture of communalism, moral truth, authority and an interpretation of freedom which was somehow lost in the West.'[10]

Identity was further complicated by its multidenominational population: Orthodox, Catholic, Muslim, Buddhist, Shamanist. When in 1439 the Russian Orthodox Church broke from Western Christianity at the Council of Florence and proclaimed Muscovy to be the Third Rome, it set itself up to be a supranational institution linked to the Russian Empire.

Russia's identity crisis was exacerbated by the historic crisis of the Russian state, which had served as an instrument of territorial expansion. One writer observed how Russia 'evolved as an empire–state rather than a nation–state, and the needs and rights of society have always been subordinated to the demands of the imperial state'. Just as importantly, 'the imperial state has been the product, as well as the cause, of much of Russian expansionary and militarist foreign policy'.[11] International relations expert Zbigniew Brzezinski has described how the Russian state 'deliberately did not conceive itself to be a purely national instrument, in the West European tradition, but defined itself as the executor of a special supranational mission'.[12]

Ambiguous state identity, to some degree, engendered indeterminate national identity. Following the USSR's disintegration, Russia's status was probed; a conclusion was that 'Of all the nationalisms in the territories of the former Soviet Union, Russian nationalism has proved to be one of the weakest.'[13] The model of cultural and ethnic assimilation into *homo sovieticus* – an ideological template obliterating difference – ceased to exist. Official Soviet nationality policy also acclaimed the goal of creating a Soviet nation, *sovietskii narod*, which would allow all nationalities to retain their formal cultural identities while injecting a socialist content and value system into them. These conceptualisations took many years to replace.

We are led back to Russia as possessing an identity that appears inescapably imperial:

> Although debates over Russia's national identity and interests have raged since the eighteenth century, the ideal of Russia as a superior civilization and a transcendent empire with a universal mission has remained. Indeed, a Russian national identity without this vision has yet to emerge.[14]

In the emotive language of Harvard professor Svetlana Boym,

> There is still, in present-day Russia, a great urge to find a single, all-embracing narrative – national, religious, historic, political, or aesthetic – to recover the single dramatic plot with devils and angels, black and white swans, hangmen and victims, that would explain Russia's Past, Present, and Future.[15]

EURASIANISM TO THE RESCUE

The most debated variant of imperial identity today is Eurasianism. It highlights the inseparability of Russians' love of vast open spaces with a communal consensus, or *sobornost'*. Through imperial rebuilding, both these values can be regained.

The Eurasian idea originated in the works of Prince Nikolai Trubetskoi and geographer Pyotr Savitskii. They

> tried in the 1920s and 1930s to give a theoretical underpinning to the identity of Russia as a non-European state. They downplayed the significance of the Urals by drawing attention to the parallel zones of humidity and the corresponding vegetation zones which characterize Siberia and European Russia but not Western Europe. They tried to derive the character of Russian society from the perennial struggle between steppe and taiga.[16]

Eurasianism has an ethnographic dimension as well: 'Eurasia is not merely a huge continent, it contains in its center a super ethnos bearing the same name.'[17] It forms part of a tripod that includes the Muslim world to the south and the Germano-Latin world to the west. The Eurasian idea asserts that 'Russians cannot exist as Russians outside a Russian state, making a multinational Russian state across Eurasia vital to the survival of Russians as a people.'[18] This point may hold true for the Russian Federation itself.

There is a mystifying feature to Eurasianism: 'Unlike Western realists who emphasize nation–states as key players of international politics, Eurasianists argue in favor of empires as the key units of action.'[19] Unlike most other contemporary narratives of Russian identity, this one begins with the belief that a Eurasian Russia must be at least the size of the former Soviet Union, possibly even greater.

Eurasianists have been divided into two factions. Modernisers emphasise restoring the USSR in some form while exploiting the vastness of the Eurasian Empire to ensure geopolitical balance and international stability. By contrast, in order to contain US imperialism, which is said to pose the principal threat to Russia, Europe and Asia, expansionists advocate further imperial enlargement of Russia beyond the old Soviet borders.[20]

For well-known Eurasian theorist Aleksander Dugin, the 'envisioned continental imperial alliance will span the Eurasian landmass from Dublin to Vladivostok, with Moscow ("the third Rome") serving as the continental capital'.[21] In 2013 the Silk Road Economic Belt, popularly known as the One Belt, One Road (OBOR) initiative, overlaps to some degree with the Russian variant since it spotlights Eurasian cooperation and connectivity. There is one problem, however: it represents a China-centred trade network.

Not all Russians are in favour of empire rebuilding. Many stress that Russia, like the USSR, has been a victim of its size. The country is so big that it represents a threat to its many neighbours – the security dilemma in which one country's resources force another's to keep pace. Nobel literature laureate Alexander Solzhenitsyn warned that Russia had to contain its geopolitical appetite: 'Should we be struggling for warm seas far away, or ensuring that warmth rather than enmity flows between citizens?'[22] He rejected both Eurasian and pan-Slavic futures for Russia, preferring to concentrate on Russia's internal makeup: 'When we say "nationality", we do not mean blood but always a spirit, a consciousness.'[23] Indeed, Solzhenitsyn ruled out building a multicultural Russia: 'Even after all the separations, our state will inevitably remain a multicultural one – despite the fact that this is not a goal we wish to pursue.'[24]

Multinational or multicultural?

Today's Russian Federation retains an enormous territory that spans eleven time zones, a population composed of over 160 ethnic groups speaking 100 languages and dialects, and a multiconfessional mixture representing all major world religions. It may be more appropriate to view the country not as a multicultural but multinational entity.

A major challenge facing the Russian state is incongruence of homeland and peoples. On the one hand, non-Russian minorities, especially Muslims, live in the Russian Federation; on the other, significant Russian diasporas are ensconced in neighbouring states.

In the late Soviet period, many Russians believed that too many foreigners lived in the USSR. Just before the country disintegrated, Russian nationalists raised the question of ethnic justice when they had become persuaded that 'small' or 'backward' peoples seemed to be receiving more than their fair share of a dwindling pool of resources. Such nationalists condemned the predatory behaviour of many non-Russians and asked why Estonians, Latvians, Armenians and Georgians enjoyed significantly higher standards of living than they did. An ethnic *kto kovo* question – who is taking advantage of whom – came to dominate relations among Soviet nations. Perceptions of unequal competition helped fuel the nationalist tide that was to overwhelm the Soviet Union.

Russian nationalists also felt that many lands that were historically Russian, like Crimea and indeed much of Ukraine, had been stolen by other nations. The Russian backlash against non-Russian titular nationalities was unambiguous. A reactive nationalism within a once-dominant nation emerged that grasped how it was losing status.

Post-Soviet Russia has therefore demonstrated the pre-eminence of the Russian titular nation. André Liebich has remarked that 'Today, for the first time in centuries, ethnic Russians represent a significant majority of the state they live in – 80 percent instead of 50 percent.'[25]

For ethno-nationalists like Solzhenitsyn, this high figure was not high enough because multicultural Russia was intolerable. Another Nobel laureate in literature, awarded the prize in 2015, Sviatlana Alexievich, was unsure that linguistic multiculturalism was valuable anywhere in the eastern Slavic states. She believed that in her homeland, Belarus, as well as in Ukraine, Russian should not be used to favour their nation building. Alexievich spoke against making Russian the official language 'in order to cement the [Ukrainian] nation. You are welcome to speak Russian, but all schools will use Ukrainian. There is no other way to create a nation.'[26]

The Russian Federation is often regarded as a multinational rather than multicultural state. With 22 ethnically defined homelands (or republics) and 63 territorially delineated regions (including the recent addition of the 'Hero City' of Sevastopol in Crimea), its asymmetrical federal structure resembles *matrioshka* nationalism, brightly painted Russian wooden dolls that enclose ever smaller dolls within them.

Seven million Tatars are scattered across Russia, making it the largest minority nation. Four million Muslims also live in the North Caucasus where mosques and *medrese*, or seminaries, had been shut down in the Soviet period but were recently rebuilt. Indeed, the collapse of Soviet power was an opportunity for re-Islamicisation of the region. Of various secessionist stirrings in the North Caucasus, Chechen president Dzhokhar Dudayev's bid for independence produced the most calamitous case of ethnic conflict in the Russian Federation to date. It was punctuated by two Russian military invasions in 1994 and 1999. In the second, Russian forces used air power and artillery indiscriminately against Chechen rebels. The wars had all the appearances of a classic confrontation between the subnationalism of an upstart, breakaway nation and the imperial nationalism of a recently humiliated great nation. Chechen independence was soon snuffed out and it remains a constituent part of Russia. Ramzan Kadyrov's selection in 2007 as its president established a *modus vivendi* with the Kremlin, which has not been untroubled.

Multiconfessionalism differentiates Muslim peoples from Orthodox Russians and other denominations. Today the revival of Russian Orthodoxy gives particular definition to the *ruskii* nation. Its psychological dimension is opportune for clergy and lay people alike: 'Most clergymen feel more at home with the [Russian] nationalists than with the liberals. The nationalists will not constantly remind them of their past collaboration with the Communist regime and demand purges in their leadership.'[27]

The canonisation in 2000 of Tsar Nicholas II and his wife Alexandra, killed by Bolsheviks in 1918, gave Orthodoxy broader appeal. Perhaps an even more momentous event, however, was Putin, after his inauguration in 2000, making the short walk through the Kremlin grounds to the Cathedral of the Annunciation for a thanksgiving service presided over by the Russian Patriarch. Aleksii II prayed that Putin would 'help us to disclose the soul of the nation'.[28]

Under Putin, the Russian Orthodox Church has returned to the status of *de facto* state religion. By contrast, 'Western' denominations like the Baptists, Adventists, Jehovah's Witnesses and Mormons have increasingly found room for proselytising limited. Of course, some religions face more repressive measures than others.

No clearer statement about the primacy of Russian Orthodoxy in the country has been given than the unflinching words of Patriarch Kiril when he still headed the Department for External Church Relations: *'Russia is Orthodox, not a multiconfessional country.'*[29]

NATIONHOOD IN FLUX

Whatever it is called in Russian, the country is drawn to an understanding of being an ethnic rather than civic nation. Ethnic Russians expect recognition for the role that they have played in its history and in nation building. By contrast, the concept of a civic nation, *grazhdanskaia natsiia*, would mark a break with Soviet-era ideals.[30] When communist ideology was discarded in the early 1990s, attempts were made to transplant Western, constructivist-inspired ideas about the nation–state on to Russian soil. The civic *rossiiane* identity is viewed with scepticism among the population because it *is* constructed. As with many other countries, however, Russia is multicultural in practice. This is particularly true in its larger cities.

Russian identity today faces challenges similar to those found in many Western countries: the pressure of economic and cultural globalisation, mass migrations, weakening of the citizen's attachment to one nation–state, dangers of extreme nationalism, and the rise of political extremism.

When immigration is condensed to movement of peoples between sovereign states, Russia does not have much immigration-based multiculturalism. But internal migration across a diverse and expansive territory does yield multicultural practices, seen in conurbations like Moscow and St Petersburg. What is the importance of recognising diversity in Russia?

A critique of multiculturalism was the focal point of Putin's 2012 article titled 'Russia: The National Question', published in *Nezavisimaya Gazeta*. Its subtitle sought to reconcile contradictory forces: 'Self-Determination of the Russian People: A Multiethnic Civilization Sealed with a Russian Core'. For the Russian leader, the

> failure of the multicultural project is caused by the crisis of the 'nation state' – namely, the state that has historically been built exclusively on the basis of ethnic identity. And it is a challenge to be faced not only by Europe, but many other regions in the world.[31]

Putin admitted that a multiethnic society was gaining ground but, inevitably, he capped it off by allotting it a Russian core.

In his annual Valdai discussion group meeting in 2013, Putin rhetorically asked a group of international Russia experts these questions: 'Who are we? Who do we want to be?' These were questions that Russians had compellingly been asking themselves over the years. He identified how ethnic Russians, the Russian language and Russian culture had become the focus of civic, state-centred identity – one of 'shared values, a patriotic consciousness, civic responsibility and solidarity, respect for the law, communion with the fate of the fatherland without losing touch with ethnic or religious roots'.[32]

Ethnic and religious groundings had become critical. The Russian Orthodox Church was an important partner in achieving Putin's political project. The Kremlin recast itself as the defender of traditional values: Russia as beacon of traditional virtues and family values, a representative of an authentic Europe, in contrast to a Europe in the grip of moral decay.

In order to reinforce Russia's self-governing character – the annexation of Crimea was still eight years away – Putin turned to confidant Vladislav Surkov to work out a doctrine that became known as sovereign democracy. Launched in 2006, its purpose has been to strengthen the sovereignty and unity of Russia and rebuild its status as a great civilisation. Consolidating Russia's identity rather than privileging separate multicultural ones within the state is its major objective.

Surkov, former deputy head of the presidential administration, regarded the nation, *natsiya*, as convening the all-encompassing supra-ethnic community of citizens in the country. It was defined not by ethnos but by citizenship, and therefore has a passing resemblance to civic nationalism.[33] But with over 80 per cent of the population being ethnic Russian, the concept of *natsiya* has left little space for expanding nationhood outwardly.

Sovereign democracy, for Surkov, reflects

> A society's political life where the political powers, their authorities and decisions are decided and controlled by a diverse Russian nation for the purpose of reaching material welfare, freedom and fairness by all citizens, social groups and nationalities, by the people that formed it.[34]

Notionally, this is akin to my understanding of nationhood.

Putin's article on the national question reshaped the concept of sovereign democracy by toeing a fine line between preventing both Russian nationalism *and* anti-Russian nationalism. He elaborated: 'I am deeply convinced that attempts to expound on the idea of building a Russian "national" mono-ethnic state are contrary to the whole of our thousand-year history.' In fact, 'it is the shortest path to the destruction of the Russian people and Russian statehood and any viable, sovereign state on our land'.[35]

The Kremlin leader warned of the danger of pandering to particular ethnic groups or, put simply, the dangers of multiculturalism. Instead he advocated that all Russians should espouse civic patriotism and conform to a single cultural code. We are drawn once again to the idea of Russian multinationalism as master signifier rather than multicultural practice.

Migration in Russia

If it were left to the majority of ethnic Russians, the Russian Federation would be *their* state, not one belonging to ethnic non-Russians. Ethnic nationalism received a boost in 2014 when Crimea was brought into the Russian Federation, part of the strong commitment since 2000 to configure Russia for the Russians. But Putin's rhetoric may only have formalised what the Russian population's perspective on ethnicity had been for a long time (Figure 4.1).

The 2010 census of the Russian Federation, confirmed in 2012, revealed that the total population had decreased from 145 million in 2002 to 142 million in 2010 (Figure 4.1). Russians who are Orthodox remain the preponderant majority at 81 per cent, in both 2002 and 2010. This fact alone may justify describing Russia as a mononational, mono-ethnic state. Neighbouring Finland is roughly similar in its ethnic profile: of the country's total population of 5.5 million at the end of 2016, 88 per cent consider Finnish their native language.

Russia's demographics are unevenly spread over the territory. In the Republic of Tatarstan, branded as the northernmost Muslim republic in

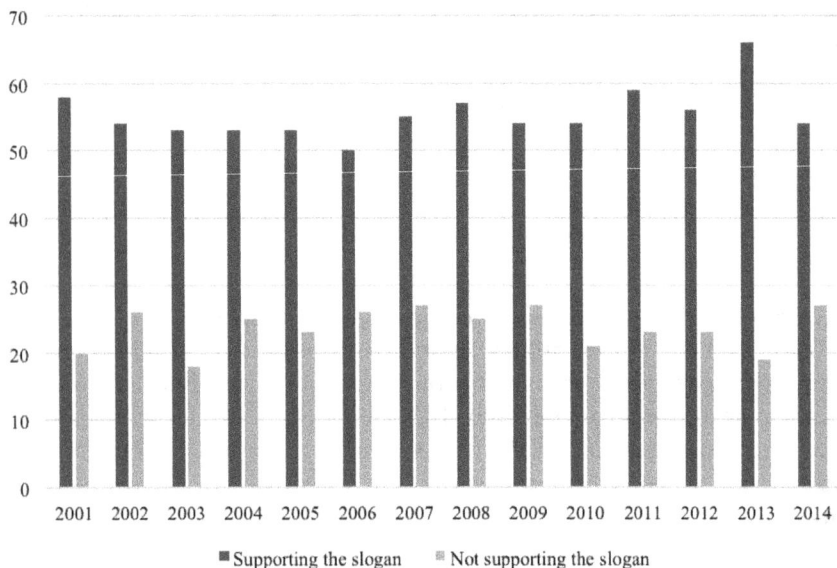

Figure 4.1 Support for the slogan 'Russia for ethnic Russians' (in percentages)

Source: Based on data from the Levada Centre (Levada-tsentr 2015, 145). Level of support is calculated based on who answered either 'I support this, it is high time to implement it' or 'It would be nice to implement, but within reasonable limits'.

the world, Russians account for 40 per cent and Tatars 53 per cent of its population. In the Chuvash Republic, Russians are an even smaller minority (27 per cent) with Chuvash making up 68 per cent. In two Russian Federation republics in the Caucasus, the minoritarian status of Russians is even more dramatic: they make up only 2 per cent in Chechnya compared to 95 per cent ethnically Chechen; and 0.8 per cent in the nearby Republic of Ingushetia.

Since the mid-2000s, the nature of migration to Russia has been changing. The share of labour migrants from Ukraine and China declined while the independent states in Central Asia – in particular, Uzbekistan and Tajikistan – together with the Caucasus region, now represent the most important sending countries. The 2010 census revealed that the Ukrainian diaspora had dropped to under two million, about one-quarter of Russia's total foreign-born population. But between 2014 and 2017, some half million registered refugees displaced by the Donbas conflict in eastern Ukraine made their way to Russia. Uncounted numbers also arrived, in part replicating historic migration patterns to the Russian Empire.[36]

The contribution of migrants to the national economy is enormous despite the low profile many of them keep. Migrant labour contributes more in taxes to the Moscow city budget than all of the oil and gas giants headquartered in the capital. Despite being a major budgetary resource for the state, migrants living and working in Russia are often regarded as a threat that requires strict regulation and control: for example, municipal residency applications.

Russia's migration management policy is designed to keep labour migrants on a short leash while extracting maximum revenue from the regulatory impediments it imposes.[37] After Putin called for more efficient adaptation and integration measures for migrants in 2016, for example, Vyacheslav Postavnin, President of the NGO *Migratsiia XXI Vek* ('21st-Century Migration'), reported that the cost and living expenses for migrants to attend integration sessions was 40,000 rubles (about US $700). Putin's goal of 'integration with the people' took a distant second place to serving as a lucrative visa service administered by the federal government.[38]

Most labour migrants can enter the country as a result of a visa-free programme with countries of the Commonwealth of Independent States (CIS); these include Armenia, Kazakhstan and Kyrgyzstan. In turn, for those states not members of the Eurasian Economic Union (EEU), Russia applies a so-called patent system regulating their labour. Initially designed to allow individual migrants to work as manual labourers or domestic workers, it has been expanded to include nearly all occupations. After listing work as the purpose of their visit, labour migrants under the patent system have thirty days after arrival to apply for a coveted work patent in order to be legally employed in Russia. Patents are issued for one year and require migrants to send in their monthly tax payments. Missing or late payments result in the permit being annulled.

Moreover, since 2015 all labour migrants must pass a mandatory Russian language, history and law test. Poor grasp of Russian was used to justify the introduction of this measure, but results showed an overwhelming 94 per cent examination pass rate. In fact, it was the testing fees that generated over 11.5 billion rubles (US $194 million) in revenue for Russian universities and affiliated partners. Rent seeking, then, was a glaring phenomenon endorsed by the state.

In response to the rise in violence that targeted immigrant vendors in 2007, the Russian government cracked down on migrants who worked in shops and markets, supposedly in the interests of public health and national security. In 2017 a ban was placed on the use of foreign drivers' licences, purportedly to improve road safety. One commentator observed how 'these restrictions legitimize racist tropes and harmful stereotypes by making them the basis of migration policy'. Furthermore, 'While many sectors of the Russian economy depend on migrant labor, Russian authorities use bans on employment and restrictions on mobility as an effective mechanism for extracting fines and bribes while also perpetuating the perception of the migrant as a threat.'[39]

Nationhood is not served by the exclusion of labour migrants through contrived regulations. To be fair, Russia's xenophobic response channelled through foreign worker patents is not dissimilar to Europe's policy concerning the Posted Workers Directive. This directive sets out rules for workers who are 'temporarily detached' from one EU member state to travel to another. Not well publicised, the programme allows companies to move employees across EU borders. They are entitled to the core labour rights in the receiving country: for example, maximum work regulations, minimum rest days, paid holidays, and access to local health, safety and hygiene standards.

The EU directive dates back to 1996, well before former communist countries joined the EU from 2004 onwards. One controversial aspect of the directive is the requirement that employers can offer only the minimum pay rate in the receiving country. This may be a boon for a posted worker from a country that has lower minimum wages. The minimum wage in France, for example, is more than three times Poland's monthly minimum. But it is much less than the pay guaranteed by French collective agreements to local workers. The race to the bottom becomes legally sanctioned when national salary structures can be undercut, as in Russia or the EU.

Critics also claim that the directive encourages cronyism in East European job placements in wealthier countries while, in turn, assuring Eastern European companies an unfair competitive advantage over local firms at home. Admittedly, ex-communist states argue that they have earned a competitive advantage because they have paid lower labour costs up to the present and now intend to make up ground after decades of communist stagnation.

Posted workers represent less than 1 per cent of the EU workforce. After Germany, France is Europe's second largest receiver of posted workers (286,000 in 2015), but it also is the third largest sender (140,000) after Poland and Germany. The phenomenon of undercutting salaries – those of Russians in this case – is widespread and often legally sanctioned. This is apart from filling state coffers with migrant money.

After winning the French presidential election, Emmanuel Macron went on record that 'The single European market and the free movement of workers is not meant to create a race to the bottom in terms of social regulations. It is exactly this that is fuelling populism and eroding confidence in the European project.'[40] In 2018 the EU ruled that posted workers would receive the same pay as locals. Russian worker patents similarly fuel populism and xenophobia.

The religious background of migrants coming to Russia is changing. About 41 per cent are Muslim or come from Muslim countries. The rural–urban character of migration is changing too: nowadays 70 per cent of migrant workers come from small towns and villages rather than large cities and capitals. This translates into a decline in their educational level: half of newcomers have no professional education. The percentage of workers who speak Russian at a basic level is declining too. Russian analysts believe that the preconditions for ethnic conflict are rooted in socio-cultural differences, not in economic competition, and that may happen under current demographics.

Increasing ethnic imbalances and lack of integration mechanisms for migrants, therefore, produce hothouse conditions for the rise in xenophobia. Russian residents demonstrate a negative attitude towards not just immigrants from outside Russia – Central Asia, Moldova, China, Vietnam, the Caucasus – but also fellow Russian citizens coming from other parts of the same country, especially the North Caucasus. A primary cause is they constitute visible minorities. According to public opinion polls, visible minorities evoke a strongly negative attitude towards newcomers in Russia generally, and the cities of St Petersburg and Moscow in particular.[41]

This was manifestly the case when in December 2010 thousands of youths, who supported Sparta Moscow football club, shouted nationalist slogans and exhibited violent behaviour at Manezhnaya Square in Moscow. The square's name became synonymous with ultra-nationalism. The Russian Public Opinion Research Centre (VCIOM) reported that, reassuringly, 65 per cent of those aware of the ethnic conflict in Manezhnaya Square said they did not support the participants, and the majority asserted that they would not take part in such actions (79 per cent).[42]

But other public opinion polls suggest that Russians, like many other outspoken groups in Europe, have decidedly mixed views about migrants; intermarriage is one. Thus a VCIOM survey on Russians' attitude towards international marriages disclosed that the most preferred marriages are between Russian couples (70 per cent). Middle-of-the-road attitudes were found regarding marriages between Russians, Ukrainians and Belarusians (45 per cent), Slavs and Europeans (44 per cent), citizens of the Baltic states (43 per cent), and Americans (41 per cent). Hostile attitudes were expressed in Russians' reactions to marriages between Russians and Chechens (65 per cent), Arabs (63 per cent), people from Central Asia (60 per cent), Caucasians (54 per cent) and Jews (46 per cent).[43]

Another survey question asked Russian citizens to identify nations and peoples that make them feel annoyance or resentment. Most often, respondents' negative emotions were directed at Caucasian peoples (29 per cent); the next most negative choice was people from Central Asia (6 per cent). Those who gave reasons for such aversion to these groups often expressed concern about terrorism (13 per cent) as well as the reluctance of newcomers to adapt to Russian norms and practices (11 per cent).[44] Not belonging accounted, therefore, for a small proportion of the sample.

Finally, VCIOM released the results of a poll on reactions to Putin's idea that stricter immigration laws should be adopted and criminal liability placed

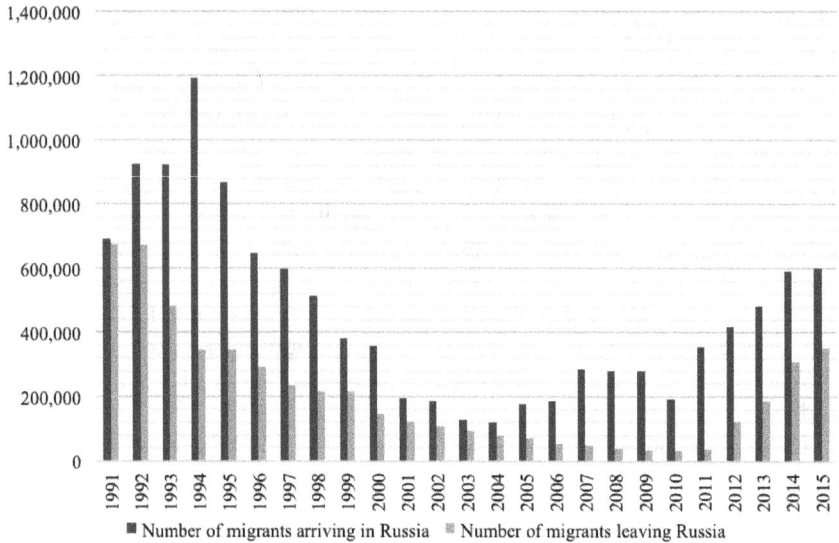

Figure 4.2 Migration to and from the Russian Federation

Source: Data from the Federal State Statistics Service, <www.gks.ru/wps/wcm/connect/ rosstat_main/rosstat/ru/statistics/population/demography/#>

on violators of rules and regulations affecting migrant registration. Seventy-seven per cent supported his view and 79 per cent endorsed his proposal to eliminate 'national enclaves' (in other words, secessionists) that might emerge on Russian territory.[45] When configured together, these attitudes show feeble support for including migrants in a bonded form of nationhood.

Hospitality towards others is rarely a given. The influx of labour migrants from Central Asia and the North Caucasus, most of whom are Muslim, has made Russia second only to the US in the number of immigrants who have become residents (Figure 4.2). Stigmatising these migrants remains plausible, given survey research. Recurrent terrorist attacks in Moscow and St Petersburg, far from Central Asia and the North Caucasus, have powered ultra-nationalist xenophobia. Indeed, the outcome of the 2013 Moscow mayoral elections told a mixed story when Alexei Navalny polled 27 per cent of the vote running against a Kremlin-backed candidate. He had run on a campaign of both anti-corruption and nationalism.

RUSSIFICATION WITHOUT NATIONHOOD

Russification is a term first used by Sergei Uvarov in 1770 and it has been used to help brand the nation. It signified that all subjects of the tsar, regardless of nationality, should be admitted into the Russian commonweal – provided they acknowledged their allegiance to the Russian state, its government and Russian Orthodoxy. Of the three components, Orthodoxy, Autocracy and Russianness, the last was most important.

When Nicholas I (1825–55) took the throne, his motto became 'Orthodoxy, Autocracy, Nationality'. Under Alexander III (1881–94), Russification was adapted so that all nationalities and cultures in the country would be replaced by Great Russians. Russification was unconcerned with small ethnic groups, given that Russia was dominant.

Variations on autocracy, nationality and Orthodoxy characterise Russia. Examining national anthems of the six countries analysed in this book can suggest which may approximate the nationhood principle and which pays no attention to it. The closest glimpse of nationhood found in Russia's national anthem is this: 'Long live our Russian Motherland, glorious and free our people are; Ages-old union of fraternal states.' But are fraternal states not already part of the motherland, and non-fraternal ones an adversary? Many Russia observers will say that Russia as autocracy, nationality and Orthodoxy is not far from the truth.

For academic Marlene Laruelle, 'as paradoxical as it may at first seem, the Kremlin interprets nationalism as an instrument in the service of Russia's triple goal: modernization, normalization and Westernization'.[46] If, historically, Russian nationalism has been associated with Russianness, today it is linked with modernisation and Westernisation too.

Rossiiskii (Russianness), a term primarily connected with state institutions, has evoked little emotional resonance in Russia.[47] Since 2012 Putin has not even used the related word *rossiiane* in his annual addresses to the Federal Assembly or in key speeches relating to national identity. He has employed the value-neutral address of *grazhdane Rossii*, 'citizens of Russia'. When *russkii* is introduced – the preferred term to describe the annexation of Crimea – it appears intimidating.

In a passionate and emotional speech at the Kremlin, Putin explained the russification of Crimea and Sevastopol as new subjects of the Russian Federation. He regretted that ethnic Russians were 'one of the biggest, if not the largest, ethnic groups in the world to be divided by borders'. He replaced the civic nationalist, state-centred *rossiiskii* adjective with the ethno-cultural *russkii*. The city of Sevastopol is *russkii*; more than 70 per cent of its population self-identify as ethnic Russians. The Black Sea Fleet is *russkii*, Crimea is native *russkaia* land (*iskonno russkaia zemlia*).[48] The speech shifted the focus of identity from state-centred to nation-centred, all but explicitly declaring Russia to be a nation–state.[49]

Crimea changed everything. It has allowed Kremlin rulers to change the story. Not just support for Putin but pride in Russia doubled. Patriotic sentiments soared and heightened society's emotional attachment to their leadership. Although coercion and control remain, 'the regime draws its power in part from its citizens', thereby incorporating the social aspect of power. Leaders stand behind the increasingly dominant narrative of a Russian people brought together by traditional values, a sense of patriotic duty, and encirclement by the West. Terms used to describe other peoples, like *russkie armiane* ('Russian Armenians') and *russkie tatary* ('Russian Tatars'), are not misnomers but new interpretations of Russian identity.

With the annexation of Crimea, Putin became a champion of Russian ethno-nationalism. Rival sub-state nation-building projects within the Federation face an uphill battle against cultural assimilation. Renewed emphasis on Russianness leaves little space for traditional Russian ethno-nationalists to mobilise against Putin.

Soft power and alluring propaganda entice both nativists and prospective immigrants:

> In today's Russia, some believe the fictions of the state because the broader social context makes it 'normal' to do so. Others are energized by a state that panders to deeply held national, patriotic, and religious identities and presents an emotionally engaging narrative. In both cases, ideological and emotional factors are outweighing economic ones.[50]

The Russian state is associated with preserving social and political order. It explicitly values power, stability and sovereignty more than freedom and democracy. There is nothing inherently anti-Western about these approaches. Russia seeks the West's recognition as partners, and accepts that 'liberal values should be established to strengthen, not weaken, the state'. But the commitment to 'the historically tested notion of a strong state' appears an institutional pillar.[51]

As discussed earlier, nationalism is not nationhood. In Russia the ethnic majority appears to reject overtures from large groups of non-ethnic Russians who may wish to join in an expanded community. Table 3.1 has hypothesised that under Putin the country's performance on inclusion and nationhood has solidified. Reluctance to recognise itself as an immigrant nation may put it at odds with other case studies that empathise with migrants on the move.

In an opinion piece published in 2017, provocatively titled 'Trump and Le Pen Would be Opposition in Russia', *Nezavisimaya Gazeta* argues how Russia's news coverage 'blasts Europe for multiculturalism, for receiving refugees from the Mideast and Africa, for tolerance to migrants', yet at home anti-immigrant policies are condemned by the authorities as 'an unacceptable form of nationalism'.[52] Survey research points to antipathy towards immigration into Russia. Is Putin, then, following other establishment leaders in the West such as Angela Merkel and advocating for immigration?

NOTES

1. Bremmer, Ian, and Raymond Taras (eds), *New States, New Politics: Building the Post-Soviet Nations* (Cambridge: Cambridge University Press, 1997), pp. 706–17.
2. Tishkov, Valery, *Ethnicity, Nationalism and Conflict in and after the Soviet Union* (London: Sage, 1997).
3. Blakkisrud, Helge, and Pål Kolstø, '*Russkii* as the new *rossiiskii*? Nation-building in Russia after 1991', in Peter Rutland and Raymond Taras (eds), *Nations and States in the Post-Soviet Space* (Cambridge: Cambridge University Press, 2019).
4 Suslov, Mikhail, '"Russian World": Russia's Policy towards its Diaspora', *Russie.Nei. Visions*, no. 103, IFRI, July 2017, available at <https://www.academia.edu/33957023/_Russian_World_Russia_s_Policy_towards_its_Diaspora_Russie.Nei.Visions_No._103_Ifri_July_2017>.
5. President of Russia, 'Meeting of the Valdai International Discussion Club', 19 September 2013, available at <http://en.kremlin.ru/events/president/news/19243>.
6. Hosking, Geoffrey, 'The Russian National Myth Repudiated', in Geoffrey Hosking and George Schöpflin (eds), *Myths and Nationhood* (New York: Routledge, 1997), p. 200.
7. Hart, Pierre R., 'The West', in Nicholas Rzhevsky (ed.), *The Cambridge Companion to Modern Russian Culture* (Cambridge: Cambridge University Press, 1998), p. 91.
8. Neumann, Iver B., 'Constructing Europe: Russia as Europe's Other', in Ulf Hedetoft (ed.), *Political Symbols, Symbolic Politics: European Identities in Transformation* (Aldershot: Ashgate, 1998), p. 259. See also his *Uses of the Other: 'The East' in European Identity Formation* (Minneapolis, MN: University of Minnesota Press, 1998).
9. Neumann, Iver B., *Russia and the Idea of Europe: A Study in Identity and International Relations* (London: Routledge, 1996), p. 200.
10. Flenley, Paul, 'From Soviet to Russian Identity: The Origins of Contemporary Russian Nationalism and National Identity', in Brian Jenkins and Spyros A. Sofos (eds), *Nation and Identity in Contemporary Europe* (London: Routledge, 1996), pp. 225–6.
11. Tuminez, Astrid S., *Russian Nationalism Since 1856: Ideology and the Making of Foreign Policy* (Lanham, MD: Rowman and Littlefield, 2000), p. 12.
12. Brzezinski, Zbigniew, *The Grand Chessboard: American Primacy and its Geostrategic Imperatives* (New York: Basic Books, 1997), p. 97.
13. Mirsky, Georgiy I., *On Ruins of Empire: Ethnicity and Nationalism in the Former Soviet Union* (Westport, CT: Greenwood Press, 1997), p. 163.
14. Prizel, Ilya, *National Identity and Foreign Policy: Nationalism and Leadership in Poland, Russia and Ukraine* (Cambridge: Cambridge University Press, 1998), p. 155.
15. Boym, Svetlana, *Common Places: Mythologies of Everyday Life in Russia* (Cambridge, MA: Harvard University Press, 1994), p. 228.
16. Dijkink, Gertjan, *National Identity and Geopolitical Visions: Maps of Pride and Pain* (London: Routledge, 1996), p. 102.
17. Gumilev, Lev N., *Ot rusi k rossii: ocherki etnicheskoi istorii* (Moscow: Ekoproc, 1992), p. 297. Quoted by Prizel, *National Identity*, p. 230.
18. Prizel, *National Identity*, p. 230.
19. Tsygankov, Andrei P., 'Hard-line Eurasianism and Russia's Contending Geopolitical Perspectives', *East European Quarterly*, XXXII, no. 3, Fall 1998, p. 318.

20. Ibid., p. 323.
21. Cited by Allensworth, Wayne, *The Russian Question: Nationalism, Modernization, and Post-Communist Russia* (Lanham, MD: Rowman and Littlefield, 1998), pp. 250–1.
22. Cited by Dijkink, *National Identity*, p. 101.
23. Solzhenitsyn, Alexander, 'Russkiy vopros v kontse dwadstatovo veka', *Novy mir*, no. 7, July 1994, p. 174.
24. Solzhenitsyn, *Rebuilding Russia: Reflections and Tentative Proposals* (New York: Farrar, Straus and Giroux, 1991), p. 19.
25. Liebich, André, *Les Minorités nationales en Europe centrale et orientale* (Geneva: Georg, 1997), p. 130.
26. Rudnik, Alesia, 'Belarusian Nobel Laureate Svetlana Alexievich Hit by a Smear Campaign', *Belarus Digest*, 11 July 2017, available at <http://belarusdigest.com/story/belarusian-nobel-laureate-svetlana-alexievich-hit-smear-campaign-29912>.
27. Laqueur, Walter, *Black Hundred: The Rise of the Extreme Right in Russia* (New York: Harper and Row, 1993), p. 243.
28. Anderson, John, 'Putin and the Russian Orthodox Church: Asymmetric Symphonia', *Journal of International Affairs*, September 2007.
29. Metropol Kiril, 'Rossia: pravoslavnaia, a ne mnogokonfessionalnaia strana', *Radonej*, 8, 2002.
30. Tolz, Vera, 'Forging the Nation: National Identity and Nation Building in Post-Communist Russia', 50, no. 6, December 1998, p. 1004.
31. Putin, Vladimir, 'Rossiya: Natsional'nii vopros', *Nezavisimaya Gazeta*, 23 January 2012, p. 1.
32. Meeting of the Valdai International Discussion Club, 19 September 2013, available at <http://en.kremlin.ru/events/president/news/19243>.
33. Mäkinen, Sirke, 'Surkovian Narrative on the Future of Russia: Making Russia a World Leader', *Journal of Communist Studies and Transition Politics*, 27, no. 2, June 2011, p. 149.
34. Transcript of speech by the Deputy Head of the Administration of the President of Russia, Vladislav Surkov, for the Centre of Partisan Study and Preparation of the Staff of United Russia, 7 February 2006, available at <https://web.archive.org/web/20061208020210/http://www.edinros.ru/news.html?id=111148>.
35. Putin, 'Rossiya', p. 1.
36. Russian Census Population Data, available at <https://www.rusemb.org.uk/russian-population/>.
37. 'Migrants Have Overtaken Oil and Gas Sector in Terms of Contributing to the Budget of Moscow', 6 August 2016, available at <http://russianeconomyportal.blogspot.com.es/2016/08/migrants-have-overtaken-oil-and-gas.html>.
38. Postavnin, Vyacheslav, cited by Mary Buckley, *The Politics of Unfree Labour in Russia: Human Trafficking and Labour Migration* (Cambridge: Cambridge University Press, 2018), p. 250.
39. Matusevich, Yan, 'Russia, Xenophobia and Profiting from Immigration Controls', *News Deeply*, 3 August 2017, available at <https://www.newsdeeply.com/refugees/community/2017/08/03/russia-xenophobia-and-profiting-from-migration-controls>.
40. 'Macron Pushes EU Labour Rule Changes on Central Europe Tour', 24 August 2017, available at <http://www.france24.com/en/20170823-france-european-union-macron-pushes-eu-labour-rule-changes-central-europe-tour>.

41. Akopov, Sergei, and Marya Rozanova, 'Migration Processes in Contemporary St. Petersburg', *NISPAcee Journal of Public Administration and Public Policy*, III/1, Summer 2010, pp. 78–9.

42. VCIOM Survey, 18–19 December 2010, based on 1,600 respondents from 138 towns from among 46 regions of Russia, available at <http://wciom.ru/index.php?id=268&uid=111221>.

43. VCIOM Survey, 3–4 July 2010, based on 1,600 people in 140 Russian towns from 42 regions of Russia, available at <http://wciom.ru/index.php?id=268&uid=13774>.

44. VCIOM Survey, 1–2 May 2010, based on 1,600 respondents from 140 towns in 42 regions of Russia, available at <http://wciom.ru/index.php?id=268&uid=13515>.

45. VCIOM Survey, 28–9 January 2012, based on 1,600 respondents from 138 towns in 46 regions of Russia, available at <http://wciom.ru/index.php?id=459&uid=112370>.

46. Laruelle, Marlene, *In the Name of the Nation: Nationalism and Politics in Contemporary Russia* (New York: Palgrave Macmillan, 2009), p. 203.

47. Rutland, Peter, 'The Presence of Absence: Ethnicity Policy in Russia', in Julie Newton and William Tompson (eds), *Institutions, Ideas and Leadership in Russian Politics* (London: Palgrave Macmillan, 2010), pp. 116–36.

48. Dreyfuss, Bob, 'Full Text and Analysis of Putin's Crimea Speech', 19 March 2014, available at <https://www.thenation.com/article/full-text-and-analysis-putins-crimea-speech/>.

49. Biersack, John, and Shannon O'Lear, 'The Geopolitics of Russia's Annexation of Crimea: Narratives, Identity, Silences, and Energy', *Eurasian Geography and Economics*, 55, no. 3, December 2014, pp. 247–69, available at <http://www.tandfon-line.com/doi/full/10.1080/15387216.2014.985241?src=recsys)>.

50. Robertson, Graeme, and Samuel Greene, 'How Putin Wins Support', *Journal of Democracy*, 28, no. 4, October 2017, pp. 90, 95, 98.

51. Tsygankov, Andrei P., *Russia's Foreign Policy: Change and Continuity in National Identity* (Lanham, MD: Rowman and Littlefield, 2010), pp. 5–6.

52. Ragozin, Leonid, 'Russia Wants Immigrants the World Doesn't', *Bloomberg*, 14 March 2017, available at <https://www.bloomberg.com/news/features/2017-03-14/russia-s-alternative-universe-immigrants-welcome>; see 'Трамп и Ле Пен в России были бы оппозиционерами', 31 January 2017, available at <http://www.ng.ru/editorial/2017-01-31/2_6916_red.html>.

CHAPTER FIVE

Multiculturalising Britain

A DEVOLVED UNITARY MONARCHY

It may be fair to say that nationhood is a characteristically British way of viewing a political society. Former empires have the incidental effect of drawing former subjects to the metropole. Over the years, the pursuit of status, wealth, education or simple employment incorporates them into an expanded nation. The concept of nationhood spawns more research in Britain than elsewhere, and Scotland is a favourite case study since, bereft of statehood, it nevertheless has virtually all the remaining attributes.[1]

At the top of the UK political system are four historic populations: English, Scottish, Welsh and Northern Irish. The English population is the juggernaut, however; in 2016 England's estimated population was 55.3 million compared to 5.4 million in Scotland, 3.1 million in Wales and 1.9 million in Northern Ireland.

Scotland had its own parliament until 1707, when, as a result of the Acts of Union, England and Scotland were 'United into One Kingdom by the Name of Great Britain' and were to be ruled over by the same monarch. Devolution in Scotland had to wait until 1997, when it was approved by a referendum, setting the stage for a Scottish Parliament in 1998. Of all the devolved entities making up the UK, this parliament has most powers, enacting primary legislation in all areas of policy not expressly reserved for the UK government and parliament. National defence and international affairs do not come under its purview. A bid to become independent in 2014 failed at a referendum where the margin was 55 to 45 per cent in favour of those opposed to independence.

Wales had been legally treated as part of England since the mid-sixteenth century. In 1997 it voted to support more limited devolution. The National Assembly for Wales was established the following year and was able to stipulate how the Welsh budget would be spent. In 2011 another referendum voted to widen its legislative powers, and popular support has strengthened for further devolution.

A Parliament of Northern Ireland was set up in 1921 but terminated in 1972 as a result of 'The Troubles' between the Catholic and Protestant populations. A Northern Ireland Assembly replaced it the following year and since then it has had many iterations, including being suspended for a time.

Other than its local government structure, England lacks self-government. The belief is that it is well represented through the Westminster system of government. Only recently have protests been voiced about the need for English rule when English affairs are before parliament. If it were not for the fact that Scottish MPs in Westminster voted overwhelmingly against it, fox hunting would have been re-established in England, a curious issue where English MPs did not get their way.

HYPER-DIVERSITY AND BREXIT

The revenge of the empire, as well as membership of the EU, has left Britain super-diverse, as experts have prosaically described it.[2] Empire ended when a series of colonies, from the Indian Raj to anglophone states in West and East Africa and the Caribbean, received their independence. The crucial date was 1947 when Pakistan came into being (on 14 August) and India followed the next day (as outlined in Chapter 7). EU membership, expected to end in 2019 if the Brexit process is successfully completed, was the result of another UK referendum. In fact, the UK only joined the European Economic Community in 1973, some time after the six founding states signed the Treaty of Rome in 1957. The UK approved it, in a referendum, in 1975, by a two-to-one margin. Significantly, yet another referendum decision put Norway against membership in 1972, foreshadowing unease with the treaty decades later.

Empire created British subjects overseas, many of whom subsequently migrated to Britain. In turn, the EU enshrined free movement of people over its frontiers, which ends in one form or another when the UK departs. These factors have driven immigration-based multiculturalism, making the country super-diverse. But multiculturalism as hyper-diverse *reality* has in recent years, paradoxically, prevented politicians from speaking about or campaigning for multicultural *policy*. Race, religion, language and culture among British subjects have been as diverse as the empire itself was broad.

Migration from former colonies was not the last stage in Britain's diversification. Free movement of people promoted by an ever-expanding EU led to a new phase of multiculturalism. The arrival in particular of large numbers of Central and East Europeans after 2004 raised the issue of whether the EU was playing fair in exporting several million people to better-paying jobs in the UK, in the process doing away with unemployment and under-employment in the poorer regions of the east. The overwhelming proportion of EU eco-nomic migrants are White, so racial preferences came into play in EU policy making.

In June 2016 a not insignificant proportion of voters in England, 53.4 to 46.6 per cent, backed Britain leaving the EU. Wales too supported Brexit, by 52.5 versus 47.5 per cent. But Scottish voters wanted to remain in the EU, by 62 to 38 per cent; these were the halcyon days of First Minister Nicola Sturgeon and her Scottish National Party (SNP). Finally, Northern Ireland, with a sizeable Catholic vote that amplified the majority sentiment of people in Eire wishing to stay, also supported the Remain side by 55.8 to 44.2 per cent.

The Brexit vote may have had at least as much to do with life in disad-vantaged English communities as it did with a 'stuff it, Brussels' mentality. According to an Ipsos Mori poll, immigration was the most important subject for voters ahead of the Brexit referendum. This was in spite of dire warnings from, for example, the British Hospitality Association, which warned how the sector faced a shortfall of 60,000 workers a year if the influx of EU workers was curtailed; 75 per cent of waiters and 37 per cent of housekeeping staff in Britain came from the EU. British farms were also heavily dependent on seasonal workers from EU countries, including 95 per cent of seasonal fruit workers. On the other hand, only 10 per cent of doctors were from the EU.[3]

Is taking part in British nationhood a major objective of immigrants from the EU? Research shows that Poles, Slovaks, Estonians, Romanians and many others are eager to integrate, even assimilate, into British society. The added value of learning English, including having their children taught it as a second language, is irresistible. The iconic image of Cool Britannia that prevails to this day, and the unique status of Britain as being not Europe *or* America, make Britain an attractive country to settle in. Of the 3.2 million EU citizens in the UK, Poles were the largest ethnic group in 2015 at 831,000, ousting the longstanding Indian population, now at 795,000.[4]

The reality that Central and Eastern Europeans were providing a reserve army of labour was not lost on disadvantaged British citizens. Though many of the newcomers are skilled, not many are given skilled jobs. Because of low professional salaries back home, they are prepared to accept more menial employment. The common perception that this drives down wages in Britain is an important factor sealing the Brexit result. It is corroborated by the fact that large-scale corporations eager to hire cheap labour were among the biggest backers of the Remain campaign.

The EU's freedom of movement clause endorsing movement – not migration – of EU citizens from Central and Eastern Europe is only partially offset by a much smaller number of British people living in the EU. Over a million have been long-time residents of other EU states. Spain was by far the top choice (over 300,000), and retirement apartments on the coast have proliferated. The next highest country for British emigration, France, had half the Spanish total.

Brexit was not just about equitable exchanges of people, however; nor was it about dislike of mostly White EU citizens arriving in the country. There has, in addition, been a general dislike of EU rules, its autocracy, perceived arrogance, democracy deficit, and the European Court of Justice that was making decisions for Britain. In other words, migration figured only incidentally in the Brexit vote. As far as international trade is concerned, many Brexiteers believe that the UK can reorganise the British Commonwealth to replace the EU as a revived UK-based trading area.

As Table 3.2 shows, Britain absorbed almost a million migrants in each of the five years ending in 2015. The trend may be weakening, I hypothesise, because of successive British governments' commitments to cut back on numbers. When commitments are not made good, other parties will vie for the vote. As in the US, irregular immigration has been high, making the government's jobs outlook more difficult (Table 3.1). Nationhood has now reached stalemate because fragile social cohesion and the state's lack of capacity to admit more migrants have made life difficult.

BRITISHNESS EXPLAINED

Nostalgia for empire is hyperbole on the part of Brexiteers. It distracts from concerns about the quality of their lives. By contrast, the hard core of the Remain campaign, the City in London, which has now expanded beyond the reaches of the Bank of England, the Stock Exchange and St Paul's Cathedral all the way to the London East postal codes and Canary Wharf, is wistful for Europe. Was London on the road to becoming Londonland? In the 2011 census, 37 per cent of London's population was foreign-born; that figure included 20 per cent from outside of Europe. In 2015 over 3 million London residents were born abroad. That year, 69 per cent of babies born in London had at least one parent born overseas.

Perceptions of the Brexit vote suggested that a narrower, more ethnicised voting block came out in its support, leaving younger Londoners who did not turn up in force at the polls in a state of shock. But largely disadvantaged people, living especially in the Midlands and north of England and left behind in terms of living standards, felt most aggrieved. They were even given scattered support from immigrant communities disenchanted with life in the UK.

In the 2016 referendum two different worlds existed, then, exemplified in Stoke-on-Trent, which had the largest number of Brexit supporters at nearly 70 per cent, and its mirror image, Lambeth, in London south of the Thames, where 79 per cent were for Remain (nine other inner London boroughs also voted Remain with figures above 70 per cent).

Conservative politician Norman Tebbit's famous cricket test (referred to in Chapter 1) may be relevant here, though with a twist. London's future does not augur well for Lord's Cricket Ground, given the trend line of ever-larger cosmopolitan populations not interested in the sport. But in the Brexit negotiations with the EU, Prime Minister Theresa May gambled that Britain could replace EU trade with worldwide and British Commonwealth-driven trade. Such a shift would mean reconnecting with the absent empire, including those cricket-loving supporters among the West Indians, Bangladeshis, Pakistanis, Indians, Sri Lankans and South Africans, in addition to Australians and New Zealanders. Hardworking, all-too-familiar EU nationals exercising the free movement principle might face a more precarious future.

In few places is the diversity of nationhood emphasised as much as it is in Britain. Multicultural theorist Tariq Modood has explained the reasons for this:

> As a theorist and advocate of multiculturalism I have always considered multiculturalism and national identity, identification and pride in a minority identity and in a British identity as mutually dependent upon each other. That is why I have argued for multicultural Britishness: a multicultural, multi-ethnic, multi-faith plural Britishness which can go hand in hand with the older idea of a multi-national Britain encompassing the nations and identities of the people of England, Scotland, Wales and Northern Ireland.[5]

With few exceptions, surveys have shown that ethnic minorities express high levels of identification with Britain and British identity. What is more, for my concept of nationhood, Modood's ideal is this: 'the Britishness that is being embraced is a Britishness capable of extension and hybridity, a country happy to accept as Britons those for whom hyphenated identities, such as Black-British, British-Muslim, British-Indian and so on are sources of pride' (Box 5.1).[6] It seems to be a ringing endorsement of enlarged nationhood.

How is nationhood forged in a kaleidoscopic, super-diverse society where rifts, cleavages and shaky social cohesion may split communities into the equivalent of 'Upstairs, Downstairs' societies? Or has banal English nationalism over several centuries produced the cement that unifies diverse migrants precisely because it is banal? Is the authority of the English language a form of bonding that pastes over differences?

A report produced for the Commission for Racial Equality in 2005 offered a definition of Britishness *sensu largo*. Focus group discussions and word associations 'showed that there was a common representation of "Britishness", organized around the following dimensions: geography, people, national

Box 5.1 *These Islands*

Indeed this ... idea paves the way for today's multicultural Britishness, for rethinking handed-down notions of our country and re-making our national identities. If this was not a realistic option we would have a problem. We cannot both ask new Britons to integrate and go around saying that being British is, thank goodness, a hollowed-out, meaningless project whose time has come to an end. This will inevitably produce confusion and will detract from the sociological and psychological processes of integration, as well as offering no defence against the calls of other loyalties and missions.

Source: Tariq Modood, 'Speech at the Launch of "These Islands"', *These Islands*, 31 October 2017, available at <http://www.these-islands.co.uk/publications/i275/tariq_speech.aspx#.Wfi6bbdYPI.facebook>.

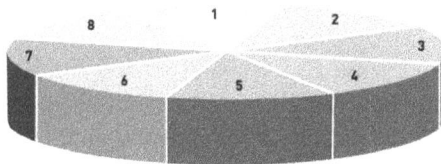

1 **Geography**
  Island nation
  Topography

2 **National symbols**
  The Union Jack
  The royal family

3 **Cultural habits and behaviours**
  Queuing
  Football, rugby and cricket
  Food and drink: fish and chips, tea, going to the pub, curry

4 **Citizenship**
  Passport

5 **People**
  English/Scottish/Welsh
  White English people
  Multicultural

6 **Values and attitudes**
  Democracy: freedom, the rule of law, fairness, tolerance and respect
  Reserve
  Pride
  Work ethic
  Community spirit, mutual help, stoicism and compassion
  Drunkenness, hooliganism and yobbishness

7 **Language**
  National language
  Accents: British, regional and class

8 **Achievements**
  Political/historical
  Technological
  Sporting
  Cultural

Figure 5.1 What is Britishness?

Source: Commission for Racial Equality (CRE), *Citizenship and Belonging: What is Britishness?* (London: ETHNOS Research and Consultancy, 2005), p. 34.

symbols, citizenship, values and attitudes, cultural habits and behaviour, language and historical achievements' (Figure 5.1). Among these, participants most strongly emphasised values and attitudes, people, and the cultural habits and behaviour of British people.[7] Admittedly, many of these word associations like democracy and freedom, tolerance and respect, tea and curry, appear as worn, archaic stereotypes of what Britishness signified not that long ago.

Of the three nations that make up Britain, 'England – in particular, White English people – was most strongly associated with Britishness.' Respondents may have only associated Britishness with White people when referring to the past. But they linked it to ethnic minorities and multiculturalism when discussing the present or the future or when they thought about citizenship.[8] Flawed methods used in this research may have yielded a Pollyanna-ish result. Nationhood does not comprise the sum of stereotypes of English people, and nationhood is shaped above all by historical memory.

God's treasured first-born

England was at a significant disadvantage when the Council of Constance ended in 1418, construing which nation should be regarded as God's first-born. French religious claims were the most influential – because they had so many dioceses. Yet it is England that has persuaded nationalism scholars to give it this distinction.[9] The persistence of Anglomania has helped it along.[10]

Already in 731 the Anglo-Saxon chronicler Bede referred to an English people, *gens anglorum*, in his ecclesiastical history of the English people. In 1362 English replaced Anglo-Norman as the language of parliament and the courts. The precocious power of English compelled a wicked medieval scholar to insist that 'whoever was unable to speak the English language was considered a vile and contemptible person by the common people'.[11]

Scotland was at that time not in union with England. In 1320 Bernard, Abbot of Arbroath, issued a legendary account forming the basis of the Scottish nation: 'The Declaration of Arbroath asserted the right of the *Scottorum nacio* to independence based not on dynastic legitimacy (which gave the king of England a strong claim), but on communal descent and a separate history of self-government.'[12] As early as seven centuries ago, then, 'The Declaration spoke for … the whole community of the realm of Scotland.' Scotland, too, intended to decouple itself from the English 'nation-in-the-making'.

The end of the Hundred Years' War, lasting from 1337 to 1453, and the rise of the House of Tudor, which reigned from 1485 to 1603, served as catalysts for the emergence of the English nation. The war had been fought on not a national but a dynastic principle, yet, indirectly, dynastic wars kindled national consciousness.

Parliamentary powers and the spread of common law were increased when England, not for the first time, abandoned the continent – an early Brexit prologue. Henry VII triumphed at the Battle of Bosworth in 1485 and brought an end to much of the fighting that had ravaged Europe. In 1509 Henry VIII rose to the thrown and established the Anglican Church, which used English as the liturgical language. He united England with Wales and added the title of King of Ireland. He uprooted the vestiges of feudal power and destroyed French Cluniac monasteries in England. English etatism began to develop around the person of the king. For Hans Kohn, 'England was the first country where a national consciousness embraced the whole people. It became so deeply ingrained in the English mind that nationalism lost its problematic character with the English.'[13] Constituting an island having a Celtic fringe, a sense of Englishness was brought into relief.

After she was crowned queen in 1553, Henry VIII's eldest daughter, Mary I, determined she would do something about the foreigners who had congregated in London. We do not have a record of polling results telling us about the prevalence of xenophobic attitudes nearly five centuries earlier, but we know that up to 12 per cent of the city's population (10,000 strong) were Protestant refugees and merchants. Most were from just across the English Channel – Holland, Flanders, Wallonia, France – but others originated in distant Spain and Italy. Queen Mary was determined to restore England to Roman Catholicism and create greater homogeneity. She made it a crime, for example, to be a stranger in London not in possession of denizen papers. Protestant refugees were soon invited to leave.

But an obstacle in her quest to expel foreigners arose. Londoners prized the guests from abroad. Indeed, according to literary historian Scott Oldenburg, 'although the English could have taken the opportunity of Mary I's reign to scapegoat strangers or aliens (the terms used in the period to refer to immigrants), the English more often seem to have valued and protected their immigrant neighbors'.[14] Her Royal Entry into the city on 30 September 1553 was countered by pageants supporting foreigners and organised by the Mayor and Aldermen. They were 'sending the message that Londoners were inextricably linked with the strangers living among them'.[15]

Popular assemblies against Mary's anti-alien policies persisted. A play whose origins may date to the fourteenth century was put on in her presence. Called *The Interlude of Wealth and Health*, it centred on a 'debate about whether Health or Wealth deserve more preeminence in England, and by extension whether decisions about strangers ought to be considered in light of the material or the spiritual interests of the realm'. Exposed to the clever rhetoric of the work, Mary learned about the trade-offs in hosting strangers. She was also made aware of the leanings of public opinion on the issue.

The relevance in mid-Tudor England to xenophobia in this quarrel between the Crown and her subjects can be exaggerated. Oldenburg prudently cautioned that these events should be viewed

> not through the lens of a transhistorical, homogenizing 'tradition of xenophobia', but within the context of tension between the state's position on immigration and the relative failure of the [anti-alien] proclamations due to the general population's lack of enthusiasm for anti-alien activities.[16]

What became evident was the split between the Court and the City of London, and the wariness of monarchs compared to the hospitality of the citizens.

Marian persecutions of religious dissenters at home proved to be much bloodier than the hounding of foreign elements. Many of Mary's policies were undone after her premature death five years into her reign. Elizabeth I, her half-sister, was to deliver more enlightened rule.

Henry VIII, father of Mary and Elizabeth, is nevertheless regarded as the godfather of the English Reformation, even of its zealousness. At the Convocation of Canterbury in 1531 he set forth a set of demands, the most significant of which was that the clergy recognise him as 'sole protector and Supreme Head of the Church and clergy of England'.

A promotional campaign accompanied this edict. Further religious imagery was constructed around Henry VIII appealing for English unity in the face of an anti-Papal conspiracy. The leading figure in the promotion of his cult was Richard Morison, who inveighed against the anti-Christ of the time – the Bishop of Rome – and appealed for English unity: 'Let us fight this one field with english hands, and english hearts, perpetual quietness, rest, peace, victory, honour, wealth, all is ours.'[17] In this struggle Henry was praised as the Lion and Chosen One. But Morison also cited Turks – a more formidable foe than the Papacy – as England's Other.[18]

Morison's was not the only voice raising the fearful spectre of the Turk. After Henry's break with Rome, Thomas More was comforted by the likelihood that the looming Turkish threat would unite England, and Europe, politically and religiously: 'all Germany, for all their divers[e] opinions, yet as they agree together in profession of Christ's name, so agree they now together in preparation of a common power in defence of Christendom against our common enemy the Turk'.[19]

In 1603, the last year of Elizabeth's reign, Arthur Dent published *The Ruin of Rome*, taking up the motif of Turks as threats. He warned that Christian brethren would be martyred under the twin persecution of 'the great Antichrist of Rome, and the cruel Turk'.[20] The Pope brought devastation with his clergy but the Mahometan religion swept across Europe with 'martial horsemen and Turkish armies' slaughtering many 'by their cruelty and barbarous inhumanity'.[21]

Cool Britannia may have had its genesis during Elizabeth's reign. England reached literary greatness, and more substance was added to English charm. A new era of scientific discovery was under way and by the seventeenth century it defined England as much as Shakespeare's plays or the High Anglican Church.

Religious and political nationalism began to develop among English inhabitants. Poet John Milton believed that England was indeed God's first-born: 'Why else was this Nation chosen before any other, that out of her as out of Sion should be proclaimed and sounded forth the first tidings and trumpet of Reformation to all Europe.'[22] The English people were identified with individual liberty. Oliver Cromwell appeared to be this great champion of liberty in the political sphere. He presided over the transition from the breakdown of religious medievalism and absolutism to widening trade interests and the awakening of the English middle class.

The new liberalism, optimism in the individual, unwavering faith in reason, and growing acquisitiveness that developed out of capitalism engendered a spirit of progress and self-assurance. John Locke (1632–1704) understood the nation as the reign of law, government by consent, and the natural rights of man. In the *Treatises of Government*, he celebrated private property and its enjoyment, and argued that liberty was founded upon property. England's rise to conscious nationhood was linked with the state's role as guarantor of individual liberty and happiness. For Kohn, then, the result was that 'A nation had come into being, directing its own destiny, feeling responsible for it, and a national spirit permeated all institutions.'[23]

Many writers have taken up the charge of defining Englishness. In his essay 'Of National Character', Scottish philosopher David Hume asserted that mixed government and the freedom enjoyed by all classes and religions were combined so that, paradoxically, the English 'of any people in the universe have the least of a national character, unless this very singularity may pass for such'.[24] Lacking a readily identifiable national character, subscribing to a low-key form of patriotism, and emphasising individual liberties over collective interests were the qualities that made England a contender for being the first-born nation.

What was there not to like about English nationalism, then? Among other matters, colonies such as India and South Africa suffered horrific nineteenth- and twentieth-century British atrocities (examined in Chapters 7 and 8). Small countries too witnessed barbaric colonisation, such as in the West Indies. In imperial times, English nationalism was simultaneously destructive and banal.

No one has better expressed this contradiction between grandiose empire and nationalist banality than social psychologist Michael Billig. He describes the violence that caused areas of the globe to launch struggles for independence. This havoc was conceptualised as 'extraordinary, politically charged and emotionally driven'.[25] Outbreaks of '"hot" nationalist passion' were located in remote or exotic parts of the world where nationalist outbursts could be confined.

Back home, Billig asks why was it that 'we' in the 'settled nations' were not categorised as nationalists and instead regarded as conducting an invisible brand of nationalism.[26] State coronations and major sporting events where flags are waved and national triumphs celebrated become classified, in contrast, as merely banal events reflecting banal nationalism. National identity is perceived as a 'form of life which is daily lived in a world of nation states'.[27] It is a form of life so entrenched and taken for granted that few even refer to it.

For Billig, it is not that national identity is no longer relevant, simply that the symbols that 'flag' the nation on a daily basis no longer register as significant. They are 'mindlessly remembered' and largely ignored.[28] What remains is the imagery of a dichotomous divide between 'our' civilised societies and 'their' violent ones.

Was Brexit, then, a flirtation with the myth of God's first-born? Colin Crouch underlines how democracy was a repository of national identity: 'while other historical bases of political identity were declining, national identity not only remained, but was being made more salient by globalization, immigration, refugee crises and Islamic terrorism'. Brexit harboured a mythical component of the British national narrative: 'National separateness ... is nearly always an illusion, because particularly in Europe there have been so many movements and mixings of people.'[29] Against the odds, it was precisely separation that Brexit backers voted for in 2014.

Nationhood exemplified: Race Equality Acts

It used to be said 'there ain't no Black in the Union Jack'.[30] Critics of British race policies may claim, however, that the country has made persistent progress to be fair to migrants of different races and religions. As early as the 1500s when Henry VIII and Mary reigned, more than 300 Black people lived in Britain. They had arrived on Spanish slave-trading ships heading for the Americas but were seized by the English navy.[31]

The British Nationality Act of 1948 granted freedom of movement to people living in British Commonwealth territories regardless of whether their passports were issued by colonial or independent states. The effect was to allow White citizens to move freely between Britain and the old dominions of Australia, New Zealand, Canada and South Africa. But migrants from the

Caribbean and South Asia who were British subjects also made use of their partial rights; they were classified as Commonwealth Citizens of the United Kingdom and Colonies with the freedom to enter and settle in the UK. Their arrival aroused apprehension; Winston Churchill in particular worried in 1954 about an influx of 'coloured workers'. A year later, he was behind an election pledge to 'Keep Britain White'.[32]

Tightening of controls on Commonwealth citizens came into force in the 1960s. The Commonwealth Immigrants Act of 1962 required Commonwealth citizens who did not have a passport issued by the UK government to apply for work vouchers; these were subject to quotas. Migration spiked as citizens rushed to 'beat the ban' that effectively was based on skin colour. In 1968 the Commonwealth Immigrants Act extended controls by introducing work vouchers for migrants whose parents or grandparents were not British citizens. The Immigration Act of 1971 repealed the automatic right of Commonwealth citizens to live in the UK. By that time many West Indian, Asian and African migrants were settling in Britain in large numbers.

Finding housing and employment for immigrants was difficult. Jamaican dub poet Lynton Kwesi Johnson wrote that 'England is a bitch; Der's no escapin' it.' Then a series of Race Relations Acts in 1965, 1968 and 1976 outlawed all forms of discrimination on the basis of race. Enoch Powell's 'Rivers of Blood' speech in 1968, calling for drastic immigration controls including repatriation, fell on largely deaf ears even if his rhetorical flourish carried on.

As minister in Harold Wilson's governments of the 1960s, Labour Home Secretary Roy Jenkins remarked how integration was 'not a flattening process of assimilation but equal opportunity accompanied by cultural diversity in an atmosphere of mutual tolerance'.[33] This has served as the immigrant standard-setter for some time.

The origins of multiculturalism, then, rest in the influx of postwar immigrants coming from diverse countries whose status on arrival in the UK was Citizens of the United Kingdom and Commonwealth. Together with subsequent British-born generations, they are recognised as ethnic and racial minorities meriting state support and differential treatment in order to overcome barriers in their exercise of citizenship.[34]

Since that time, the state has integrated minorities into the labour market and other areas of British society through the promotion of equal access: that is, equality of opportunity. A series of Race Relations Acts have displayed government commitment to this norm.

The 1976 Race Relations Act strengthened state support of race equality by recognising the fact of indirect discrimination. It imposed a statutory public duty to promote good race relations, applying them to public and private institutions. The EU's 2000 Racial Equality Directive was shaped by the UK's anti-discrimination legislation. It requires member states having no national legislation on racial discrimination to enact this directive as national law. The directive concerned only race, not nationality or religion, so many plaintiffs contesting citizenship on the basis of religious discrimination did not qualify for its judicial remedies.

The EU's 2000 Employment Equality Directive prohibited discrimination in employment and occupation on grounds of religion and belief, age, disability and sexual orientation. The Equality Act of 2006 extended the injunction to religious forms of discrimination involving the provision of goods, services and facilities. The Equality Act of 2010 went further and mandated public bodies to tackle not just religiously based discrimination but other kinds too: age; race and ethnicity; gender; disability; sexuality; and religion and belief. In this way the ban on religious discrimination has attained the same level of protection as racial discrimination.[35]

To be sure, Race Relations Acts have not allowed for positive discrimination or affirmative action favouring a particular racial group. In legal terms, this would represent discrimination on racial grounds and so would be deemed unlawful.

The sum of these Acts represents a defining British quality to the integration of minorities. It entails the institutionalisation of redress against racially structured barriers to participation. Racial discrimination has not been done away with. For a Black British MP, 'many non-white people felt that while it was possible to be in Britain it was much harder to be *of* Britain'.[36]

In terms of legislative representation, have non-Whites made progress in gaining seats in the venerated House of Commons? The 2017 election may have eroded Theresa May's majority, but across the board a record number of ethnic minority MPs were elected. Fifty-two non-White parliamentarians were returned compared to 41 in the last Parliament. Of these, 32 (12 per cent) of 261 Members were seated on the Labour benches. Nineteen (6 per cent) out of 315 Members were Conservatives. Liberal Democrats had one ethnic minority MP (8 per cent) out of a total of 12. Thirty years on, this tells a positive story about Black representation since the breakthrough year of 1987.

There were twelve new 'Class of 2017' ethnic minority MPs. Of the 41 ethnic minority MPs who stood again in this election, 40 were re-elected (23 for Labour, 17 for the Conservatives). Two Sikh MPs joined the House of Commons. Scotland did not elect any ethnic minority MPs, though one stood for office. In the Scottish Parliament, 2 Members of Pakistani origin have served in Holyrood since 2015 (1 SNP, 1 Labour), and in the Welsh Assembly two members remain (1 Tory, 1 Labour).

Diane Abbott was the first Black British MP to be elected and has held the seat for the Labour benches since 1987. Black MPs have increased in numbers so that after the 2017 elections, in addition to 12 Black MPs,

114

there were 5 mixed Black–White British sitting Members (3 Labour, 2 Conservative).

Neither 'God Save the Queen' nor 'Rule, Britannia' acknowledges nations other than Britons. It goes without saying that 'Britons never, never, never shall be slaves'. But the House of Commons has now been pried open by Black and mixed-race politicians, a testament to the march of race directives. To be sure, slavery has not been defeated and today it can target different racial groups. As journalist Felicity Lawrence writes,

> Since the Modern Slavery Act of 2015, British companies over a certain size have been required to report on slavery in their supply chains. Their statements are both shocking and admirable. Shocking because they make clear that the incidence of slavery has become normalised once again – and not just in criminal operations such as the illegal drugs trade or trafficking for prostitution, but in the mainstream economy.... They are admirable, however, in that transparency must be the first step to tackling this phenomenon.[37]

Modern slavery is not a British problem alone, though transparency is a mainly British innovation.

ATTITUDES TOWARDS MINORITIES

What are the British attitudes towards different groups of Black people regarded as visible minorities? Specifically, is there evidence of political exclusion and inequality of opportunity, or is there redress for discriminatory practices? My focus is on British attitudes towards Blacks and South Asians who emigrated some time ago (with a few more recent migrants) from their countries of origin. According to research conducted by five British-based academics, these findings 'may have serious and neglected implications for social cohesion and disaffection'.[38]

The main established ethnic minorities surveyed were Indian, Pakistani, Bangladeshi, Black Caribbean and Black African (Muslim groups were not distinguished). Results were compiled after the 2010 elections and subsumed 2,787 respondents. Among Afro-Caribbean Commonwealth nations, 60 per cent originated in Jamaica, 6 per cent in Barbados and 4 per cent in Trinidad and Tobago. For African Commonwealth states, Nigeria accounted for 27 per cent of immigrants and Ghana for 14 per cent. The remainder came from other nationalities.

Fluency in English was striking; it was 100 per cent among Black Caribbean immigrants. Black Africans came next with 85 per cent, Indian 80 per cent, Pakistani 70 per cent and Bangladeshi 63 per cent. On average, immigrants were better educated than those who remained in their countries of origin. Overall they had positive views about British political life. Moreover, across generations there was evidence of convergence with British norms, and there was less ethnic bonding with their own group. These immigrants generally avoided the trap of leading separate lives from British citizens.[39]

When asked if non-Whites were held back by prejudice, the Negritude of respondents appeared to be a factor: 58 per cent of Black Caribbean and 53 per cent of Black African persons of immigrant origin agreed prejudice was present. For Pakistani, Indian and Bangladeshi respondents, on the other hand, prejudice was in the 38–41 per cent range.[40]

Acquiring UK citizenship was unproblematic for 89 per cent of first-generation Caribbean and 99 per cent of second-generation respondents. Language proficiency and knowledge of Britain account for this. Figures were lower for people growing up in non-English-speaking environments, such as first-generation Bangladeshi (76 per cent), Pakistani (74 per cent), Black African (58 per cent) and Indian (51 per cent).

Were people from immigrant communities satisfied with British democracy? Figures were nearly the reverse of ease of those for acquiring citizenship: Indian, Pakistani, Bangladeshi and Black Africans expressed support for democracy in the 73-7 per cent range. White British were more sceptical (59 per cent), but Black Caribbeans (52 per cent) and those with a mixed Black/White background (47 per cent) were most critical.[41]

The authors offered only a general assessment of Muslim communities. 'Ethno-religious cultural concerns distinguish Muslim groups from other minorities,' they wrote. They did not elicit much sympathy from the British public.[42] Typical 'Muslim' issues such as dress left many British people indifferent or uncaring.

British Muslims

In defending the British approach to diversity, Tariq Modood contends that Race Relations Acts *do* add up to flexible *British* multiculturalism that rejects integration based on unity that would be achieved through cultural assimilation of migrants. Despite their strong identification with Britain and pride in being British, debates about Muslim identity often allege the little loyalty they have to the country.

Nasar Meer and his co-authors claim that some journalists and politicians stoke these anxieties by portraying Muslims as having difficulty feeling British. They reinforce a sense that many Muslims are outsiders and do not belong.[43] In one poll, 52 per cent of British respondents claimed that Muslims created problems, 47 per cent saw them as a threat, and 45 per cent believed Britain had admitted too many Muslims.[44] Another study based on group interviews with English-born Whites observed that Whites saw themselves as the rightful symbolic owners of the British nation.[45]

116

The Economist reported in 2017 that attitudes towards Muslims were hardening. In England about 4 people in 10 acknowledged that they have become more suspicious of Muslims following terrorist attacks in London and Manchester. While there was tolerance of diversity, attitudes to Islam were the exception. About half the respondents apparently thought that Islam posed a 'threat to Western civilization', and a quarter regarded it as a 'dangerous' religion because of its capacity to incite violence.[46] Race Relations Directives could not undo the framing of Muslims as outcasts.

Another major research project on Muslims was carried out between 2009 and 2012 by a consortium of six European universities. Known as EURISLAM, it investigated the socio-cultural integration of four different ethnic Muslim communities in Europe: Turks, Moroccans, ex-Yugoslavs (or Bosniaks) and Pakistanis. Six European states figured in the study: Belgium, France, Germany, Netherlands, Switzerland and the UK. Let me examine the UK results.

The survey asked national majority and Muslim minority samples a series of questions about religiosity, loyalty and belonging. On the role of religion in society, Table 5.1 gives data on whether Muslim respondents shared quite similar or very similar views with the majority population. In the UK considerable dissonance occurred between the British majority and the large Pakistani community.

Belonging signifies identification with, pride in and acceptance by the country in which one is resident. Muslims in the Netherlands identified most closely with their country of residence, but those in the UK identified least. A feeling of being recognised as fellow citizens was also highest in the Netherlands as well as France, but again it was lowest in the UK.

A related question concerned levels of interaction between Muslim minorities and the majority population. The greatest amount of interethnic contact took place in the Netherlands; again, the UK stood out as having the least amount of contact. When asked whether they were proud to be members of the national community of their country of residence, Turkish disenchantment was highest in Germany (70 per cent) and the UK (60 per cent). Conversely, all four minority Muslim groups exhibited very low rates of expressing the sentiment 'proud to be English'. Pakistanis were least likely to say this – just 14 per cent – when very strong and strong expressions of pride were combined.

The EURISLAM survey also examined Muslims' feelings of acceptance by the majority group. French respondents were best disposed towards Muslims, the other five countries being less inclined to accept Muslims as fellow citizens. Consistent with and possibly helping explain the finding that few minority group members felt proud to be English, no minority group in the UK believed that the people of the UK *regarded* them as English. Pakistani

117

Table 5.1 Subjective perception of distance to outgroup with regard to the role of religion: combined percentage of 'quite similar' and 'very similar' answers

	Netherlands	Germany	Switzerland	UK	Belgium	France
National majority group	29	16	22	7	17	30
Ex-Yugoslavia group	49	49	50	35	53	56
Turkish group	29	14	29	28	16	26
Moroccan group	27	32	41	24	32	27
Pakistani group	28	23	36	15	28	36

Source: 'Final Report Summary – EURISLAM: Finding a Place for Islam in Europe: Cultural Interactions Between Muslim Immigrants and Receiving Societies)', 18 July 2014, available at <http://cordis.europa.eu/result/rcn/59098_en.html EURISLAM>.

respondents came closest with about one-third sharing this view. A much stronger feeling of being accepted as Muslims occurred in the other five states with positive ratings exceeding 50 per cent. The picture of British welcoming is alarming, therefore. Significantly, the EURISLAM survey took place before the 2014 EU referendum.

The most divisive issue for non-Muslim majorities was the division of roles between men and women in the household. By contrast, for Muslim groups this issue was either non-divisive or of secondary importance. The perceived separation between the non-Muslim majority and resident Muslim minorities is related to the position of women and less so to purely religious practices.[47] In this respect, the UK can take comfort in perceiving the status of women as not a polarising issue.

A 2017 survey of European Muslims used different methodologies to analyse the Muslim experience in Europe. The Second European Union Minorities and Discrimination Survey faced the habitual criticism that it was intended to make the EU look good. But the research was impressive none the less, receiving responses from 10,527 respondents who identified themselves as Muslim when asked about their religion.[48]

Significantly, the majority of Muslim respondents (76 per cent) feel strongly attached to their country of residence. They are open towards other groups and feel comfortable having neighbours of different religious backgrounds (92 per cent). However, 23 per cent feels uncomfortable with having lesbians, gays or bisexuals as neighbours. With regard to belonging, some 76 per cent selected a value of 4 or 5, indicating a tendency to feel strongly attached to an EU state; only 2 per cent mention not feeling attached at all to their country of residence.

In the case of Britain, a high level of attachment (4.3) was recorded when compared to the fifteen other countries surveyed. Britain also scored very high in the absence of discrimination towards Muslims based on three specific grounds: skin colour, religion, and ethnic origin/immigrant background. These ranged from just 8 to 10 per cent. The EU-MIDIS II report placed Britain in the middle of rankings of Muslims who believe that discrimination is very or fairly widespread in the receiving society.

The EU-MIDIS II survey emphasising attachment to Britain is at odds with the EURISLAM study revealing little Muslim pride in being English. It is the nature of survey research to delineate the specific time, place and respondent group that differentiates surveys. Who commissions the research also plays an important role.

After Brexit

In the eleven years between mid-2005 and mid-2016, the population of the UK increased by just over 5 million people. The previous increase of 5 million had taken thirty-five years, occurring from mid-1970 to mid-2005. The 5 million added before that appeared over a seventeen-year period between mid-1953 and mid-1970. The push and pull of migration is not easy to predict, but in the UK significant increases to population size have been a regularity since World War II. It is not just the baby boom that has been responsible.

Immigration to Britain hit record levels just before Brexit – one that was skilfully exploited by anti-EU UK Independence Party (UKIP) leader Nigel Farage. About 650,000 immigrants, the highest ever, arrived before June 2016, spearheaded by a historically high 284,000 EU citizens (Figure 5.2). This was more than three times the government's target seeking to reduce annual net migration to below 100,000 a year.

After the Brexit vote, Home Office figures indicate that the backlog of EU citizens who applied to secure their right to UK residence rose in the three pre-Brexit months. The figures for applications for permanent residence cards alone jumped 83 per cent during the six months bracketing the referendum campaign and the vote itself. Joining British nationhood was an undeniable incentive.

In contrast, data after the Brexit vote suggested that migration to the UK decreased. Net migration – the difference between those entering and leaving the UK – fell by 81,000 to 246,000 in the year up to March 2017, marking the lowest migration rate in three years. Figures reveal a sharp rise of 17,000 in departures of citizens back to the Czech Republic, Estonia, Hungary, Latvia, Lithuania, Poland, Slovakia and Slovenia.

National insurance data also confirmed that Poles and other East European

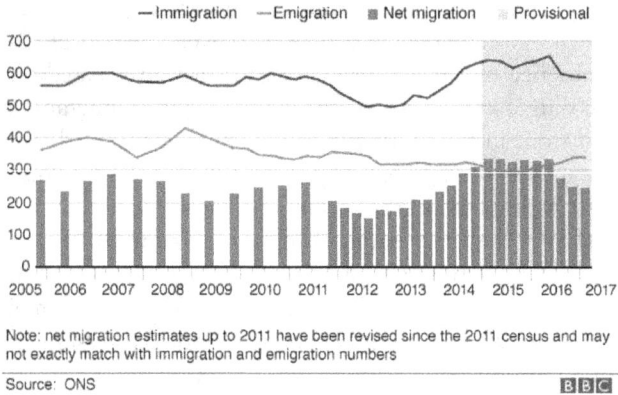

Figure 5.2 Long-term international migration to the UK (thousands)

Source: Office for National Statistics.

migrants registering to work in Britain dropped by 17 per cent in the twelve months up to September 2016. On the other hand, 11 per cent growth was recorded in Romanians and Bulgarians registering for national insurance. Overall, the signs that post-Brexit Britain is becoming a less attractive place for EU migrants to live and work have been unmistakable.

The proportion of EU citizens coming to work in Britain without having a specific job offer rose to a record high of 43 per cent, but 57 per cent had received a definite job offer. Despite Europe's refugee crisis, the number of Syrians claiming asylum in the UK fell by 317 to 2,298; the largest group were Iranians. EU migrants from Eastern Europe, then, not asylum seekers from Syria and Iraq, benefited disproportionally from the freedom of movement principle.

The UK government has published its first 'exit checks' – a count of all people who were known to have left the UK. For the year to March 2017, data showed that 97 per cent of international students from outside the EU with a visa to enter the UK either complied with their visa requirements by extending them or left the UK.

Brexit may have targeted 'excessive' immigration to the UK led by East Europeans, but there already were measures that could have reduced these numbers without pulling the UK out of the EU. Under pre-Brexit rules, citizens of other EU states could be removed after six months if they had not found a job, had no realistic possibility of finding one or required social welfare. Admittedly, well-networked EU migrants could find ways around these hurdles.

A criticism levelled at Prime Minister Tony Blair was that while in office he had agreed in 2004 to give Central European enlargement states immediate access to British labour markets at a time when Germany and France purposefully delayed access. It was ironic, then, that in 2017 his Institute for Global Change offered ways of reforming free movement rules without jeopardising the UK's membership of the EU single market.

Blair's proposal required that EU nationals should already have offers of work when they arrived. Those who did not receive permission to stay would be banned from claiming benefits, opening bank accounts or renting a home. Free healthcare would be available only to employed migrants. Universities could charge EU nationals tuition fees that were higher than for UK students. Free movement could be retained even while it imposed restrictive rules on access to benefits.

As part of extricating the UK from the free movement clause, the Blair recommendation appears reasonable. But it came too late to tip the Brexit balance. If anyone was responsible for enticing Eastern Europeans to the UK, the argument is made, it was the Blair government.

Then there is Scotland and its pointed reference to nationhood. According to Michael Higgins, President of Ireland, 'its Scottish expression, through thinkers such as Adam Smith and David Hume, affirmed that mutual sympathy – the capacity to imagine ourselves in the place of others – and natural sociability constitute the heart of human motivations'.[49] This is a moving way to understand nationhood. What about its practicalities, then?

Not for the first time, former Chief Minister Alex Salmond has railed about how, 'as a nation', Scotland has the right to determine its own future: 'There are many people who may have questions about Scottish independence, but ask them the fundamental question: does Scotland have the right to decide? Of course the answer is "yes", because anything else undermines Scottish nationhood'.

Charging Prime Minister May with 'finger wagging at Scotland', he warned that her efforts to block a second independence referendum would 'backfire spectacularly'. Salmond added: 'no self-respecting Scot will take a Westminster Prime Minister doing that'. In fact, 'Theresa May will rue the day when she edged towards telling the Scottish people what they can and can't do in expressing their nationhood.'[50]

NOTES

1. Bell, Ian A. (ed.), *Peripheral Visions: Images of Nationhood in Contemporary British Fiction* (Cardiff: University of Wales Press, 1995); Canovan, Margaret, *Nationhood and Political Theory* (Cheltenham: Edward Elgar, 1998); Davidson, Neil, *The Origins of Scottish Nationhood* (London: Pluto Press, 2000); Grant, Alexander, *Independence and Nationhood: Scotland 1306–1469* (Edinburgh: Edinburgh University Press, 1991);

Kenney, Michael, *The Politics of English Nationhood* (Oxford: Oxford University Press, 2014); Kidd, Colin, *British Identities before Nationalism: Ethnicity and Nationhood in the Atlantic World, 1600–1800* (Cambridge: Cambridge University Press, 2006).

2. For specific reasons bearing on Irish history, I exclude Northern Ireland from this analysis.

3. Kottasová, Ivana, 'Why Britain Needs the Immigrants It Doesn't Want', *CNN*, 18 October 2017, available at <http://money.cnn.com/2017/10/18/news/economy/brexit-immigration-uk-eu/index.html>.

4. Garapich, Michal P., *London's Polish Borders: Transnationalizing Class and Ethnicity among Polish Migrants in London* (New York: Ibidem Press, 2016).

5. Modood, Tariq, 'Speech at the Launch of "These Islands"', *These Islands*, 31 October 2017, available at <http://www.these-islands.co.uk/publications/i275/tariq_speech.aspx#.Wfi6b-bdYPI.facebook>.

6. Ibid.

7. Commission for Racial Equality, *Citizenship and Belonging: What is Britishness?* (London: ETHNOS Research and Consultancy, 2005), pp. 18, 33.

8. Ibid., p. 22.

9. Greenfeld, Liah, *Nationalism: Five Roads to Modernity* (Cambridge, MA: Harvard University Press, 1993), Ch. 1.

10. Buruma, Ian, *Anglomania: A European Love Affair* (New York: Vintage, 2000).

11. Hertz, Friedrich Otto, *Nationality in History and Politics: A Study of the Psychology and Sociology of National Sentiment and Character* (London: K. Paul, Trench, Trubner & Co., 1945), p. 83.

12. Gat, Azar, *Nations: The Long History and Deep Roots of Political Ethnicity and Nationalism* (Cambridge: Cambridge University Press, 2012), p. 231.

13. Kohn, Hans, *The Idea of Nationalism: A Study in its Origins and Background* (London: Macmillan, 1948), p. 178.

14. Oldenburg, Scott, 'Toward a Multicultural Mid-Tudor England: The Queen's Royal Entry Circa 1553, *The Interlude of Wealth and Health*, and the Question of Strangers in the Reign of Mary I', *ELH (English Literary History)*, 76, 2009, p. 100.

15. Ibid., p. 107.

16. Ibid., pp. 114, 120.

17. Morysen, Richarde, *An Exhortation to Styrre All Englysh Men to the Defence of Theyr Countreye* (Amsterdam: Theatrum Orbis Terrarum, 1972), p. d8r.

18. Ibid., p. a3r.

19. More, Thomas, *A Dialogue of Comfort against Tribulation* [1535], ed. by Frank Manley (New Haven, CT: Yale University Press, 1977), p. 40.

20. Dent, Arthur, *The Ruin of Rome or an Exposition upon the Whole Revelation* (London: T. Kelley, 1841), p. 71.

21. Ibid., p. 115.

22. Cited by Kohn, *The Idea of Nationalism*, p. 171.

23. Ibid., p. 183.

24. Cited by Frederick Hertz, *Nationality in History and Politics* (London: Routledge and Kegan Paul, 1966), p. 44.

25. Billig, Michael, *Banal Nationalism* (Thousand Oaks, CA: Sage, 1995), p. 44.

26. Ibid., p. 47.

27. Ibid., p. 68.

28. Ibid., p. 144.
29. Crouch, Colin, 'Nations are Political Constructs', *Social Europe*, 19 May 2017, available at <https://www.socialeurope.eu/2017/05/nations-political-constructs/>.
30. Gilroy, Paul, *'There Ain't No Black in the Union Jack': The Cultural Politics of Race and Nation* (Chicago, IL: University of Chicago Press, 1991).
31. Qureshi, Sadiah, 'We Prefer Their Company', *London Review of Books*, 39, no. 12, 15 June 2017, p. 40, available at <https://www.lrb.co.uk/v39/n12/sadiah-qureshi/we-prefer-their-company>.
32. Smith, David, 'What Churchill Said about British Immigrants', *The Guardian*, 5 August 2007, available at <https://www.theguardian.com/uk/2007/aug/05/race.past>.
33. Cited by Adonis, Andrew, and Keith Thomas (eds), *Roy Jenkins: A Retrospective* (Oxford: Oxford University Press, 2004), p. 142.
34. Thomassen, Lasse, *British Multiculturalism and the Politics of Representation* (Edinburgh: Edinburgh University Press, 2017).
35. Meer, Nasar, Claire Dwyer and Tariq Modood, 'Beyond "Angry Muslims"? Reporting Muslim Voices in the British Press', *Journal of Media and Religion*, 9, no. 4, 2010, pp. 216–31.
36. Olusoga, David, 'The Reality of Being Black in Today's Britain', *The Guardian*, 30 October 2016. See also his *Black and British: A Forgotten History* (London: Pan Macmillan, 2016), available at <https://www.theguardian.com/commentisfree/2016/oct/30/what-it-means-to-be-black-in-britain-today>.
37. Lawrence, Felicity, 'How did we let modern slavery become part of our everyday lives?', *The Guardian*, 2 April 2018, available at <https://www.theguardian.com/commentisfree/2018/apr/02/modern-slavery-daily-life-exploitation-goods-services>.
38. Heath, Anthony, Stephen D. Fisher, Gemma Rosenblatt, David Sanders and Maria Sobolewska, *The Political Integration of Ethnic Minorities in Britain* (Oxford: Oxford University Press, 2013), p. 12.
39. Ibid., pp. 28, 53–4.
40. Ibid., p. 115
41. Ibid., p. 198.
42. Ibid., p. 75.
43. Meer, Nasar, Varun Uberoi, and Tariq Modood, 'Nationhood and Muslims in Britain', in Nancy Foner and Patrick Simon (eds), *Fear, Anxiety, and National Identity: Immigration and Belonging in North America and Western Europe* (London: Russell Sage Foundation, 2015), pp. 173–83. See also Nasar Meer, *Key Concepts in Race and Ethnicity* (Thousand Oaks, CA: Sage, 2014).
44. Heath et al., *The Political Integration of Ethnic Minorities in Britain*, p. 60.
45. Foner and Simon, *Fear, Anxiety, and National Identity*, p. 18.
46. Erasmus, 'Attitudes to Islam in Europe Are Hardening', *The Economist*, 1 September 2017, available at <https://www.economist.com/blogs/erasmus/2017/09/inter-faith-relations>.
47. 'Final Report Summary – EURISLAM: Finding a Place for Islam in Europe: Cultural Interactions Between Muslim Immigrants and Receiving Societies', 18 July 2014, available at <http://cordis.europa.eu/result/rcn/59098_en.html>.
48. European Union Agency for Fundamental Rights, *Second European Union Minorities and Discrimination Survey: Muslims – Selected Findings* (Luxembourg: Publications

Office of the European Union, 2017), available at <http://fra.europa.eu/en/publica tion/2017/eumidis-ii-muslims-selected-findings>.

49. Higgins, Michael D., 'Restoring Social Cohesion: A Project for 2018 and Beyond', *Social Europe*, 12 January 2018, available at <https://www.socialeurope.eu/restoring-social-cohesion-project-2018-beyond>.

50. Peterkin, Tom, 'Alex Salmond: Blocking indyref will "backfire spectacularly"', *The Scotsman*, 16 March 2017, available at <http>.

CHAPTER SIX

Immigrant America

HOW NEW A WAY TO NATIONHOOD

It was in America that many of the European ideals of the age of Enlightenment were put into practice. In 1770 Abbé Raynal praised the liberty, prosperity and religious tolerance of the British colonies. The English tradition of rational law and active engagement in the commonweal had brought prosperity to the colonists and an emerging sense of nationhood. The colonies revolted against Britain not so much because they felt oppressed but more because they wanted to expand the considerable freedoms they had already acquired. The American Revolution was the result less of a reaction to English tyranny and more of the fact that the settlers were already among the freest of people. These are the mythical foundations of the birth of the United States.

Key factors shaped the character of the new nation. The English tradition of common law and constitutional liberties was one. The colonists underscored universal and natural rights that had been developed in English and Scottish political thought. The arrival in America of immigrants from the continent, often of lower-class background and a multiplicity of religions, inhibited the growth of class and religious hierarchies. Many were from nations that held an antipathy towards England, such as the Scots, Irish and Germans. Initially, the diverse background of settlers held back the process of integration because locally branded loyalties, creeds and racial strains remained influential. In the 1770s little territorial unity existed, with different colonies squabbling and insisting on their autonomies.

The struggle for civic liberty against a purportedly oppressive colonial power – whether it was reality or myth – begot a new nation that reflected the will of its people, or so it was supposed. Not common ancestry, loyalty to a monarch, or geographical compactness held it together. Americans emancipated themselves from their European past. Benjamin Franklin eloquently

---

Box 6.1 Saving the Union or sowing secessionist seeds?

In his 'Notes on Debates in Congress' that immediately preceded the Declaration of Independence on 4 July 1776, Thomas Jefferson displayed a pragmatic side to his dealings with colonial England. He inscribed a politically indispensable change at the last moment. When New York, the last holdout, agreed to this text, which required the removal of the critique of slavery and the slave trade from the Declaration of Independence, it passed unanimously.

> Congress proceeded the same day [2 July] to consider the declaration of Independance, which had been reported & laid on the table the Friday preceding, and on Monday referred to a commee. of the whole. the pusillanimous idea that we had friends in England worth keeping terms with, still haunted the minds of many. for this reason those passages which conveyed censures on the people of England were struck out, lest they should give them offence. the clause too, reprobating the enslaving the inhabitants of Africa, was struck out in complaisance to South Carolina & Georgia, who had never attempted to restrain the importation of slaves, and who on the contrary still wished to continue it. our Northern brethren also I believe felt a little tender under those censures; for tho' their people have very few slaves themselves yet they had been pretty considerable carriers of them to others.

Source: Thomas Jefferson, 'Notes on Debates in Congress', 2–4 July 1776, Ch. 15, Document 18, Papers 1:314, available at <http://press-pubs.uchicago.edu/founders/documents/v1ch15s18.html>.

---

testified to this: 'Here individuals of all nations are melted into a new race of men, whose labors and posterity will one day cause great changes in the world.'[1]

Because of its diversity, excluding slaves, a centralising power had to manage American federalism. Alexander Hamilton designed strong national government that infused the US with 'a national character and policy'. The 1789 Constitution overcame separation of the Thirteen Colonies and created the basis for commerce and prosperity. It forged a nation based on truths held 'to be self-evident, that all men are created equal, that they are endowed by their Creator with certain unalienable Rights, that among those are Life, Liberty and the Pursuit of Happiness' (Box 6.1).[2]

Even though Hamilton was himself an immigrant, he opposed the open immigration policies that President Thomas Jefferson had recommended in his first annual message to Congress in 1801. Jefferson viewed it as a way to secure the pre-eminence of his own Democratic–Republican party, also endorsed by James Madison, over Hamilton's centralising Federalists. Precociously, the US system was shaped by the primacy of electoral politics.

Hamilton was convinced that Jefferson's proposal for unrestricted immigration would lead to the triumph of the radical principles of the French Revolution over those of its more sensible American counterpart. He noted that 'foreigners will generally be apt to bring with them attachments to the persons they have left behind; to the country of their nativity, and to its particular customs and manners'.

Hamilton argued too that 'it is unlikely that they will bring with them that temperate love of liberty, so essential to real republicanism'. He concluded: 'To admit foreigners indiscriminately to the rights of citizens, the moment they put foot in our country, as recommended in [Jefferson's] message, would be nothing less than to admit the Grecian horse into the citadel of our liberty and sovereignty.'[3]

For his part, Jefferson gave the new nation an ideological foundation to complement its independence. Opposing conservative and centralising groups that hoped to re-establish the rigid social order prevailing in European states, he advocated a new brand of egalitarianism and popular democracy. A representative of the liberal, humanist nationalism of the late eighteenth century, Jefferson stressed public allegiance to the national idea as the basis for its existence. His patriotism was devoid of exclusionary practices and he stressed the strength of diversity – even if slavery tarnished his romantic vision. Britain had passed the Slavery Abolition Act in 1833 but it was only during the Civil War in 1863 that Abraham Lincoln launched his Emancipation Proclamation.[4]

As a Southerner, Jefferson shared the views of Northern advocates of emancipation and accepted that the slave trade had to stop. He also recommended a more liberal, compassionate policy towards native Indians even as charges of genocidal acts became apparent. Agriculture was, for him, the foundation of the new nation's economic life and he cherished the ideal of self-contained communities imbibed with civic virtue and moral happiness. For Jefferson, America's nationhood also had universal significance: its form of government was 'a standing monument and example for the aim and the imitation of the people of other countries'.[5]

No nation is ever created as purely the result of a national language, but few can do without one. Noah Webster was keen on developing an American language and an American 'fashion'. This was the reverse of Europe, where culture and ideology had preceded national independence.

In short, as Daniel Bell's seminal work illustrated,

The saving grace, so to speak, of American politics, was that all sorts of groups were tolerated, and the system of the 'deal' became the pragmatic counterpart of the philosophic principle of toleration. But in matters of manners, morals, and conduct ... there has been a ferocity of blue-nose attitudes unmatched by other countries.[6]

This moralism emerged out of an evangelism intimately linked to puritan culture, a current still influencing American life.

The demographics of nations are historically more complicated than they seem. Thomas Paine remarked how in the US 'not one third of the inhabitants are of English descent'. Accordingly, 'Europe, and not England, is the parent country of America.'[7] Much later Samuel Huntington focused on this aspect of political elitism: 'The American people who achieved independence in the late eighteenth century were few and homogeneous: overwhelmingly white (thanks to the exclusion of blacks and Indians from citizenship), British, and Protestant, broadly sharing a common culture'.[8] To be sure, in the Thirteen Colonies, up to 20 per cent of the population were Black slaves.

Jumping forward, in the year 2000 Americans had multiplied about 100 times and they were now a multiracial society: 69 per cent White, 12 per cent Hispanic, 12 per cent Black, 7 per cent other. Americans had also become multiconfessional: 63 per cent Protestant, 23 per cent Catholic, 14 per cent other or no religion. And society was multiethnic, with no majority group in a position of power.

Diversity can be a smokescreen for elitism. Liav Orgad, author of a book on the liberal theory of majority rights, suggested that, even assuming Western societies are diverse, the policy making elite may essentially remain unchanged. In the case of the US citizenship test,

The manner in which new Americans are created is a political decision. 'We' are those who define who 'we' are, what nation 'we' want to be, what number and kind of people 'we' allow to join our community, and what rules apply to our naturalisation process.[9]

The purpose of citizenship tests is, then, to forge similar mindsets with elites and to develop attachement to them.

Moreover, the most persuasive explanation for preserving the *status quo ante* of an earlier elite is that 'cultural defense policies are implemented in order to preserve the cultural hegemony of the majority, whose members have an interest in adhering to their culture and sustaining it. The value of culture is intrinsic, not just instrumental.'[10] Culture is only secondarily symbolic or identitarian, challenging today's social constructivism. As reviewed in more detail below, White Anglo-Saxon Protestant (WASP) *culture* in the US has not disappeared even if some of its WASP prerequisites have.

A NATIONAL DIALECT

The 1776 Declaration of Independence was written in the flowery language of that period, and people assumed that colonists spoke with the same British accents that their families had emigrated with. When did Americans start sounding different to English ears?

For linguist Chi Luu,

> By the time America was ready to consciously uncouple itself from the mother country, it had long since achieved a kind of linguistic independence. Thanks to a remarkable kind of linguistic melting pot process, early Americans spoke with a standard dialect all their own.[11]

Indeed, Americans spoke in a national dialect that had emerged at least two generations before 1776 (Box 6.2).

In 1770 an English traveller to the New World observed that

> The colonists are composed of adventurers, not only from every district of Great Britain and Ireland, but from almost every other European government.... Is it not therefore reasonable to suppose that the English language must be greatly corrupted by such a strange admixture of various nations?

The very reverse was true:

> Far from being peopled with only British and European immigrants and their accompanying speech habits as some might assume, there was a robust and growing population of Americans, with a homegrown American variety of English that had not only been born by this time, but had already prospered through a few

---

Box 6.2 Did Shakespeare sound more American than British?

Far from being an isolated community, the American colonies developed culturally and linguistically while being in constant, vibrant contact with the outside world and with a healthy flow of immigrants from Britain, Europe and other countries – as well as each other, as American colonists were apt to move more than their British counterparts as land was being settled. There was an urgent need to interact with people from many different backgrounds and social class in an effort to form a self-sustaining community.

Source: Chi Luu, 'When did Colonial America Gain Linguistic Independence?', available at <https://daily.jstor.org/colonial-america-gain-linguistic-independence/?utm_source=marketing&utm_medium=social&utm_campaign=twitter>.

---

generations of native-born speakers, long before the Declaration of Independence was written.[12]

At this point immigration made a decisive difference to manner of speaking. A common mode of speech consisting of language learned through the contact of two mutually intelligible dialects (called *koine* from its Greek name) established colonial American English. Communication practices removed strong dialectical features as people moved from one place to another and had to make themselves understood. Cultural and social influences also meant that newcomers wanted to achieve higher social status and mobility. A 'prestige' dialect, much like diglossia today, therefore emerged.

An American *koine* was established, then, by newer generations of Americans who adopted it while code switching back to their own regional dialects. Soon they would even abandon their native tongue in order to nativise and assimilate into a wider American linguistic community.[13] The origins of American English, therefore, rest squarely with immigrants.

MANIFEST DESTINY AND EXCEPTIONALISM

American nationalism was upbeat before the War of 1812. An aggressive nationalism was reflected in James Madison's stark exhortation to conquer Canada because it entailed 'a mere matter of marching'. This second war against Britain heightened American national consciousness even though their armies were driven out of Canada and their new capital, Washington, was burned down.

The wars against Britain, as well as the annexation of the Republic of Texas in 1845 and the follow-up US–Mexican war of 1846–8, which led to conquest of about one-third of Mexican territory since it gained independence in 1821, strengthened nationalism further while remaking US borders. Not long after, the Civil War of 1861–5, won by Union troops, raised fears that British North America would again be a target. It led to Canadian Confederation in 1867. There was nothing unusual about war as a means of determining national borders:

> It is hard to think of any nation–state, with the possible exception of Norway, that came into existence before the middle of the twentieth century which was not created, and had its boundaries defined, by wars, by internal violence, or by a combination of the two.[14]

From the outset, economic interests structured American nationalism. The Jeffersonian ideal of self-contained, self-governing rural communities became an anachronism and a strong national economy was put in its place. Advocacy of manufacture, commerce and tariffs as the basis for creating a strong economy boosted immigration.

The conquest of the West after 1815, and mass killings and ethnic cleansing of Indians over subsequent decades, in the view of some historians, was almost genocidal in scope.[15] In turn, the Louisiana Purchase reflected secretive diplomacy as well as undemocratic measures; inhabitants – many French-speakers with a distinct culture and lifestyle – were not asked their opinion about annexation.[16] In contrast to European nation making, then, the American nation arose not as the product of blood, soil and natural borders or as a result of shared memories, but as a universal ideal, which meant that everyone could be included in it, even if some ethnicities were threatened by this expansion.

The American Revolution had a far-reaching impact on other countries. The political and national awakening of the French nation followed closely on the heels of the US Declaration of Independence. In Central Europe, Poland attempted in 1792 to stave off partition by drafting a democratic constitution in the spirit of the American document. Jean-Jacques Rousseau believed that large independent states with recognisable national communities had the right to remain independent: 'It is making fools of people to tell them seriously that one can at one's pleasure transfer peoples from master to master, like herds of cattle, without consulting their interests or their wishes.'[17]

Manifest destiny and American exceptionalism went hand in hand. They were refracted in the national anthem written at a time when Britain and the US were locked in sea combat in the Battle of Baltimore in 1814. It venerates the battle, enquiring: 'O say does that star-spangled banner yet wave, o'er the land of the free and the home of the brave?' This is an eloquent testament to nationhood – of that time.

For John Torpey, two versions of American exceptionalism exist, a good and a bad one. Alexis de Tocqueville's enduring classic, *Democracy in America*, had mapped out the first: the US is a 'shining city on a hill' that has a providential historical mission to be exemplary and do good. Bad exceptionalism, by contrast, highlights the absence of a European-style welfare state. It can even come down to the question why is there no socialism in America. As de Tocqueville observed, voluntary associations now took the place of the welfare state and the reason was American individualism.[18] For Torpey, Tocqueville's concern about the malady of individualism in American life spawned a series of sociological best-sellers on the topic, from *The Lonely Crowd* to *Habits of the Heart* to *Bowling Alone*. He claimed that 'self-absorption and self-seeking had gained the upper hand and overwhelmed concern for the commonweal. The tension between state strength and individual freedom has been a perennial theme since the founding of the republic.'[19]

Whether through self-selection or assimilation into American values, many immigrants to the US display the 'rugged individualism' earlier Americans pioneered. At the same time, this individualism may blind some Americans from focusing on an intermediary American identity that is sandwiched between rugged individuality on the one hand and extraordinary ventures of the nation–state on the other. Yale law professor Amy Chua makes the credible argument that

> Humans are tribal. We need to belong to groups. In many parts of the world, the group identities that matter most – the ones that people will kill and die for – are ethnic, religious, sectarian, or clan-based. But because America tends to see the world in terms of nation–states engaged in great ideological battles – Capitalism vs. Communism, Democracy vs. Authoritarianism, the 'Free World' vs. the 'Axis of Evil' – we are often spectacularly blind to the power of tribal politics.[20]

Perhaps framing politics in this Manichean way has more to do with how US political elites function rather than how average Americans understand the world. 'Tribal' is, in any case, not a term most Americans would use about their own society.

ELITISM AND EXCLUSION

Sociologist Seymour Martin Lipset believed that the US was an outlier when compared to Western Europe or Canada. Initially its value system was biased in favour of Nordic Protestants:

> The passage of this law in 1924 [Table 6.1] eliminated the universalistic and egalitarian principle which asserted that anyone had a right to become an American, that to become one required only that one wanted to be an American, not that one be lucky in having chosen one's parents.... The fact remains that to have imposed particularistic ethnic and religious restrictions on immigration constituted a fundamental violation of traditional American values.[21]

But WASP domination irked him. Lipset had called the US the first new nation based on its liberty, egalitarianism, individualism, republicanism, democracy and *laissez-faire* economic system. The US was given a unique mission to transform the world and Americans had a duty to ensure that 'government of the people, by the people, for the people, shall not perish from the earth'. But nothing could be further from these attributes than WASP-ishness:

> The crusade to keep America Protestant by imposing ascetic norms on the total population and by barring massive non-Protestant immigration is actually almost as old as the United States itself.... There was an association between conservative politics, efforts to impose ascetic Protestant morality on the lower classes – often viewed as largely immigrant in composition – and attempts to limit immigration of (or to withhold equal rights from) the foreign-born.[22]

132

Table 6.1 A timeline of US policy on immigration and naturalisation: What First New Nation?

1790	Congress adopts uniform rules so that any free White person can apply for citizenship after two years of residency
1798	Alien and Sedition Acts require fourteen years of residency before citizenship and provided for deportation of dangerous aliens
1819	First federal legislation on immigration includes reporting requirement
1846	Irish of all classes emigrate to US
1857	Dred Scott decision declares a Negro cannot be a citizen
1864	Contract Labor Law allows recruiting of foreign labour
1868	African Americans gain citizenship with 14th Amendment
1875	*Henderson v. Mayor of New York* decision declares all state laws governing immigration unconstitutional; Congress must regulate foreign commerce. It prohibits convicts and prostitutes from entering country
1880	More than 5.2 million immigrants enter country between 1880 and 1890
1882	Chinese Exclusion Act suspends Chinese immigration for ten years and bars Chinese in US from citizenship. Also bars convicts, lunatics and others unable to care for themselves from entering. Head tax placed on immigrants
1885	Contract Labor Law makes it unlawful to import unskilled aliens from overseas as labourers
1888	For first time since 1798, provisions are adopted for expulsion of aliens
1890	Foreign-born in US make up 15 per cent of population. More arrive from southern and Eastern Europe ('new immigrants') than northern and western states ('old immigrants')
1891	Bureau of Immigration established under Treasury Department. More classes of aliens are restricted, including those monetarily assisted by others for their passage. Steamship companies are ordered to return ineligible immigrants to countries of origin
1892	Ellis Island is opened to screen immigrants entering on east coast. Angel Island screens those on west coast. Ellis Island officials report that women travelling alone must be met by a man or they are immediately deported
1902	Chinese Exclusion Act is renewed indefinitely
1903	Anarchists, epileptics, polygamists and beggars are ruled inadmissible
1906	Knowledge of English becomes a basic requirement
1907	Head tax is raised. People with physical or mental defects, tuberculosis, and children unaccompanied by a parent are added to exclusion list. Japan agrees to limit emigrants to US in return for eliminating segregation of Japanese in San Francisco schools
1917	Immigration Act provides literacy tests for those over sixteen and establishes an Asiatic Barred Zone banning all immigrants from Asia
1921	Quota Act of 1921 limits immigrants to 3 per cent of each nationality present in US in 1910. A non-quota category is established: wives, children of citizens, learned professionals and domestic servants are not counted in quotas

Table 6.1 continued

1922	Japanese are made ineligible for citizenship
1924	Quotas are changed to 2 per cent of each nationality based on 1890 numbers. While 82 per cent of all immigrants come from Western and northern Europe, 16 per cent are from southern and Eastern Europe, and 2 per cent from rest of world. As no distinctions are made between refugees and immigrants, this limits Jewish émigrés during 1930s and 1940s. Despite protests from many settlers, Native Americans are made citizens of US
1929	Annual quotas of 1924 Act are made permanent
1943	Chinese Exclusion Laws are repealed but China's quota is set at a token 105 immigrants annually
1946	Procedures facilitate immigration of foreign-born wives, fiancé(e)s, husbands and children of US armed forces personnel
1948	Displaced Persons Act allows 205,000 refugees over two years
1950	Grounds for exclusion and deportation are expanded. Aliens are required to report their addresses annually
1952	Immigration and Nationality Act eliminates race as a bar to immigration or citizenship. Japan's quota is set at 185 annually, China's at 105, and other Asian countries at 100. Northern and western Europe's quota comprises 85 per cent of all immigrants. Tighter restrictions are placed on immigrants coming from West Indies
1965	Hart–Celler Act abolishes national origins quotas. Categories of preference are based on family ties, critical skills, artistic excellence and refugee status
1978	Separate ceilings are set for Western and Eastern hemispheric immigration
1980	Refugee Act removes refugees as a preference category
1986	Immigration Reform and Control Act provides for amnesty for many illegal aliens and introduces sanctions for employers hiring illegals
1990	Immigration Act of 1990 limits unskilled workers to 10,000 a year. Skilled labour requirements and immediate family reunification are major goals. It continues to promote nuclear family model
2001	USA Patriot Act amends Immigration and Nationality Act to broaden scope of aliens ineligible for admission or deportable due to terrorist activities
2012	Deferred Action for Childhood Arrivals (DACA, or 'Dreamers') offers temporary reprieve from deportation to nearly 800,000 unauthorised immigrants who entered US before age 16
2017	President promises to build US–Mexico border wall to halt illegal immigration. Visas are restricted for select Muslim majority countries. DACA is suspended

Source: Adapted from Elise Guyette, Fern Tavalin and Sarah Rooker, *The Flow of History*, available at <http://www.flowofhistory.org/themes/movement_settlement/uspolicytimeline.php>.

The fact that no socialist tradition was implanted in the US permitted it to escape political convolutions during the twentieth century unscathed. But invocation of WASP-ishness and, with it, the exclusionary policies that followed were serious fault lines. One writer chronicled the exclusionary politics of the period from 1924 to 1965 after the national origins quota system had been implemented by the Act of 1924:

> The Johnson–Reed Act was certainly not the nation's first restrictive immigration law. The exclusion of Chinese, other Asians, and various classes of undesirable aliens (paupers, criminals, anarchists, and the like) in the late nineteenth and early twentieth centuries signaled the beginnings of a legal edifice of restriction. But the 1924 act was the nation's first comprehensive restriction law. It established for the first time numerical limits on immigration and a global racial and national hierarchy that favored some immigrants over others.[23]

New ethnic and racial categories and hierarchies of difference were drawn in this era. The concept of race itself changed, from late-nineteenth-century race science, which centred on physiognomic differences, to twentieth-century racial thought linking race to physiognomy and nationality.

Historian Mae Ngai writes exasperatedly that 'The illegal alien is an "impossible subject", a person who cannot be and a problem that cannot be solved. Even as Congress abolished quotas based on national origin in 1965, it preserved the principle of numerically limiting immigration.'[24] The myth of immigrant America is closely connected to the narrative of American exceptionalism. This myth

> shores up the national narrative of liberal consensual citizenship, allowing a disaffected citizenry to experience its regime as choiceworthy, to see it through the eyes of still enchanted newcomers whose choice to come here ... reenact[s] liberalism's ... fictive foundation in individual acts of uncoerced consent.[25]

Ngai points out that in the 1920s the legal traditions that justified racial discrimination against African Americans were frequently extended to apply to other ethno-racial groups. Immigration law introduced euphemisms such as 'aliens ineligible to citizenship' and new categories of identity such as 'national origins', which are now used to juxtapose Asian and Latino immigrant success narratives with 'undisciplined' African Americans. Thus, 'the strategy deploys immigrant exemplars of hard work, thrift and self-reliance against an alleged 'culture of poverty' among native-born minorities (African Americans as well as Puerto Ricans) to explain the persistence of unemployment and poverty among the latter.[26]

A paradigmatic shift occurred with the Immigration Act of 1965, which promoted at the same time greater inclusions and exclusions. The national origins quota system was abolished so that Eastern and southern Europeans, who had been the principal objects of exclusion in the Immigration Act of

1924, now could enter the US in the same numbers as northern and Western Europeans. Today's migrants 'travel with the ghosts of migrants past as they, too, traverse boundaries, negotiate with states over the terms of their inclusion, and alter the future histories of nations and the history of our world'.[27] Agreeing with Homi Bhabha, Ngai does not believe that immigrants are external to the nation but 'the migrants, the minorities, the diasporic come to change the history of the nation'.[28] This enhances a more complete understanding of nationhood.

Anthony Appiah phrases this sentiment in a negative way. Dividing humanity into nation–states means that

> all individuals in the world are obliged, whether they like it or not, to accept the political arrangements of their birthplace, however repugnant those arrangements are to their principles or ambitions – unless they can persuade somebody else to let them in.[29]

This brings us to the 2016 US election.

In the result one political analyst noted a contrary meaning of exceptionalism:

> Trump and the broader wave of populist anger that he rode to office reflect the fact that we are living in an 'age of disruption' in political, social, and economic terms that is altering the course of American exceptionalism as traditionally understood.[30]

His connections with right-wing movements, White supremacists and anti-immigrant lobbies (focusing on Mexicans and Muslims) convinced Trump that what he was elected to do was represent 'Pittsburgh, not Paris'.

A different perspective on why the Republican candidate won the election was given by geopolitical analyst Ian Bremmer:

> The American people have elected a president who made very clear that the United States does not want to have the burdens of global leadership, it doesn't want to be the world's policeman, it doesn't want to be the architect of global trade, and it doesn't want to be the exceptionalist power that promotes its values all over the world.[31]

This benign symbiosis of Trump and his electorate equated isolationist policy with xenophobic anger. It rolled back US nationhood as it has existed for nearly 250 years.

A grudging recognition of nationhood can be found in a country musician's paean to Texas. Lyle Lovett captured the differences between fear-mongering and hospitality, between nativism and outsiderness, in this refrain:

> That's right you're not from Texas
> You're right you're not from Texas

That's right you're not from Texas
But Texas needs you anyway.

Immigrant Americans

If England was God's first-born nation, then as a long-existing immigrant society the US may be the first to have achieved modern nationhood. It became a united commonweal of communities having different racial, ethnic and religious backgrounds. The melting-pot process helped forge American nationhood in a distinctive way, different from a vertical mosaic model that created Canadian nationhood, and multiculturalism that carved out its modern German counterpart.

In the 1780s an obscure writer, Hector St John de Crèvecœur, had put forward the argument that 'individuals of all nations are melted into a new race of men', which was a 'mixture of English, Scotch, Irish, French, Dutch, Germans, and Swedes'. Such an immigrant left 'behind him all his ancient prejudices and manners, receives new ones from the new mode of life he has embraced, the new government he obeys, and the new rank he holds'.[32] Much later, following the production of his play in Washington in 1909, Israel Zangwill broadened the racial mix beyond northwestern Europeans to subsume 'Celt and Latin, Slav and Teuton, Greek and Syrian, black and yellow – Jew and Gentile'.[33] Nationhood was in its expansive phase, even allowing Hamilton to be depicted as a particularly illustrious immigrant in the eponymous musical.

Culture does make a difference, writes sociologist Nathan Glazer, 'But it is very hard to determine what in culture makes the difference.'[34] In melting into American life, the great traditions of a culture were not necessarily the best place to find them.

> Ethnic and racial groups in the United States are not randomly drawn from the large populations that bear or are characterized by a culture. The million Chinese in the United States do not represent a China a thousand times larger; and similarly with the million Asian Indians in the United States. This is the case with every ethnic or racial group in the United States.[35]

For Glazer, then, 'it was rare that the elite bearers of the great tradition were among the immigrants'. A purposeful reductionism was required and 'culture in the large must be disaggregated to the very specific variants that characterize American immigrants, who came from distinct provinces, classes, and subgroups of the large culture'.[36]

Gat's assimilationist argument about immigrants is noteworthy. He agreed that immigrants retain a distinct appreciation of their origin and cultural roots in the first generation after immigration, but they also were trading their language, values and much else: 'Within a few generations, they merge into a shared, amalgamated American culture, to which they also variably contribute.' From the third generation on, as cultural differences are reduced and common denominators become stronger, intermarriages among immigrant ethnic groups increase and shared kinship emerges.

Despite the estimable rhetoric of multiethnicity affirming new norms of respect for group heritages, Gat is insistent about unique Americanness:

> There exists a very distinct American culture and identity, widely shared by the large majority of Americans and characterized by a common English language and all-pervasive folkways. These encompass mores, symbols, social practices, public knowledge, and a sense of common historical tradition; popular tastes, images, and heroes; music, sports, cuisine, public holidays, and social rituals.

It is a fusion culture drawing from many different immigrant sources, traditions and kinship networks. American history and tradition become distinctively theirs and 'there are plausible reasons for referring to the American national community in ethnic terms'. The majority identity in America is American and this bridges original ethnic identities as members lose touch with their often mixed countries of origin and their ancestral identities. 'The American nation was created by immigrants, its population is multiethnic, and immigration remains central to the nation's experience, ethos, and identity.' Moreover, 'The new people's self-perception as a community of culture and, to some degree, also kinship (intermarried, adopted) becomes very recognizable,' so 'there are plausible reasons for referring to these new kin-culture national communities in ethnic terms'.[37] In the memorable words of Stanley, who rails against ethnic stigmatisation in Tennessee Williams's celebrated play A Streetcar Named Desire, 'I'm not a Polack. People from Poland are Poles, not Polacks. But what I am is one hundred per cent American, born and raised in the greatest country on earth and proud as hell of it.'[38]

Finally, while Americans are bound together by citizenship, allegiance to their adopted country and adherence to its Constitution, that is not identical with nationhood:

> The precept that nationhood equals citizenship is very far from being universally applicable. The notion that different ethnicities in a country should remain together and count as a nation even if they do not perceive themselves as such, or do not get along, is partly derived from the erroneous view that nationhood and ethnicity are entirely different concepts.[39]

In fact they are intertwined.

Immigration writ large and small

The US faces legal and illegal immigration challenges to its migration policy but under President Trump it is defiant (Table 3.1). Restrictions on travel from Muslim-majority states are decided in the courts. Deportations of people from El Salvador granted Temporary Protected Status because of an earth-quake at home are occurring. Yet these changes are predictable, given past US immigration history.

In 2012 the US was home to an astonishing 11.7 million undocumented immigrants, up from 3.5 million in 1990. Irregular immigrants comprised more than a quarter of the total foreign-born population of around 40 million. Eight million either work or are looking for work.[40] How did this dramatic increase come about and what are its consequences?

The sequel to the controversial *The Clash of Civilizations and the Remaking of World Order*[41] dealt with American understanding of *Who Are We?* From the outset, Samuel Huntington made clear what US goals should be:

> Americans should recommit themselves to the Anglo-Protestant culture, tradi-tions, and values that for three and a half centuries have been embraced by Americans of all races, ethnicities, and religions and that have been the source of their liberty, unity, power, prosperity, and moral leadership as a force for good in the world.[42]

To be sure, he distinguished 'an argument for the importance of Anglo-Protestant culture, not for the importance of Anglo-Protestant people'. The Harvard political scientist even resigned himself to the fact that 'America will still be America long after the WASPish descendants of its founders have become a small and uninfluential minority.'

His view was not shared by Nathan Glazer and Daniel Moynihan, who had written a seminal book earlier. In *Beyond the Melting Pot*, penned in the 1960s, the authors were unsure that Irish identity would (ironically) cement WASP identity. In New York they still enjoyed the prestige of representing 'the majority' and still dominated the large banks, insurance companies and corporations. But 'Young people flock to the city to work ... and discover they have become WASPs.' The term had served as a 'created identity'.[43]

At the time Huntington was writing, in the first years of this century, a par-ticular core group was resisting assimilationist pressures that in the past had been neutralised by immigrants arriving from around the world. Huntington took aim at immigration from Mexico because of its *uniqueness*: 'No other First World country has a land frontier with a Third World country, much less one of two thousand miles.' American images of immigrants derive from 'crossing several thousand miles of ocean', not from crossing a porous border. In fact, 'Mexican immigration is leading toward the demographic *Reconquista* of areas Americans took from Mexico by force in the 1830s and 1840s.'[44]

The influx of Mexicans was increasing exponentially: from 640,000 legal migrants in the 1970s to 2,250,000 in the 1990s. It made up one-quarter of all legal migration to the US. A different study discovered that Mexicans represented 74 per cent of immigrants admitted under the provisions of the 1986 Immigration Reform and Control Act, which applied to illegal immigrants living in the country before January 1982.[45] Substantial illegal entry into the US was a post-1965 Mexican phenomenon, reported Huntington. Their concentrated immigration profile was assisted by high fertility rates among Hispanics.

Huntington marshalled further data in his critique of Mexican migration. In 2000 about 75 per cent of the foreign-born population representing the top five countries in the US was Mexican: there were 7.8 million Mexicans but only 1.4 million Chinese, 1.2 million Filipinos and 1 million Indians. They were concentrated in southern California but were spreading to other areas.

Mexicans were 'persistent' in making it to the US. Huntington cited Myron Weiner's assertion: 'If there is a single "law" in migration, it is that a migration flow, once begun, induces its own flows.' Chain migration follows.[46] The implication was, then, that 'the longer migration continues, the more difficult politically it is to stop it' since NGOs lobby to expand migrant rights and benefits, promoting ever more immigration. With such high numbers, 'sustained high-level immigration retards and can even obstruct assimilation'.

Huntington also threw into the mix below-average rates of linguistic assimilation, weaker educational results, lower occupational and income performance, higher probability of living in poverty, lower citizenship naturalisation rates, less frequent intermarriage rates (he was tentative about this), a fourth generation that had not advanced beyond the second generation, and finally, 'weak identification with America on the part of Mexican immigrants and people of Mexican origin'. For good measure, he added a 1990 survey that found Hispanics to be less patriotic than Jews, Asians and Southern Whites. Huntington referred to people smuggling into the US, though not to narco-traffickers. Huntington's ambivalent conclusion was: *Uncle Sam no es mi tío*.[47]

Huntington's critique did not take into account whether Mexicans and other Hispanics insisted on a status as racialised minority. Research by Richard Alba and Nancy Foner described how Mexican immigrants were noted for their low rates of education, high rates of poverty, and sizeable proportion of undocumented workers. Perceptions claimed they are 'stigmatized as inferior, illegal, and foreign and seen as nonwhite'. Some social scientists, therefore, labelled them a racialised ethnic group that were 'targets of prejudice and discrimination because of nativism'.[48] Skin colour affected their

140

socio-economic standing as well as their status: foreignness and the right to be in the country were challenged.

Canadian contrast?

Trump's praise for the immigration model of his neighbour to the north may suggest that he values pragmatism more than race or ethnicity. At one point he demanded a 'total rewrite' of the US immigration system into a merit-based one. Canada's programme has been remarkably rational and it claims to comprise the world's most successful, prosperous immigrant population anywhere. Its foreign-born population is better educated, works harder, creates more business opportunities and uses fewer welfare dollars than even its native-born compatriots.[49]

About one-half of Canadian immigrants arrive with a college degree; the US figure is 27 per cent. Immigrant children in Canadian schools read as well as native-born; the gap is enormous in the US. Canadian immigrants are 20 per cent more likely to own their own home and 7 per cent less likely to live in poverty than their American equivalents.

Canada has one of the highest per capita immigration rates in the world, three times higher than the US. More than 20 per cent of Canadians are foreign-born, almost twice the American total, including US undocumented migrants.

Recent Canadian polls show that 82 per cent of respondents believe immigration has a positive effect on the economy. The vertical mosaic model, where immigrants are encouraged to retain their own language and are supported by Department of Heritage public funding programmes, plays a crucial role in positive Canadian perceptions of immigrants. Foreign-born children in Canada are likely to speak two or more languages.

The way that immigrants to Canada are chosen, however, reflects a hard-nosed approach. About 65 per cent in 2015 were admitted on purely economic grounds, prioritising the skilled economic migrant. A nine-point rubric assessing migrant applications ignores race, religion and ethnicity and instead looks at such factors as age, education, job skills and language ability. Individuals willing to make major investments in the country (as in some other countries) are welcome. Between 2018 and 2020, Canada plans to accept close to 1 million more immigrants. For a country of nearly 37 million with the world's second largest surface area, that seems practical.

Canada's refugee policy is, by contrast, modest and even grudging. About 48,000 Syrians arrived in 2016 and 2017, to much nation-branding ballyhoo that featured Prime Minister Justin Trudeau. There is also the 'echo effect' – the surge in families and relatives who want to be reunited with recently resettled refugees. Furthermore, Ottawa places limits on the number of refugees that can be resettled by sponsorship groups each year; there were only 16,000 private sponsorship spots in 2017. In addition, in January 2018 Canada announced a lottery system for migrants uniting with parents and grandparents abroad. It replaced one that was said to be too litigious. It was subsequently scrapped.

A final point is that Immigration and Refugee Protection Regulations (IRPR) refers to medical refusals and inadmissibility for migration. The regulations define excessive demand as 'a demand on health services or social services for which the anticipated costs would likely exceed average Canadian per capita health services and social services costs over a period of five consecutive years'. Excessive demand would add to existing waiting lists and would increase the rate of mortality and morbidity in Canada as a result of an inability to provide timely services to Canadian citizens or permanent residents.[50] Canada's health service has received much praise and it is sometimes used to define what a Canadian is. Medical inadmissibility rejecting immigrant applications has not been uncommon but is now under reconsideration.

In the US, by contrast, in 2015 nearly two-thirds of immigrants were admitted under a family reunification programme. Their fate depends on whether they already have relatives in the country. For a *New York Times* author, 'Family reunification sounds nice on an emotional level – who doesn't want to unite families? But it's a lousy basis for government policy.'[51] Rethinking US immigration policy is urgent but immigration deadlock has been scuttling most of the ambitious plans.

IDENTITIES AND DIVISIONS

Is the US in the process of unmaking nationhood? Will the bar be raised for immigrants from other countries who wish to be attached to this country? Just as importantly, are Americans splintering and feeling they have a more tenuous bond with compatriots? Is the sense of nationhood in this quintessential country of immigration being downsized?

In Mark Lilla's view, splintering may be the product of divisive identity politics. It consists of 'a pseudo-politics of self-regard and increasingly narrow and exclusionary self-definition'. It is bipartisan in that both political parties are pandering to particular identities, whether related to gender, sexual orientation, ethnicity, body type, disability or chronic medical condition.[52]

> What's extraordinary – and appalling – about the past four decades of our history is that our politics have been dominated by two ideologies that encourage and even celebrate the unmaking of citizens. On the right, an ideology that questions the existence of a common good and denies our obligation to help fellow citizens, through government action if necessary. On the left, an ideology institutionalized

in colleges and universities that fetishizes our individual and group attachments, applauds self-absorption, and casts a shadow of suspicion over any invocation of a universal democratic we.[53]

If Americans are not divided, they at least pursue narrow, identity-related interests. Vietnam war protests or civil rights marches in the 1960s and 1970s unified citizens on the basis of ideology. But today they are a distant memory, and a reason why identity politics may be replacing them. E pluribus unum does not follow from compartmentalised identity politics.

> If you frame 'identity politics' as a self-indulgent distraction from the vital business of creating a shared vision of America that all Americans can believe in, you're not only taking identities of gender or race or sexuality out of play; you are also taking for granted what it means to be 'American'.[54]

An America exists isolated from identity politics.

> You need to visit, if only with your mind's eye, places where wifi is non existent, the coffee is weak, and you will have no desire to post a photo of your dinner on Instagram. And where you'll be eating with people who give genuine thanks for that dinner in prayer. Don't look down at them.[55]

This observation may exaggerate the prevalence of weak coffee in small-town America, but red–blue, Republican–Democratic divides have deepened, also splitting who belongs or does not.

The US is an economically divided society in which post-tax income inequality spikes. Seventy per cent of countries have more equal income distribution than the US. The top 1 per cent accounts for over 20 per cent of income, but perceptions can be misleading. The average American estimates that the current ratio of Chief Executive Officer (CEO) to unskilled worker pay is 30 to 1 and their preference is for about 7 to 1; yet the actual CEO to unskilled wage ratio in America is 354 to 1.[56]

Intersectionality is a sociological theory that describes multiple threats of discrimination when an individual's identity overlaps with other marks of disadvantage such as race, gender, age, ethnicity and health. It recognises multiple forms of oppression and exploitation, and the resultant need for solidarity. But complex multivariate analysis will find it difficult to compare the plight of Black, Muslim or White women facing disadvantage.

The political consequences of inequality for campaign funding are clearly expounded by former President Jimmy Carter.

> Millionaires, billionaires can put in unlimited amounts of money directly into the campaign. In a way, it gives legal bribery a chance to prevail, because almost all the candidates, whether they're honest or not, and whether they're Democratic or Republican, depend on these massive infusions of money from very rich people in order to have money to campaign.[57]

143

Legal bribery of politicians, programmes and policies fractures nationhood and voting has little relevance or impact.

Emotions matter in politics and one of them is anxiety. 'Emotions are motivating, meaning that they cause us to want to act. In particular, anxiety motivates individuals to avoid danger, seek protection, and create a safer environment.'[58] Concerning immigration debates, 'Anxiety leads citizens to support policies that deny others rights in times of crisis and to support leaders who may continually provoke anxiety to maintain power and support for favored policies.'[59] Anxiety has also found its way to the streets of cities and towns.

RACE AND ANXIETY

The US is exceptional for the high degree of physical separation that occurs between Blacks and Whites. Racial categories and migrant opportunities go hand in hand. But separation goes beyond physicality and affects forms of behaviour: 'African Americans typically raise their children to protect themselves against a presumed hostility from white teachers, white police officers, white supervisors, and white co-workers.'[60]

Whether immigrant or native-born, Blacks frequently are residentially segregated from Whites (in contrast to their cohorts in Western Europe). Rates of Black–White intermarriage are lower in the US than in countries like Britain, France and the Netherlands. It is not only those categorised as Black who are seen through the prism of colour-coded racism.[61] Defensive about racism, President Barack Obama implored Black audiences to be mainstream: 'a standard portion of Obama's speeches about race riffed on black people's need to turn off the television, stop eating junk food, and stop blaming white people for their problems'.[62] When viewed as non-White or people of colour, Latinos and Asians suffer from the same stereotypes.

Racial roles appeared to change when a Black President was inaugurated in January 2009. Ta-Nehisi Coates notes how 'The symbolic power of Barack Obama's presidency – that whiteness was no longer strong enough to prevent peons taking up residence in the castle – assaulted the most deeply rooted notions of white supremacy and instilled fear in its adherents and beneficiaries.'[63]

Towards the end of his presidency, Obama went so far as to put the subject of reparations to Black people on the table. 'Theoretically, you can make obviously a powerful argument that centuries of slavery, Jim Crow, discrimination are the primary cause for all those gaps,' Obama said, referencing the gap in education, wealth and employment that separates Black from White America. 'That those were wrongs to the black community as a whole, and black families specifically, and that in order to close that gap, a society has

144

a moral obligation to make a large, aggressive investment, even if it's not in the form of individual reparations checks but in the form of a Marshall Plan.'[64]

Ta-Nehisi Coates's *We Were Eight Years in Power* argues that America did not need to worry that a Black president would derail American greatness; just the opposite happened. He conjectures that Obama turned one of America's greatest fears into reality. Referring to Reconstruction-era Black politicians, W. E. B. Du Bois had said, 'If there was one thing South Carolina feared more than bad Negro government, it was good Negro government.' That was what Obama assured.

But the militarisation of the police and 'stand your ground' laws increased in step with good Negro government. *The Guardian* compiled a list of police killings showing how Blacks were more than three times as likely to be killed by police as Whites. In 2015 (and 2016), 1,146 people were killed (1,093 in 2016), of whom 27 per cent (24 per cent in 2016) were Black. Respective figures for Hispanics were 17 percent in both years.[65] Using a different source, at the end of December 2017 27 per cent of 1,147 people killed by the police were Black.[66]

Radical critic Cornel West has taken issue with the defanged fight-back politics proposed by Coates:

> He represents the neoliberal wing that sounds militant about white supremacy but renders black fightback invisible. This wing reaps the benefits of the neoliberal establishment that rewards silences on issues such as Wall Street greed or Israeli occupation of Palestinian lands and people.

West railed that, like Coates' worldview, 'Wall Street power, US military policies, and the complex dynamics of class, gender, and sexuality in black America is [sic] too narrow and dangerously misleading.' He reported that

> Coates praises Obama as a 'deeply moral human being' while remaining silent on the 563 drone strikes, the assassination of US citizens with no trial, the 26,171 bombs dropped on five Muslim-majority countries in 2016 and the 550 Palestinian children killed with US supported planes in 51 days.[67]

While it is clear that 'the buck stops here', it remains unclear how much real authority Obama had to make a difference.

Aspiring to look like a militant organisation, Black Lives Matter is criticised as having barely touched on other problems affecting Black people. For instance, large disparities occurred in sentencing cases. At school Blacks were expelled, suspended or otherwise disciplined more frequently than White cohorts; White students could play their 'puppy cards' longer than Blacks. Perceptions of Blacks were that they seemed older, more experienced, more threatening.

Whistling Vivaldi may be of no help when Black suspects are cornered

---

Box 6.3 The new normal

[Americans] are building a custom-made utopia, all of us free to reinvent ourselves by imagination and will.... The exciting parts of the Enlightenment idea have swamped the sober, rational, empirical parts.... we Americans have given ourselves over to all kinds of magical thinking, anything-goes relativism, and belief in fanciful explanation – small and large fantasies that console or thrill or terrify us. And most of us haven't realized how far-reaching our strange new normal has become.

Source: Kurt Anderson, 'How America Lost its Mind', *The Atlantic*, September 2017, available at <https://www.theatlantic.com/magazine/archive/2017/09/how-america-lost-its-mind/534231/>.

---

by police officers. Based on the story of an African American walking in a Chicago park, the book of the same name documents how Whites reacted fearfully when they walked past him. When, however, he whistled tunes by, incongruously, eighteenth-century Baroque composer Antonio Vivaldi, White passers-by seemed to relax; some even smiled. Social psychologist Claude Steele explains how contextual factors, not individual characteristics or personal beliefs motivated by prejudice, explain the racial and ethnic stereotypes that make us fearful.[68] The Vivaldi ruse, though inventive, is unlikely to work where Black Americans face danger. Has America lost its mind when Vivaldi is being asked to protect us?

HAS AMERICA LOST ITS MIND?

Writing in *The Atlantic*, Kurt Anderson decried how 'The American experiment, the original embodiment of the great Enlightenment idea of intellectual freedom, whereby every individual is welcome to believe anything she wishes, has metastasized out of control.'[69] Political leaders understand that citizens do not always heed rational precepts when they vote. In fact, they realise that 'voters *resent* the judicious study of discernible reality. Keeping those people angry and frightened won them elections.'[70]

   The idea of the US as a land of promise and opportunity, and equality for all has been dented. President Trump's policy was ambiguous about the Deferred Action for Childhood Arrivals (DACA) programme and even offered a reprieve from deportation to 800,000 unauthorised immigrants who had entered the US as children before the age of 16. Deporting 'Dreamers' may be the end of the American Dream, the end point for aspirations to nationhood.

Anderson also paid a damning tribute to the President's insincerity: 'Donald Trump took a key piece of cynical wisdom about show business – the most important thing is sincerity, and once you can fake that, you've got it made.' Trump did more than that: 'His actual thuggish sincerity is the opposite of the old-fashioned, goody-goody sanctimony that people hate in politicians.'[71] It may be too alarming to view American nationhood as crumbling after nearly 250 years. But that is the consequence of spreading the myth that Americans can be anything (Box 6.3).

NOTES

1. Cited by Kohn, Hans, *The Idea of Nationalism: A Study in Its Origins and Background* (New York: Macmillan, 1969), p. 276.
2. *The Declaration of Independence*, available at <http://www.ushistory.org/declaration/document/>.
3. Hamilton, Alexander, 'The Examination', Number VIII, [12 January 1802], available at <https://founders.archives.gov/documents/Hamilton/01-25-02-0282>.
4. On the South as pathogen, see Drew Gilpin Faust (ed.), *The Ideology of Slavery: Proslavery Thought in the Antebellum South, 1830–1860* (Baton Rouge, LA: Louisiana State University Press, 1981).
5. Cited by Kohn, *The Idea of Nationalism*, p. 310.
6. Bell, Daniel, *The End of Ideology: On the Exhaustion of Political Ideas in the Fifties* (New York: Free Press, 1961), p. 112.
7. Paine, Thomas, *Common Sense, the Rights of Man, and Other Essential Writings*, Sydney Hook (ed.) (New York: Meridian, 1984), pp. 39, 50.
8. Huntington, Samuel P., *Who Are We? The Challenges to America's National Identity* (New York: Simon and Schuster, 2005), p. 11.
9. Orgad, Liav, 'Creating New Americans: The Essence of Americanism under the Citizenship Test', *Houston Law Review*, 47, no. 5, 2011, p. 1296, available at <https://ssrn.com/abstract=1586531>.
10. Orgad, Liav, *The Cultural Defense of Nations: A Liberal Theory of Majority Rights* (Oxford: Oxford University Press, 2015), p. 160.
11 Luu, Chi, 'When did Colonial America Gain Linguistic Independence?', available at <https://daily.jstor.org/colonial-america-gain-linguistic-independence/?utm_source=marketing&utm_medium=social&utm_campaign=twitter>.
12 Ibid.
13. Longmore, Paul K., '"They … Speak Better English than the English Do": Colonialism and the Origins of National Linguistic Standardization in America', *Early American Literature*, 40, no. 2, 2005, pp. 279–314, available at <http://www.jstor.org/stable/25057400>.
14. Howard, Michael, *The Lessons of History* (New York: Oxford University Press, 1991), p. 40.
15. Novack, George, *Genocide against the Indians* (New York: Pathfinder Press, 1970).
16. For the consequences, see Alfred O. Hero, *Louisiana and Quebec: Bilateral Relations and Comparative Sociopolitical Evolution, 1673–1993* (Lanham, MD: University Press of America, 1995).

17. Rousseau, Jean-Jacques, 'Political Writings', cited by Alfred Cobban, *The Nation State and National Self-Determination* (New York: Crowell, 1970), p. 32.

18. Torpey, John, 'The End of the World as We Know It? American Exceptionalism in an Age of Disruption', *Sociological Forum*, 32, no. 4, December 2017, pp. 701–25, available at <http://onlinelibrary.wiley.com/doi/10.1111/socf.12372/full>.

19. Ibid.

20. Chua, Amy, *Political Tribes: Group Instinct and the Fate of Nations* (New York: Penguin Books, 2018).

21. Lipset, Seymour Martin, *The First New Nation: The United States in Historical and Comparative Perspective* (New York: Anchor Books, 1967), pp. 389–90.

22. Ibid.

23. Ngai, Mae M., *Impossible Subjects: Illegal Aliens and the Making of Modern America* (Princeton, NJ: Princeton University Press, 2004), p. 4.

24. Ibid., p. 5.

25. Ibid., p. 8.

26. Ibid., p. 268.

27. Ibid., p. 270.

28. Ibid., p.14; see also Homi K. Bhabha, *The Location of Culture*, 2nd edn (London: Routledge, 1994), p. 320.

29. Appiah, Kwame Anthony, 'Citizenship in Theory and Practice: A Response to Charles Kesler', in Noah M. J. Pickus (ed.), *Immigration and Citizenship in the Twenty-First Century* (Lanham, MD: Rowman and Littlefield, 1998), p. 41.

30. Torpey, 'The End of the World', p. 701.

31. Ibid., pp. 714–15.

32. St John de Crèvecœur, J. Hector, *Letters from an American Farmer and Sketches of 18th Century America* (New York: Penguin, 1981), pp. 68, 70.

33. Zangwill, Israel, *The Melting Pot: A Drama in Four Acts* (New York: Arno Press, 1975), p. 184.

34. Glazer, Nathan, 'Disaggregating Culture', in Lawrence E. Harrison and Samuel P. Huntington (eds), *Culture Matters: How Values Shape Human Progress* (New York: Basic Books, 2000), p. 230.

35. Ibid., p. 222.

36. Ibid., pp. 223–4.

37. Gat, Azar, *Nations: The Long History and Deep Roots of Political Ethnicity and Nationalism* (Cambridge: Cambridge University Press, 2012), p. 268.

38. Williams, Tennessee, *A Streetcar Named Desire* (New York: New Directions, 2004).

39. Ibid.

40. Passel, Jeffrey S., and D'Vera Cohn, 'Unauthorized Immigration Population Stable for Half a Decade', *Pew Research Center*, 21 September 2016, available at <http://www.pewresearch.org/fact-tank/2016/09/21/unauthorized-immigrant-population-stable-for-half-a-decade/>.

41. For the twentieth anniversary edition, see *Foreign Affairs*, 21 August 2013, available at <https://www.foreignaffairs.com/articles/united-states/1993-06-01/clash-civilizations>.

42. Huntington, *Who Are We?*, p. xvii.

43. Glazer, Nathan, and Daniel P. Moynihan, *Beyond the Melting Pot: The Negroes, Puerto*

Ricans, Jews, Italians, and Irish of New York City (Cambridge, MA: MIT Press, 1970), pp. xxxi–xxxii.

44. Huntington, *Who Are We?*, pp. 221–45.

45. Brimelow, Peter, *Alien Nation: Common Sense about America's Immigration Disaster* (New York: Harper Perennial, 1996), p. 309.

46. Weiner, Myron, *The Global Migration Crisis: Challenge to States and to Human Rights* (New York: HarperCollins, 1995), p. 21.

47. Huntington, *Who Are We?*, pp. 221–45.

48. Alba, Richard, and Nancy Foner, *Strangers No More: Immigration and the Challenges of Integration in North America and Western Europe* (Cambridge: Cambridge University Press, 2015), p. 107.

49. Teppermanjune, Jonathan, 'Canada's Ruthlessly Smart Immigration Policy', *New York Times*, 28 June 2017, available at <https://www.nytimes.com/2017/06/28/opinion/canada-immigration-policy-trump.html?action=click&pgtype=Homepage&clickSource=story-heading&module=opinion-c-col-right-region&region=opinion-c-col-right-region&WT.nav=opinion-c-col-right-region&_r=0>.

50. Government of Canada, 'Medical Refusals and Inadmissibility', available at <https://www.canada.ca/en/immigration-refugees-citizenship/corporate/publications-manuals/operational-bulletins-manuals/standard-requirements/medical-requirements/refusals-inadmissibility.html>.

51. Teppermanjune, 'Canada's Ruthlessly Smart Immigration Policy'.

52. Lilla, Mark, *The Once and Future Liberal: After Identity Politics* (New York: Harper, 2017).

53. Ibid.

54. Meek, James, 'Against Passion', *London Review of Books*, 39, no. 23, 30 November 2017, p. 22, available at <https://www.lrb.co.uk/v39/n23/james-meek/against-passion>.

55. Ibid.

56. 'Why Is America More Tolerant of Inequality Than Many Rich Countries?', *The Economist*, 18 December 2017, available at <https://www.economist.com/blogs/democracyinamerica/2017/12/capital-question?cid1=cust/ddnew/email/n/n/20171218n/owned/n/n/ddnew/n/n/n/nNA/Daily_Dispatch/email&etear=dailydispatch>.

57. Interview with John Humphrys, 'Jimmy Carter: US Campaign Funding is "Legal Bribery"', *BBC*, 3 February 2016, available at <http://www.bbc.co.uk/programmes/p03hd981>.

58. Albertson, Bethany, and Shana Kushner Gadarian, *Anxious Politics: Democratic Citizenship in a Threatening World* (Cambridge: Cambridge University Press, 2015), p. xx.

59. Ibid., p. 156.

60. Coates, Ta-Nehisi, 'My President was Black', *The Atlantic*, January–February 2017, available at <https://www.theatlantic.com/magazine/archive/2017/01/my-president-was-black/508793/>.

61. Gilliam, Jr, Franklin D., *Farther to Go: Readings and Cases in African-American Politics* (Fort Worth, TX: Harcourt, 2002).

62. Coates, 'My President was Black'.

63. Coates, Ta-Nehisi, *We Were Eight Years in Power: An American Tragedy* (New York: One World, 2017).

64. Ibid.
65. 'The Counted: People Killed by Police in US', *The Guardian*, available at <https://www.theguardian.com/us-news/ng-interactive/2015/jun/01/the-counted-police-killings-us-database>.
66. 'Mapping Police Violence', available at <https://mappingpoliceviolence.org/>.
67. West, Cornel, 'Ta-Nehisi Coates is the Neoliberal Face of the Black Freedom Struggle', *The Guardian*, 17 December 2017, available at <https://www.theguardian.com/commentisfree/2017/dec/17/ta-nehisi-coates-neoliberal-black-struggle-cornel-west>.
68. Steele, Claude M., *Whistling Vivaldi: How Stereotypes Affect Us and What We Can Do* (New York: W. W. Norton, 2011).
69. Anderson, Kurt, 'How America Lost its Mind', *The Atlantic*, September 2017, available at <https://www.theatlantic.com/magazine/archive/2017/09/how-america-lost-its-mind/534231/>.
70. Ibid.
71. Ibid.

CHAPTER SEVEN

Multinational India

MAJORITY AND MAJORITY

India is immense in every way. Its national anthem, written by Nobel laureate Rabindranath Tagore, aspires to nothing less than this: 'Thou art the ruler of the minds of all people.' The country has more than twenty official languages, twenty-nine states and 1.2 billion people. Before independence it spanned more territory, had two enormous confessional groups and spoke even more languages. It is the leading country in the world in terms of sending migrants to other countries – over 15 million in 2015. But it ranks twelfth in taking in migrants (Table 3.2). Despite these large numbers, I hypothesise that India is not engaged in expanding nationhood (Table 3.1).

With perceptible growth of Hindu nationalism, many minorities feel insecure. Supporters of Prime Minister Narendra Modi are typed as intolerant amid religious tensions with the Muslim 'minority'. Due to India's size, minority can signify a vast population and about 180 million make up its Muslim 'minority'.

Can demographic diversity and territorial size translate into far-reaching nationhood for an entire subcontinent? Muhammad Ali Jinnah's theory of two nations served as the ideological basis for the partition of the British Raj into Muslim and Hindu states. But each of these countries is diverse in its own right. What are the normative, institutional and identitarian structures that make up nationhood? A proposition I examine is whether a multinational state can aim to create singular nationhood.

THE BRITISH RAJ AND INDIAN NATIONALISM

A Cambridge historian argued that 'British rule in India became the most spectacular case of imperialism in modern times.'[1] This jewel in Queen

Victoria's crown became, after London, the second centre of British world power:

> By the later nineteenth century the Indian Empire covered a sub-continent of one and a half million square miles, inhabited in 1881 by some 256 million people. More than one-third of India was composed of native states, with a population of fifty-six millions. In the remainder, the British directly ruled over two hundred million subjects.[2]

Modern Indian nationalism emerged in the late nineteenth century and for the next fifty years it struggled against British imperialism, emerging victorious in 1947 when an independent, if partitioned, Indian state was proclaimed. The character of Indian nationalism was shaped by British rule. As one Indian scholar noted, it 'emerged against the background of changes associated with British imperialism, notably as they impinged upon the political structure, economy and education of the country'.[3]

When the British seized power from Mughal rulers in the eighteenth century, the social, economic and political conditions prevailing in India did not encourage national consciousness. Religious, linguistic, ethnic and caste divisions hindered the emergence of pan-Indian identity. The vast majority of the population lived in villages comprising hermetic self-sufficient systems having little social, economic and intellectual contact with the outside world. The caste-stratified village structure insulated and isolated much of the population.[4]

Pre-British India had negligible political unity and was divided into unconnected kingdoms and principalities. Mughal rule was unable to bring the territory of India under its control and after the death of its emperor in 1707 it began to fall apart. India had enjoyed a rich tradition of the arts, literature and education, but they were limited to urban centres. Most of the population remained illiterate and uneducated.

The absence of a national consciousness, together with social, economic and political divisions, was the reason why the British seized power with relative ease. The English East India Company had begun trading on the subcontinent in the seventeenth century when it was under the Mughals, but the Battle of Plassey in 1757 gave the Company, and England, effective control over the key province of Bengal.

The pursuit of economic gain underlay the expansion of British rule. Unwittingly, this was to create the conditions for the development of Indian nationalism that ultimately drove them out of the country. The Raj, as India was known under British rule, comprised territories ruled directly, first by the East India Company, then after 1857 by the British Crown. Alongside direct rule were many princely states led by hereditary princes and monarchs who enjoyed substantial autonomy in return for loyalty to the British.

Probably the most famous reform implemented by British rule was the political, administrative and legal unification of the country. Replacing the traditional legal system based on customary law, the British introduced common law. It assumed the equality of all citizens before the law. A cen-tralised bureaucracy took over the administrative powers overseeing villages. A new education system, patterned on the one in England, introduced schools and colleges that produced graduates to staff the vast administrative machinery and economic infrastructure. Key administrative posts remained in British hands but local support was needed to manage a growing economy.

English schooling created a well-educated class of Indians whose members became familiar with Western democratic political ideals. They subsequently spearheaded the movement for India's freedom. But the colonisers used various strategies to deflect demands for autonomy, ranging from outright annexation of territory, collusion with local rulers in return for British pro-tection, creation of loyal classes (such as the *zamindars*), setting up religious divisions through the policy of divide and rule, and use of brute force and coercion where necessary.

Many sections of Indian society awoke to the drawbacks of alien rule:

> The industrial bourgeoisie found in the absolute control of India by Britain an obstacle to carry through its program of unfettered industrial development. The educated classes found in the monopoly of key posts in the state machinery by the British an obstacle to their just ambition to secure jobs. The peasantry found in the new land and revenue systems introduced by Britain the basic cause of their progressive impoverishment. The proletariat found in the British rule a foreign undemocratic agency preventing it from developing class struggles for improving their conditions of life and labor and finally for ending the wage system itself under which they were exploited.[5]

These grievances formed the basis for the rise of anti-colonialism. An underlying paradox emerged. The ideas of national self-determination and liberal nationalism arose in the West, and Indian nationalists viewed them as progressive, but they recognised how they originated in an alien culture and had to be adapted to India's culture. A double rejection followed: first, of the Western intruder – though not necessarily of some Western ideas and prac-tices seen as progressive; second, of one's own traditional culture, especially beliefs, customs and practices seen as obstacles to progress.

How were these two conflicting imperatives reconciled? Partha Chatterjee argues that, characteristic of its cultural foundations, Indian nationalists separated 'the world of social institutions and practices into two domains – the material and the spiritual'.[6] The material consisted of the outside world – of the economy, political institutions, and science and technology where the imperial power had to be confronted but where superiority of Western ideas and achievements had to be replicated. The spiritual domain contained the essential markers of India's cultural identity. The greater the success in imitating Western skills in the material domain, the stronger was the need to preserve the distinctness of India's spiritual culture.

Two components of Indian nationalism emerged together. At the material level, it involved political struggle against British imperialism, though not against Western political and economic ideas nor against Western discourses on modernity. At the spiritual level, it required the consolidation of a distinct modern and syncretic Indian national culture.

What role did the division of this culture into Hindu and Muslim traditions play? One specialist believed that 'antagonistic Hindu and Muslim nations existed before the nineteenth century'. Then, Hindu and Muslim movements began 'to transform a plethora of religious communities, which indeed were often antagonistic, into Hindu and Muslim nations'.[7] If the political manifestation of Indian nationalism was responsible for ending British imperialism, the spiritual dimension partitioned the subcontinent when independence was proclaimed.

MUTINY AND NATION

The Indian national movement began as an elitist, secular, non-confrontational programme having limited goals. In time it evolved into a mass movement that employed radical but generally non-violent means of political activity to achieve independence. It was accompanied by a concurrent rise in the strength of Muslim nationalism. By the late 1930s, it called for a separate state for India's Muslims.

Facing this intractable double challenge, the ability and will of the British government to rule India started to decline.

The first nationalist uprising took place in 1857. Called the *Sepoy* (or Soldiers') Mutiny, cavalry units of the Bengali Army revolted against their British officers. This first nationalist spark coloured 'the way that the participants were imbued with the sense of a common nationhood and were fighting for their country and freedom'.[8] The Mutiny had at least three major political consequences for the British role in the Raj.

First, the shock value of the *Sepoy* revolt, also known as the Indian Mutiny or India's First War of Independence, on the British was unexpected. Not just the murderous Mutiny but also the cruel British response to it rocked the political system. Before the rebellion, 50,000 British troops commanded about 300,000 *sepoys* serving in the East India Company military. But in May 1857 *sepoys* of the British East India Company's army revolted against British officers. The trigger was ammunition supplied for the new rifles they had to use. Cartridges in the rifles had to be bitten open. Muslims were angry because they believed unclean pig fat was used in them; Hindu soldiers were upset because they were convinced they were laced with cow fat.

Both Hindu and Muslim sides cooperated with each other. For Tariq Ali, 'The bulk of the fighting against the British in 1857 was actually carried out by Hindu and Muslim soldiers.... Afterwards, many religiously unified divisions were separated to prevent a repeat performance.'[9] The siege of Cawnpore, in particular, proved traumatic. The besieged British company and civilian compatriots were unprepared and had to surrender to rebel forces. Nana Sahib, an Indian *Peshwa* who had economic grievances with the British, promised the besieged safe passage. But their evacuation turned into a massacre and most of the men were killed. Sahib was accused of the atrocity and fled to the hills of Nepal. More shocking was the fact that 120 British women and children captured by *sepoy* forces were killed, and their bodies thrown down a well so as to hide the evidence. Following the British recapture of Cawnpore and the discovery of the massacre, the outraged forces, inspired by the war cry 'Remember Cawnpore', exacted brutal retribution on captured rebel soldiers and local civilians.

Historian Andrew Ward has remarked on the unprecedented character of the rebellion and its aftermath. *The Times* of London wrote how the Cawnpore massacre was 'the crowning atrocity – for it can hardly be surpassed – of native India, comprising in one deliberate act its pagan and infidel rulers and conquerors'.[10] Benjamin Disraeli, burgeoning champion of the British imperial ideal, wrote:

> I am persuaded that our soldiers and our sailors will exact a retribution which it may, perhaps, be too terrible to pause upon.... I protest against meeting atrocities by atrocities. I have heard things said and seen things written of late which would make me almost suppose that the religious opinions of the people of England had undergone some sudden change, and that instead of bowing before the name of Jesus we were preparing to revive the worship of Molech.[11]

British atrocities were recognised and no less a figure that Queen Victoria announced a Day of Humiliation 'so both we and our people may humble ourselves before Almighty God, in order to obtain pardon of *our* sins'. Of all the fallen stations in India, Britain had heard 'a wail come across the ocean from the well of Cawnpore'.

A second consequence was that responsibility for British India was transferred from the East India Company to the British Crown. By the Act of 1858, governance of India was assigned to the Secretary of State in London, and to the British Governor-General in Calcutta, the Viceroy, who symbolised British supremacy over the princes.

A third upshot was that the British abandoned their policy of forcible territorial annexation of princely states. These important states contrived to prolong their existence by being cajoled into becoming loyal subjects of the Crown.

Nearly three decades later, in 1885, nationalism as an organised political movement was launched with the formation of the Indian National Congress. From the beginning, the Congress projected itself as a secular, all-India institution concerned with national politics but steering clear of issues that could give rise to religious or social conflicts. It strove for limited political and economic reforms that would give Indians greater say in the legislative councils, wider entry into the Indian Civil Service (ICS), and more equitable land taxes. Congress liberals wished 'to convince the British of the justness of the demands of the Indian people and of their democratic duty to meet them'.[12]

The call for greater militancy arose from the conviction that India's spiritual greatness was being short-changed. Unlike the secular outlook of liberals, militants invoked indigenous symbols associated with Hinduism and claimed that India was the land of Hindus. Its greatness came from the Hindu religion, especially the teachings of the Vedas, Puranas, Upanishads and the *Bhagavad Gita*. For a Hindu nationalist leader writing in the 1920s, 'A Hindu means a person who regards this land of Bharat Varsha, from the Indus to the Seas, as his Father-Land as well as his Holy-Land that is the cradle of his religion.'[13] Hindu-ness, or *Hindutva*, conflates religious and national identity. But it is silent about non-Hindus.

Identification of part of the Congress party with Hinduism had a major impact on Hindu–Muslim relations and contributed to the growth of Muslim separatism. The Muslim community had mixed feelings about the Congress. On the one hand, Indian nationalism provided the opportunity to regain the pride that had been lost when the British wrested power from the Mughals in the eighteenth century. On the other hand, 'the doctrine of nationalism and the general realization among the Muslims that the triumph of this ideology would reduce them to a state of permanent political subjugation by the more numerous Hindus' produced a sense of fear.[14] Indeed, religious polarisation was embedded in the construction of homelands on the subcontinent. According to one historian, 'nation building is directly dependent on religious antagonism, between Hindus and Muslims, between Sikhs and Hindus, between Buddhists and Hindus'.[15]

Some scholars reject this explanation for Muslim separatism and argue that Indian Muslims' attitudes were formed by the teachings of their own religion: in particular, the supremacy of *umma*, the community of believers in Allah, over *watan*, the fatherland or territorial nation. Others believed that Indian Muslims' rejection of Hindu nationalism was the result of deep-rooted cultural cleavage between the two communities, which was reinforced under the Raj. Yet another viewpoint questioned whether Indian Muslims formed a monolithic community. What is clear is that by the turn of the twentieth century the growth of Hindu extremism within the Congress and the loss of Muslim confidence in the British Government's commitment to protect their rights convinced them of the urgency to set up a separate Muslim political organisation.

Under pressure from Hindu communities, in 1898 the British government recognised Hindi (the language spoken mainly by Hindus) alongside Urdu (that mostly spoken by Muslims) as languages of administration in the predominantly Muslim United Province. But the British then backtracked on their decision in 1905 to partition Bengal and annulled the two-language decision in 1911. In the interim, in 1906 they decided to establish the Indian Muslim League. Apart from some Western-educated Muslim leaders like Mohammad Ali Jinnah, most pan-Islamic conservatives and religious elites remained hostile to Indian nationalism.

Towards partition

A turning point in India's history was the rise of Mahatma Gandhi to the Congress leadership in 1920. He quickly turned it into a mass movement with a distinctive ideology and strategy. His inclination was for radical political action carried out non-violently; non-violence, with its emphasis on self-suffering, was an act of courage differing from mere passive resistance. In 1928 the Congress issued an ultimatum that if dominion status was not conceded by the British within a year, a civil disobedience campaign would begin, aimed at *Purna Swaraj*, or complete independence. The British dissembled and in 1930 Congress launched the Civil Disobedience Movement. The Muslim League's reaction was again hostile and viewed it as a Hindu plot to oust the British from India.

In Britain, under Labour Party leader Ramsay MacDonald, the government took a small constitutional step forward. In 1935 it proposed a federal constitution encompassing British India and the princely states. It also contained provisions for separate electorates for Muslims in all the provinces.[16] But the Government of India Act was condemned by both Conservative Party leader Winston Churchill and Gandhi's Indian National Congress. While Churchill, not without foundation, saw the Act as 'the beginning of the dissolution of the Empire',[17] Congress condemned it for providing parliamentary quotas for Muslim minorities.

After the 1937 elections, the political thinking of the Muslim League changed. Its electoral performance, especially in Muslim-majority provinces, was dismal. Jinnah determined that the Congress had little concern for Muslim interests and, not without a grain of truth, he accused it of seeking to establish a Hindu Raj. The inescapable conclusion was that a separate state

157

needed to be created for India's Muslims, and this was formally embraced by the Muslim League in 1940.

Jinnah's justification for an independent Pakistan was based on the concept of two separate nations. Indian Muslims were defined not merely as a separate but also as a 'self-determining political community'. It formed a separate nation smaller than, but equal to, the Hindus. This was the core of the 'Two Nation' theory under which Jinnah called for the creation of Pakistan.

FAMINE

The catastrophic standoff between the Raj and Britain may owe a lot to one person's prejudices. The Bengal Famine of 1943–4 represented the worst disaster to have hit the subcontinent in the twentieth century. Close to 4 million Indians died as a result of a famine that was fabricated by the British government. It was a man-made holocaust since Churchill's policies were directly responsible.

In 1942 Bengal had an abundant harvest, but on Churchill's orders the British government sent food grain from India to Britain, worsening the massive food shortage in present-day West Bengal, Odisha, Bihar and Bangladesh. Scholar Madhusree Mukerjee interviewed survivors of the famine and heard harrowing stories. 'Parents dumped their starving children into rivers and wells. Many took their lives by throwing themselves in front of trains.' People were too weak to cremate their loved ones. Dogs and jackals feasted on dead bodies in Bengal's villages. Wheat was judged too precious a food to expend on non-Whites.

For Mukerjee, those who escaped the famine were men who migrated to Calcutta for jobs, and women who turned to prostitution to feed their families: 'Mothers had turned into murderers, village belles into whores, fathers into traffickers of daughters.'[18] By 1943 hordes of starving people poured into Calcutta, where they encountered well-fed White British soldiers. But Churchill turned down appeals for assistance from two successive Viceroys, his own Secretary of State for India, and the US President. His excuse that in wartime Britain could not spare ships to transport emergency supplies was phoney; Mukerjee discovered official records showing that ships carried grain from Australia on their way to the Mediterranean – and bypassed India. Future Prime Minister Jawaharlal Nehru aptly called it 'the final judgment on British rule in India'.[19]

Famines were not new to India. Mike Davis writes of famines that killed 29 million Indians; they were people, he claims, who were murdered by British state policy in 1876, 1877–8 and the 1890s. In the latter decade alone, 19 million lives were lost. All this occurred even as grain was exported in record amounts to England. Life expectancy in India, Davis calculates, fell by 20 per cent between 1872 and 1921.[20]

Amartya Sen, Nobel Prize laureate in economics, published a seminal work in 1981, which revolutionised policies on how international organisations and governments had to manage food crises. Using India as a historical case in *Poverty and Famine*, he demonstrates that famine was not a consequence of nature but an avoidable economic and political calamity. A decline in food production often precedes drought and flooding but it rarely accounts for famine, Sen notes. Typically, even if many thousands die, there is enough food in the country to go around, or enough money to import it. Disaster strikes when the poorest people can no longer afford to buy food because they have lost their jobs or because food prices have increased. In the wartime Bengali famine in which close to 4 million perished, India's food supplies were not low. But colonial rulers, immune to democratic pressures, stood by and allowed people to starve.[21] These cyclical disasters demonstrated that Britain's banal nationalism at home was anything but banal in running its empire.

HINDU NATIONALISM TRIUMPHANT

Other than man-made famine, nationalist politics in India from 1940 to 1947 were marked by increasing communal unrest caused by diverging programmes of the Muslim League and the Congress party (Box 7.1). The Congress view of the Muslims was best articulated by Nehru:

> The Moslem nation in India – a nation within a nation, and not even compact, but vague, spread out, indeterminate. Politically, the idea is absurd; economically it is fantastic; it is hardly worth considering. To talk of a 'Moslem nation', there-fore, means that there is no nation at all but a religious bond.[22]

For Nehru, religion could not serve as the basis for separate nationhood because 'Almost always it seems to stand for blind belief and reaction, dogma and bigotry, superstition and exploitation, and the preservation of vested interests.'[23] A commitment to follow a more secular way could have laid the foundations for a multireligious, multicultural state, but it would perforce exclude the 'Moslem nation'.

In 1942 Churchill dispatched a member of his War Cabinet to work out a solution for India's future but it proved unacceptable to both Congress and the Muslim League. In the British elections of 1945 Churchill was defeated by Clement Attlee, head of the Labour Party, which was sympathetic towards the Indian national movement. Public opinion in England also favoured an early pullout from India. In the US, too, President Franklin D. Roosevelt was 'unquestionably opposed to imperialism'[24] while taking care not to antago-nise Churchill.[25]

In 1946, a Cabinet Mission was sent to India to negotiate between the

---

Box 7.1 Jinnah justifies Pakistan

It is extremely difficult to appreciate why our Hindu friends fail to understand the real nature of Islam and Hinduism. They are not religions in the strict sense of the word, but are, in fact, different and distinct social orders, and it is a dream that Hindus and Muslims can ever evolve a common nationality and this misconception of one Indian nation has gone beyond its limits and is the cause of most of your troubles and will lead India to destruction if we fail to revise our notions in time. . . . The present artificial unity of India only dates back to the British conquest and is maintained by the British regime.

Source: Quoted in Sumit Ganguly, *The Origins of War in South Asia: Indo-Pakistani Conflicts Since 1947* (Boulder, CO: Westview Press, 1994), pp. 20-1.

Congress and the Muslim League. The Muslim League, 'while reiterating its desire for an independent Pakistan, agreed to cooperate in the constitution-making process because the Mission Plan had grouped the Muslim provinces together, thus forming the basis for Pakistan'.[26] Friction between the two over the Interim Government arose immediately. Jinnah played on Muslim apprehensions about Hindu domination and called for Direct Action to achieve it. Communal violence erupted on the day of Direct Action (16 August 1946) and cost many lives, especially in Bengal. Frustrated by the failure to bring the two sides together, in February 1947 Attlee announced to the House of Commons that 'His Majesty's Government wish to make it clear that it is their definite intention to take necessary steps to effect the transference of power to responsible Indian hands by a date not later than June 1948.'[27]

Lord Louis Mountbatten was appointed to serve as Viceroy of India to work out the plan that would transfer power to India. He soon realised that the gulf between the two nationalist movements was unbridgeable. But key Congress leaders, including Nehru, were persuaded that partition of the country was inevitable and notified the Viceroy that

> The point has now been reached at which the Congress must reluctantly accept the fact that the Muslim League will never voluntarily come into a Union of India. Rather than have a battle we shall let them have their Pakistan, provided you will allow the Punjab and Bengal to be partitioned in a fair manner.[28]

Jinnah and the League reluctantly accepted the idea of a truncated Pakistan.

On 3 June 1947, Mountbatten formally announced the Partition Plan, which would create two countries. The latter would comprise provinces with Muslim majorities while Bengal and Punjab would be divided. Six weeks later

160

the Partition Plan received royal assent and became the Indian Independence Act of 1947. The Partition Plan displaced over 10 million people living on the subcontinent. About 6 million Indian Muslims were forced to move to the new Pakistan, and 4.5 million Hindus and Sikhs had to find refuge in an abridged India. Over 1 million people were killed, often in brutal confessional massacres. The political status of the Princely States locked the two countries again into conflict, particularly over Kashmir.[29] Mountbatten was able to ensure a peaceful transfer of power elsewhere.[30]

A different political actor emerged at that time. Insisting on Kashmir's accession to India, the militant Hindu organisation Rashtriya Swayamsevak Sangh (RSS) had served as a radical body organising a training school for Hindu cadres. The RSS has developed into the ideological parent of the governing Bharatiya Janata Party (BJP).

There are even similarities between Prime Minister Modi and President Trump.

It seems as if Modi, just like US President Donald Trump and many other world leaders, has hit on a political recipe in which nationalism is used as a way to maintain and increase power while challenging democratic values. Modi's style of nationalism may be more subtle than some others. He often talks about unity and development, but the underlying rhetoric of Hindu nationalism threatens to displace secularism as the founding principle of the country. India's democracy, and the values that come with it, will be tested as nationalism grows.[31]

FLAWED NATIONHOOD

The partition of British India marked the end of nationalist struggles against British rule. The cost of independence was massive. Communal violence racked cities and towns on the eve of partition, millions of refugees fled their homes as a result of partition, and bitterness between the two new countries boiled over. In a short time, each of these new states faced serious ethnonationalist and secessionist challenges of their own, often with the support of its rival.

Seventy years after partition, writers from both sides of the divide have different views about the division of the subcontinent. For Indian essayist Pankaj Mishra, both Hindu and Muslim movements have been corrupted:

Narendra Modi and his mob are completing the unfinished business of partition: the unification of a political community through identification and persecution of internal and external enemies. In conforming to this grimly familiar historical pattern, India has outpaced Pakistan, where regional differences serve to check a ruthlessly homogenizing nationalism (and Islamism), and no single ideological movement is able to colonize all key institutions of the state and civil society.[32]

Also apprehensive about Hindu nationalism is Salman Rushdie. 'The country is rapidly being pulled in the direction decreed by the proponents of "Hindutva", Hindu nationalism, and away from the secular ideals of the founding fathers.'[33] US-based Indian novelist Kiran Desai underscored that 'The political wing of the RSS, the organization to which Gandhi's assassin was once a member, is the party that runs the country now, and it exults in the same vocabulary of violence now as then.'[34] For Pakistani novelist Kamila Shamsie, the most important consequence of partition was the violation of minority rights in both states.

> These were nations born as a result of a heroic opposition to imperial rule, but their birth was also marked by hatred and bloodshed. Contemporary conversations often focus on what that bloodshed means for India and Pakistan's relationship to each other, but increasingly as I look at both nations, now so mired in violence towards their own minorities, I wonder what it means for each nation's relationship to its own history, its own nature. There was never a reckoning for the violence of partition; that would have got in the way of the narrative of a glorious independence. Instead it became easier to blame the other side for all the violence, and pretend that at the moment of inception both India and Pakistan didn't wrap mass murder in a flag and hope no one would notice the blood stains.[35]

The partition was an unimaginable disaster, causing bloodshed and suffering that uprooted millions across both sides of the border. There could be no question that what was once a heterogeneous subcontinent that might have experimented with developing a sense of nationhood came to be haunted by heartbreak (Box 7.2).

Focusing on today's India, a major concern is to prevent the emergence of separatist movements, whether endogenous or aided by Pakistani support. A specialist has identified four ways that ethnic conflicts would not spread to separatist ones:

1. No secessionist movements can be tolerated and where necessary they should be suppressed by force.
2. Given a commitment to secularism, 'no demand for political recognition of a religious group can be considered'.
3. No 'capricious concessions would be made to the political demands of any linguistic, regional or other culturally defined group'.
4. '[N]o political concessions to cultural groups in conflict would be made unless they had demonstrable support from both sides.'[36]

Partly due to these strictures, President's Rule – allowing the central government to take over the administration of a state in peril – was invoked sixty-five times up to 1982. Yet political mobilisation of ethnic groups has

162

Box 7.2 A writer from northeastern India

The boundary commission headed by the barrister Cyril Radcliffe finished preparing their maps only on 12 August, although these maps would not be made public until 17 August, two days after partition. By then, the ethnic cleansing was well under way. Over a million were killed, thousands raped and abducted, and between 12 and 20 million displaced in the process. Trains criss-crossed the landscape with carriages filled with corpses. Those escaping on foot travelled in columns that were sometimes 45 miles long. None of this violence and pain has really worked its way into the official histories of Britain, India, Pakistan or Bangladesh. This is surely one reason why the partition shows an uncanny ability to replicate itself through the decades, in mini partitions, mini pogroms and the steady marginalization and brutalization of minorities that has become the governing spirit of nationalism in south Asia.

Source: Siddhartha Deb, 'Partition, 70 Years On', 5 August 2017, *The Guardian*, <https://www.theguardian.com/books/2017/aug/05/partition-70-years-salman-rushdie-kamila-shamsie-writers-reflect-india-pakistan>.

remained a matter of concern for Indian politics. Among those who have mobilised are Assamese, Sikhs, Kashmiri Muslims and, in northeast India alone, Bodo, Naga, Kuki, Mizo, Manipuri and Tripura insurgent groups.[37]

CLIMATE REFUGEES

In 2015 climate research found that conflict in Syria had been preceded by record drought. It had led to lower agricultural yields, forcing farmers to migrate to urban areas. Drought was an added stressor in the war. In Pentagon jargon, climate change breeds a 'threat multiplier'.

It is not enough to explain causes of migration purely in terms of a desire to improve economic opportunities. Persecution and war are the chief reasons for seeking political asylum but exogenous weather fluctuations are a factor too. Localised shocks to agricultural production were found to increase EU asylum applications from affected regions; a change from an agriculture-optimum level of 20°C (70°F) – a rise in global temperatures of about 1.8°C now makes this inevitable – will produce 28 per cent more asylum seekers. At the present rate of temperature increases – up to 4.8°C – applications will go up 188 per cent: that is, there will be 660,000 more applicants every year.[38]

The UN's World Meteorological Organization weather agency reported in 2016 that carbon dioxide concentrations in the atmosphere increased at record-breaking speed. Carbon dioxide (CO_2) was 50 per cent higher than the average of the past ten years – driving it to the highest level in 800,000 years. A Test Match between India and Sri Lanka in Delhi in December 2017 was stopped with reports that many players were vomiting. The same happened in Sydney, Australia, in January 2018 because of record heat. Rapid declines in levels of CO_2 and other greenhouse gases are needed to avoid dangerous temperature growth by 2100 that would overwhelm the climate targets set in the 2015 Paris accords. But how international migration is affected by these gases is anyone's guess.

Deaths caused by pollution topped 9 million in 2015 – three times those from AIDS, tuberculosis and malaria combined, and fifteen times more than war and other forms of violence. Mining and manufacturing have shifted to poorer countries where environmental regulations are lax. Not surprisingly, 92 per cent of pollution-related deaths occur in low- or middle-income developing countries. India is atop the list with 2.5 million deaths. These days, construction workers in New Delhi are more exposed to air pollution and less able to protect themselves as they walk, bike or take the bus to workplaces.[39] Climate refugees affect Indian society profoundly.

Naomi Klein and Arundhati Roy have both been fierce critics of capitalism and staunch supporters of environmental activism – two sides of the same coin. In her 2014 book *This Changes Everything: Capitalism vs. the Climate*, the Canadian critic asserted that it was becoming impossible to ignore the real-life consequences of global warming as extreme weather events become more prevalent. The battle between 'capitalism and the planet' requires radical changes to the economic system in order to lower fossil-fuel emissions. But lower emissions 'fundamentally conflict with deregulated capitalism, the reigning ideology for the entire period we have been struggling to find a way out of this crisis'.[40] For Klein, air pollution will be a game changer, particularly in India and China where action on climate change is urgent. *The Lancet*, one of the world's oldest general medical journals, issued a chilling report on health and climate change in 2017.[41] The knock-on effect on mobility will be far-reaching.

For essayist and sometime novelist Roy, the capitalist point of departure is similar to Klein's: 'Violating human rights is integral to the project of neoliberalism and global hegemony.' But she also offers a paean in praise of passion: 'If we were to lose the ability to be emotional, if we were to lose the ability to be angry, to be outraged, we would be robots. And I refuse that.'

India's identity is a puzzle to Roy.

Which India? ... The land of poetry and mad rebellion? The one that produces haunting music and exquisite textiles? The one that invented the caste system

164

and celebrates the genocide of Muslims and Sikhs and the lynching of Dalits? The country of dollar billionaires? Or the one in which 800 million live on less than half-a-dollar a day? Which India?'

The violence done to indigenous peoples and low-caste Dalits is her special concern.

To annihilate indigenous populations eventually paves the way to our own annihilation. They are the only people who practice sustainable living. We think they are relics of the past, but they may be the gatekeepers to our future.

Roy focuses on an often-overlooked subject that has grave implications for mobility – dams. In India the Sardar Sarovar dam was transformed from a dispute over a river valley to a debate over the entire political system. Who owned the land, its rivers, forests and fish (a question Canadian First Nations have been asking)? 'Big dams started well, but have ended badly,' Roy argues. Big dams have inspired writers to create poetry, but in the First World they are now regarded as the main cause of floods, water-logging, salinity and disease. The First World has deemed them obsolete and decommissions them. So they are exported to the Third World – in the name of development.

Mobility is a crucial issue when dam reservoirs displace large populations, leaving them homeless and destitute. The Indian Institute of Public Administration determined that fifty-four large dams resulted in an average of 44,182 people being displaced by each. Since 3,300 were constructed in 1999 when Roy wrote her essay, by her calculation 33 million were displaced in the past fifty years.

'What has happened to all these millions of people? Where are they now? How do they earn a living? Nobody really knows.' Roy reports that tribal people displaced by the Nagarjuna Sagar Dam were selling their babies to foreign adoption agencies. Most tribal people have no formal title to the land. Even if some illiterate men received petty cash payments, women got nothing. Roy concludes: 'The millions of displaced people don't exist anymore. When history is written they won't be in it. Not even as statistics.'[42]

Significantly higher temperatures, CO_2, pollution and dam construction are among the major causes of population displacements. These can be life-threatening and mobility-causing events; nationhood is of little importance in this context. The caste system in India should be added to these events, and also to nationhood.

Tribal communities are divided into about fifty groups, many of which are low-caste, impoverished and illiterate. The Constitution of India recognises historically discriminated communities, which are designated as Scheduled Castes and Scheduled Tribes. In modern accounts they are referred to as Dalits (or Untouchables). According to the 2011 census, they comprise 17 per cent of the total population of India. Half of them are concentrated in four states including Uttar Pradesh, the most populous one. A separate list of Hindu Scheduled Tribes makes up 9 per cent of the population.

These groups are the most vulnerable – educationally, economically and ecologically – to losing lands that they inhabited from long ago. Catastrophic disasters in these lands include tsunamis, hurricanes, tropical storms, flooding, volcanic eruptions and the like. More gradual erosive processes comprise deforestation, drought and famine. Epidemics causing mobility may follow outbreaks of malaria, cholera and HIV infection. Industrial causes too are the result of pollution, toxic substances, explosions and forest fires. Finally, complex emergencies are caused by human factors: wars, domestic conflicts, ethnic cleansing and violations of human rights.

Developmental causes are less chronic but more acute. Invasion and expropriation of lands is an example. Mobility caused by factory closures or their transfers to other regions, especially affecting agricultural workers, is a second. Housing shortages or expropriation of lands is a third. Low calorie and protein intakes force mobility too. Unsafe drinking water, common to India and other developing states, together with bacterial infections and microbiological transmissions, should be included. Loss of forests, pastures and grasslands, also widespread in India and other underdeveloped areas, forces people to move elsewhere.

In India's case, scattered data show that climate change contingencies increase migration flows. Flooding, uneven rainfalls and storms can raise tensions between communities. As men go out in search of work, women are exposed to different risk factors – raising children, caring for the elderly, and looking after households, cattle and farms in difficult conditions. Sometimes they make young women vulnerable to sex traffickers.[43]

According to the 2011 census, just under half of the country's 1.2 billion citizens migrate for work, marriage, education or other reasons, and settle in a place different from their previous location. Over 25 per cent of men migrate for work and a small percentage of women do too, but 70 per cent of women migrate for marriage while less than 5 per cent of men do. This may be changing: the UN climate science panel's 2014 study noted that unpredictable rainfall, sea level rises and heat waves across India and Bangladesh will probably intensify as global temperatures rise higher.

In 2015 and 2016 alone, severe drought in India caused over 300,000 people to move permanently from their homes. Displacement due to erratic or extreme weather has affected millions of others. Flooding in Jammu and Kashmir in 2015, in Uttarakhand in 2013 and in Assam in 2012 displaced 1.5 million. Even though the National Disaster Management Authority maps natural disasters, migration statistics are not tracked. Data on how many people move because of climate change around the world is therefore scarce.

166

Typically, due to extreme weather events, communities near coastlines and those relying on agriculture are most likely to move.[44]

Climate research has predicted that South Asia will be hard hit, leading to significant migration from drought-impacted regions and disruptions caused by severe weather. Warmer temperatures, rising sea levels, and more intense and frequent cyclonic activity in the Bay of Bengal, coupled with high population density, will generate large-scale migration, primarily to cities. Emergent urban areas absorbing inward migration will come under severe strain.

Bangladesh's Sunderbans – one of the last mangrove homes of the Bengal tiger – is particularly prone to regular flooding. Land and water are increasingly contaminated by salt-water intrusion from rising sea levels, cyclones and storm surges. This has been documented as the cause of hypertension, poor maternal health and pregnancy difficulties. High salinity of water and lack of sanitation cause conception problems as well as urinary tract infections.[45]

We should not overlook, lastly, a standard reason for mobility in South Asia: ethnic conflict. Bangladesh, and indirectly India, were affected by a refugee relocation crisis that was not the result of climate. In 2016, Myanmar border police were gunned down by fighters from an armed Rohingya group in neighbouring Myanmar, the Arakan Rohingya Salvation Army (ARSA). Ethnic cleansing ensued after Myanmar government troops poured into villages in Rakhine State, expelling Muslims and burning their homes and fields.

The ethnic group calling themselves Rohingya, but described by locals as Bengali Muslims, lived for centuries in majority-Buddhist Myanmar. But they were not included among the country's 135 official ethnic groups; not belonging and denying them nationhood were the results. Since 1982 they have become stateless, as they could not identify as Rohingya, only as naturalised citizens. Nobel Peace laureate Aung San Suu Kyi and her government regarded Rohingya as not being an ethnic group and so violence in Rakhine was ascribed to 'terrorists'.

The issue is complicated by the fact that up to 1948 the British administered Myanmar as an Indian province. This meant that migration was considered internal within India, rather than cross-national between India, Bangladesh and Myanmar. Buddhists in what was then Burma opposed the UK-sanctioned migration of Muslim labourers to their country.[46]

In Bangladesh, and India too – Kolkata is 500 miles from the Myanmar border – concerns were expressed that resettling 600,000 Muslim refugees throughout Bangladesh, rather than interning them in cholera-prone refugee camps, heightens the Muslim terrorist threat in South Asia. It is another international crisis of ethnic cleansing that confronts the UN High Commissioner for Human Rights.

BJP RISING

States in India harbouring secessionist claims hold that New Delhi is respon-sible for sowing discontent within the empire. The benefits of economic development have not reached groups on the periphery, whether due to nepotism, corruption, waste or bureaucracy. The central government's indif-ference to minorities' fears of assimilation has sparked discontent. To what extent is India's secular nationalism inclusive, then?

Some experts see the clash between secular nationalism and religious com-munalism as contrived.[47] But the Congress party, the purported instrument of secular nationalism, 'imagines a common ethnic culture of India in terms of religious pluralism. In this moderate view the different communities that populate the nation have to be represented in the state.'[48]

In reality, equal treatment of all religions puts religion squarely in the middle of discourse on the homeland. Since 80 per cent of citizens are Hindu, the notion recognises its hegemonic position.[49] Gandhi's legacy can be inter-preted to mean 'religious transnationality in "Hindu spiritualism" and in the Muslim *umma*'.[50] In practice, religions do not enjoy equal status.

Communal conflict between Hindus and Muslims has been an intermit-tent feature of Indian political life since independence. Muslims make up 14 per cent of the Hindu-majority nation but conflict is focused on certain parts of the country. One study found that less than 4 per cent of deaths in communal violence between 1950 and 1995 occurred in rural India, where the majority of Indians live. Therefore 'Hindu–Muslim violence turns out to be primarily an urban phenomenon.' It is concentrated in eight cities, where 46 per cent of all deaths in communal violence took place.[51] Gujarat state is one of these.

Under Congress party rule, this state fostered a myth of religious ecumen-ism. But the state has not been secular. Rather, 'it promotes a specific view of "religion" as a universal characteristic of Indian ethnicity. The different religions are only refractions of one great Indian spirituality.'[52]

The rise of the BJP since the 1980s is seen as a backlash against the long-ruling Congress party's pseudo-secularism and support instead for the confes-sional Hindu state. In the 1996 elections to parliament (the Lok Sabha), the BJP emerged as the country's largest party, receiving over one-fifth of the vote. If in 1984 it had 2 seats in parliament, in 2001 it held 182.

The rise of the BJP is associated with popular support for making the Hindu homeland strong, a phenomenon also encountered in Russia and the US. The party stresses *Hindutva*, a Hindu nationalism arguing for an Indian identity centred on its historic culture and religion – not politics. There is the expectation that a single community will be created through the assimilation of groups around common Hindu symbols. To this end, the BJP

168

ceased to be a party dominated by high-caste Hindu traders and even began recruiting Muslims to senior executive positions.[53] More moderate ideas were proposed and 'regional parties were uncomfortable with the perceived extremism of the Hindu nationalist party. In return for an electoral alliance and later support in government, they expected the BJP to moderate its policies.'[54]

But communal violence appeared unavoidable with a party of that character on the rise. In 1992 a Hindu mob destroyed the historic Babri mosque at Ayodhya, which had been built in 1528 by a Muslim general, on the site of a temple that marked the supposed birthplace of Lord Ram, the ubiquitous reincarnation of the divine. The BJP did not have a direct hand in its destruction but it gained notoriety from the communal conflict. It promoted attacks on other allegedly reprehensible influences undermining Hindu culture, such as Western fast food.

The most serious communal violence this century was the pogrom of Muslims in Godhra in Gujarat state. The riots started when sixty Hindu pilgrims died after a train they were on was set on fire. Since Godhra was 40 per cent Muslim, the supposed perpetrators became easy to target. Over 1,000 people were killed in violence that began in February 2002 and lasted two months. Some 20,000 Muslim homes and businesses and 360 places of worship were destroyed; 150,000 Muslims were displaced.

What was most significant about these riots was the fact that the Gujarati Chief Minister – and future Prime Minister – Narendra Modi was implicated in the anti-Muslim riots. Modi was quoted as saying that the Muslim community had to be taught a lesson following the attack on Hindu pilgrims.[55] A wave of Hindu support led to his reappointment as Gujarat Chief Minister later in 2002. On the other hand, foreign countries saw his sinister hand in the violence and Modi was subjected to a diplomatic boycott in Britain up to 2012 and in the US until 2014.[56]

Back in the 1980s and 1990s, the *Hindutva* movement in Gujarat had mobilised in support of the Narmada dam, a controversial project that was finally approved by the Supreme Court in 2001, months before Modi took over power. The Delhi Supreme Court and many NGOs had delayed its construction for several decades. With Supreme Court backing, Modi projected himself as the defender of Gujarati interests.[57]

His anti-establishment, identitarian politics were signalled in a confrontation with what he termed the Nehru–Gandhi 'Delhi Sultanate'. Characterising himself as *aam aadmi*, or son of the soil, against a cosmopolitan, privileged Nehru–Gandhi family with little connection to the Gujarat state, he lashed out at Congress leader Sonia Gandhi, labelling her a foreigner while insisting he was 'from this country only'. He stressed his Hindu identification and rhetorically asked: 'What kind of people are these

Congressmen? They can regard an Italian woman as their own but they find a son of the soil like me an outsider.' He countered: 'I was born and grew up there. I don't require your certificate of nationalism.'[58]

As Gujarat leader, Modi declared that 'Cultural nationalism is once again leading our country on the right path that was shown by saints and sages centuries ago.' The BJP made good on his rhetoric by not nominating Muslim candidates in the 2007 and 2012 elections. During the 2012 campaign, he associated himself further with Hinduism. Replying to a derogatory remark by a Congressman, he scolded: 'A Congress leader recently called me a monkey. Probably he hasn't read the Ramayana or he would have known about the power of monkeys. I am Hanuman and ... Gujaratis are my Ram whom I serve.'[59]

When he took over the national reins, however, Modi metamorphosed from one of the most divisive figures in Indian politics to consensus-building leader, and from pariah to Prime Minister. Nominated as BJP candidate in 2013, he changed his image as Hindu hardliner. For the 2014 elections, he assiduously avoided the language of *Hindutva* and instead embraced neutral-sounding issues like development and the investor-friendly climate he had established as Gujarat leader. He invoked the 'Vibrant Gujarat' summits starting in 2003 that attracted investment by prominent Indian and foreign business leaders. He stressed the unifying narrative of *vikas*, or development, and the 'Clean India' sanitation campaign.[60] These policies had a symbolic dimension.

But the makeover of Modi has not whitewashed his legacy in the anti-Muslim riots. In 2017 Gujarat steered on a determinedly *Hindutva* course and elected a new leader: he 'represents the rise of a muscular, Hindu India' and offers an opportunity to revise 'years of official policy going too far to accommodate India's Muslim minority'.[61]

When a leader is chosen on the basis of *Hindutva*, an India that excludes its large Muslim population is in the making. Some extremist leaders not only believe that Indian Muslims should go to Pakistan, but also set a condition that Muslims can stay only if they renounce Islam and convert to Hinduism.[62] Modi

> may not care about convincing his detractors that he is not spearheading a move-
> ment to turn India into the unified Hindu nation his supporters want to create. But
> he should care about respecting and preserving the religious tolerance to which
> India has always aspired in spite of its unmanageable diversity.[63]

Bengali scholar and iconoclast Nirad Chaudhuri once questioned whether Hindu spirituality has ever existed.[64] If that is so, by what contortions can *Hindutva* fabricate something that is its opposite – inclusive nationhood in a multinational Indian state?

Notes

1. Seal, Anil, *The Emergence of Indian Nationalism: Competition and Collaboration in the Later Nineteenth Century* (Cambridge: Cambridge University Press, 1971), p. 1.
2. Ibid., p. 25.
3. Desai, A. R., *Social Background of Indian Nationalism*, 4th edn (Bombay: Popular Prakashan, 1966), p. 44. See also G. Aloysius, *Nationalism Without a Nation in India* (New Delhi: Oxford University Press, 1999).
4. Desai, *Social Background*, pp. 11–13.
5. Ibid., pp. 307–8.
6. Chatterjee, Partha, *The Nation and Its Fragments: Colonial and Postcolonial Histories* (Princeton, NJ: Princeton University Press, 1993), p. 6.
7. Van der Veer, Peter, *Religious Nationalism: Hindus and Muslims in India* (Berkeley, CA: University of California Press, 1994), p. 201.
8. Masselos, Jim, *Indian Nationalism: An History* (New Delhi: Sterling Publishers, 1991), p. 24.
9. Ali, Tariq, 'Could It Have Been Avoided?', *London Review of Books*, 39, no. 24, 14 December 2017, <https://www.lrb.co.uk/v39/n24/tariq-ali/could-it-have-been-avoided>.
10. Ward, Andrew, *Our Bodies are Scattered: The Cawnpore Massacre and the Indian Mutiny of 1857* (New York: Henry Holt and Company, 1996), p. 512.
11. Ibid., pp. 514–15.
12. Desai, *Social Background*, p. 322.
13. Savarkar, V. D., *Hindutva* (Poona: S. R. Date, 1942), p. 1.
14. Suntharalingam, R., *Indian Nationalism: An Historical Analysis* (New Delhi: Vikas Publishing House, 1983), p. 187.
15. Van der Veer, *Religious Nationalism*, p. 2.
16. Suntharalingam, *Indian Nationalism*, p. 377.
17. Masselos, *Indian Nationalism*, p. 185.
18. Mukerjee, Madhusree, *Churchill's Secret War: The British Empire and the Ravaging of India during World War II* (New York: Basic Books, 2011), p. 243.
19. Simha, Rakesh Krishnan, 'Remembering India's Forgotten Holocaust', *Tehelka Daily*, 13 June 2014, 25, no. 11, <http://www.tehelka.com/2014/06/remembering-indias-forgotten-holocaust/>.
20. Davis, Mike, *Late Victorian Holocausts: El Niño Famines and the Making of the Third World* (Brooklyn, NY: Verso, 2017).
21. Sen, Amartya, *Poverty and Famine* (Oxford: Oxford University Press, 1981).
22. Nehru, Jawaharlal, *Toward Freedom: The Autobiography of Jawaharlal Nehru* (New York: John Day, 1941), p. 292.
23. Ibid., p. 240.
24. Hess, Gary R., *America Encounters India, 1941–1947* (Baltimore, MD: Johns Hopkins University Press, 1971), p. 31.
25. Venkataramani, M. S., 'Roosevelt, America, and the Indian Freedom Struggle: Some Reflections', in Venkataramani and B. K. Shrivastava, *Roosevelt, Gandhi, Churchill: America and the Last Phase of India's Freedom Struggle* (New Delhi: Radiant Publishers, 1983), p. 315.
26. Ibid., p. 24.

27. Cited by Manmath Nath Das, *Partition and Independence of India: Inside Story of the Mountbatten Days* (New Delhi: Vision Books, 1982), p. 13.
28. Ibid., p. 88.
29. Lamb, Alastair, *The Kashmir Problem: A Historical Survey* (New York: Frederick Praeger, 1966), p. 35.
30. Hasan, K. Sarwar (ed.), *Documents on the Foreign Relations of Pakistan: The Kashmir Question* (Karachi: Pakistan Institute of International Affairs, 1966), pp. 11–16.
31. Facsar, Fanny, '#NewNationalism: "Turn India into a Hindu state"', *Deutsche Welle*, 21 August 2017, <http://www.dw.com/en/newnationalism-turn-india-into-a-hindu-state/a-40171737>.
32. 'Partition, 70 Years On', 5 August 2017, *The Guardian*, <https://www.theguardian.com/books/2017/aug/05/partition-70-years-salman-rushdie-kamila-shamsie-writers-reflect-india-pakistan>.
33. Ibid.
34. Ibid.
35. Ibid.
36. Singh, Gurharpal, 'Ethnic Conflict in India: A Case Study of Punjab', in John McGarry and Brendan O'Leary (eds), *The Politics of Ethnic Conflict Regulation* (London: Routledge, 1993), p. 86. See also Paul Brass, 'The Punjab Crisis and the Unity of India', in A. Kholi (ed.), *India's Democracy* (Princeton, NJ: Princeton University Press, 1987).
37. Taras, Raymond, *Liberal and Illiberal Nationalisms* (Houndmills: Palgrave, 2002), pp. 95–9.
38. Missirian, Anouch, and Wolfram Schlenker, 'Asylum Applications Respond to Temperature Fluctuations', *Science*, 358, no. 6370, 22 December 2017, pp. 1610–14, <http://science.sciencemag.org/content/358/6370/1610.full>.
39. Das, Pamela, and Richard Horton, 'The Lancet Commission on Pollution and Health', *The Lancet*, 19 October 2017, <http://www.thelancet.com/commissions/pollution-and-health>.
40. Klein, Naomi, *This Changes Everything: Capitalism vs. the Climate* (New York: Simon and Schuster, 2014), p. 18.
41. 'Health and Climate Change', *The Lancet*, 390, no. 10107, <http://www.thelancet.com/climate-and-health>.
42. Roy, Arundhati, 'The Greater Common Good', Friends of River Narmada, April 1999, <http://www.narmada.org/gcg/gcg.html>.
43. King, Ed, 'India "Lacks Plan" to Cope with Climate-Linked Migration,' *Climate Change News*, 22 December 2016, <http://www.climatechangenews.com/2016/12/22/india-lacks-plan-to-cope-with-climate-linked-migration/>.
44. Lal, Neeta, 'Climate Migrants Lead Mass Migration to India's Cities,' *Relief Web*, 27 July 2016, <https://reliefweb.int/report/india/climate-migrants-lead-mass-migration-india-s-cities>.
45. Ibid.
46. 'Myanmar: Who are the Rohingya?', *Al Jazeera*, 28 September 2017, <http://www.aljazeera.com/indepth/features/2017/08/rohingya-muslims-170831065142812.html>.
47. Bose, Sugata, and Ayesha Jalal (eds), *Nationalism, Democracy, and Development: State and Politics in India* (New Delhi: Oxford University Press, 1999).
48. Van der Veer, *Religious Nationalism*, p. 23.

49. Vanaik, A., *The Painful Transition: Bourgeois Democracy in India* (London: Verso, 1990).

50. Van der Veer, *Religious Nationalism*, p. 202.

51. Varshney, Ashutosh, 'Ethnic Conflict and Civil Society: India and Beyond', *World Politics*, 53, no. 3, April 2001, p. 371–2, Table 1.

52. Van der Veer, *Religious Nationalism*, p. 23.

53. See Graham, B., *Hindu Nationalism and Indian Politics: The Origins and Development of the Bharatiya Janata Party* (New Delhi: Cambridge University Press, 1990).

54. Wyatt, Andrew, 'Two Steps Forward, One Step Back: The BJP and the General and State Assembly Elections in India, 1999–2000', *Asian Affairs*, 31, no. 3, October 2000, p. 291.

55. Majumder, Sanjoy, 'Narendra Modi "allowed" Gujarat 2002 anti-Muslim riots', *BBC News*, 22 April 2011, <http://www.bbc.com/news/world-south-asia-13170914>.

56. 'Timeline of the Riots in Modi's Gujarat', *New York Times*, 19 August 2015, <https://www.nytimes.com/interactive/2014/04/06/world/asia/modi-gujarat-riots-timeline.html#/#time287_8514>.

57 Jaffrelot, Christophe, 'Narendra Modi between Hindutva and Subnationalism: The Gujarati Asmita of a Hindu Hriday Samrat', *India Review*, 15, no. 2, 2016, p. 197, <http://dx.doi.org/10.1080/14736489.2016.1165557>.

58. Ibid., p. 200.

59. Ibid., pp. 203, 210.

60. Sen, Ronojoy, 'Narendra Modi's Makeover and the Politics of Symbolism', *Journal of Asian Public Policy*, 9, no. 2, 7 April 2016, pp. 98–111, <http://www.tandfonline.com/doi/full/10.1080/17516234.2016.1165248>.

61. Mandhana, Niharika, 'Modi Picks Hindu Nationalist to Lead India's Most Populous State', *Wall Street Journal*, 20 March 2017, <https://www.wsj.com/articles/modi-picks-hindu-nationalist-to-lead-indias-most-populous-state-1489934500>.

62. 'Those Who Want Beef Should Go to Pak: Mukhtar Abbas Naqvi', *The Hindustan Times*, 22 May 2015, <http://www.hindustantimes.com/india/those-who-want-to-eat-beef-should-go-to-pak-mukhtar-abbas-naqvi/story-kTyciMp58MrUhrWJfp5kFK.html>.

63. Seervai, Shanoor, 'The Rising Tide of Intolerance in Narendra Modi's India', *Kennedy School Review*, 27 July 2016, 16, pp. 101–8.

64. Chaudhuri, Nirad C., *Hinduism: A Religion to Live By* (Oxford: Oxford India University Press, 1997). See also Almond, Ian, *The Thought of Nirad C. Chaudhuri: Islam, Empire and Loss* (Cambridge: Cambridge University Press, 2015).

CHAPTER EIGHT

Multiracial South Africa

TROUBLED LEGACY

For three centuries South Africa was ruled by colonial powers, then by an apartheid regime. When the first democratic elections were held in 1994, South Africa represented one of the most inegalitarian societies in the world. The White population making up 13 per cent of the country's inhabitants owned 86 per cent of the land and over 90 per cent of its wealth. By contrast, of the 30 million Blacks, 50 per cent were unemployed, lived below the poverty line, were illiterate or semi-literate, and under twenty years of age. One in ten had no home and many resorted to squatting. The result was that 'in a state such as South Africa, the social identities such as race, culture and language remain stronger than national identity'.[1]

When South Africa emerged from nearly a century of oppressive racist apartheid, many questioned whether this multiethnic state would be riven by racial and ethnic strife, weak state structures and iron-fisted political leadership. Few political systems anywhere had ever been based so profoundly on racial and ethnic categories as that of South Africa. To be sure, the apartheid assumption was that Black communities living in bantustans would eventually mature into nations, like the Afrikaans and English-speaking Whites had done. Until then, Blacks had to live in designated tribal homelands (or language areas) and townships even though, as a result of wars, uprooting and relocation, few ever possessed an ancestral home.

The demographic composition was finely balanced among diverse communities. The largest of the Black African groups, amounting to about 75 per cent of the total population, was made up of 8.5 million Zulu speakers. Next were 6.6 million Xhosa and 6.3 million Sotho. The White population (14 per cent) consisted of 5.8 million Afrikaners (Dutch speakers) and 3.5 million English. Mixed race, or Coloureds, totalled nearly 9 per cent while those originating from India were 2.5 per cent.

174

Black-majority rule eliminated the homelands but created new ethnic fault lines and rivalries. Attempts to use the rhetoric of the so-called Rainbow Nation have been unconvincing. Despite the country's fixation on national identity and nationhood, this chapter shows that South Africa remains a long way from Rainbowism.

In addition, immigration to South Africa, primarily by people from other poorer southern African states, has not been well received and has been reduced since 2010 (Table 3.2). Xenophobia, often of a non-racial kind, has spiked in spite of government agencies and NGOs that want to include outsiders. Have the policies of the South African state expanded nationhood to other groups beyond those recognised as constituting parts of the Rainbow Nation? Or, in the case of all of Africa, have we learned that nation building may be a divisive process in which people revolt against state efforts imposing on them an identity that they did not want? That is, 'African governments should be cautious in their attempts to create a common national bond among their citizens.'[2] In South Africa, should the government proceed with the development of a Rainbow Nation or heed the advice against nation building?

THE VIOLENCE OF COLONIALISM

The Office of the United Nations High Commissioner for Refugees (UNHCR) Statistical Database on Refugees and Internally Displaced Persons reveals that over 9 million people were killed in all of Africa's conflicts since the end of the Cold War. The death toll in the Democratic Republic of Congo has been ten times higher than that in the Israeli–Palestine conflict. In Angola 3 million refugees were driven from their homes by the quest for blood diamonds and offshore oil, and the civil war that reached its height in the 1980s.[3]

In ironic fashion, South African Nobel Peace laureate Desmond Tutu has proffered a cruel observation: 'When the missionaries came to Africa they had the Bible and we had the land. They said, "Let us pray." We closed our eyes. When we opened them we had the Bible and they had the land.' Not everyone was persuaded, however, when Tutu added 'And we got the better deal.'[4]

The Berlin Conference of 1884–5 partitioned Africa. Because there was no natural footprint to divide Africa up, colonial administrators invented African traditions and peddled them to sections of the native population. In addition, customary law, land rights and political structures were all invented following colonial codification. Just as every European was said to belong to a nation, a continent-sized vastness – sometimes organised as a theme park – was created where every African had to belong to a tribe. This comprised

175

a cultural unit having a common language, a single social system and time-honoured customary law – so it was proclaimed.

British colonialism in Africa promoted local hierarchies based on malleable, cooperative and corrupt local chiefs. When colonists abandoned empires starting in the 1960s, they left behind loyal elites that continued to siphon off Africa's wealth. To this day, Africa serves as a profitable dumping ground for nations and arms manufacturers anxious to sell off a Cold War era inventory of weapons stocks. Not just the usual culprits like the US and Russia but also liberal international nations like Canada and Sweden have raced to sell arms on the continent.

Africa's ancient history is demonstrated by 'Lucy', a hominid of the *Australopithecus afarensis* species that lived in Ethiopia 3.2 million years ago. Africa had its own empires all over. The empire of Ghana ruled from 750 to 1078; the medieval Sahelian kingdoms, which included Mali, governed after 1235 and peaked in the 1350s; the Jolof empire in West Africa lasted from 1350 to 1549; the Songhai in the 1500s stretched from the Cameroons to North Africa; and an Islamic empire, the Sokoto caliphate, which conquered the Hausa in Nigeria, was dominant throughout the nineteenth century – until the arrival of the Europeans (Box 8.1).

The first symbolic steps in overhauling South Africa's apartheid system came in 1992. A series of banknotes replaced the likeness of Jan van Riebeeck (on the face of the South African rand since 1921) with the Big Five animals of Africa: lion, rhinoceros, leopard, cape buffalo and elephant.

In 1996 a new national anthem was proclaimed that combined the Xhosa hymn *Nkosi Sikelel' iAfrika* ('God Bless Africa') with the Afrikaans anthem *Die Stem van Suid-Afrika* ('The Call of South Africa'). Using four different languages, the last stanza was composed in English to emphasise the ideal of unity in the pursuit of freedom. The anthem begins with a Xhosa invocation for the Lord to bless all of Africa, then it privileges the Sesotho lyrics: 'Lord we ask you to protect our nation, Intervene and end all conflicts.' The hymn represents a metaphorical key to enlarging South Africa's nationhood.

In 2000 a new national coat of arms highlighted the democratic change in South Africa and a new sense of patriotism.[5] Added to the national emblem is a motto, written in the Khoisan language, meaning 'diverse people unite' and committing the government to 'unity in diversity'. However, these platitudes conceal political interests: 'nation-building is a smokescreen to advance the interests of the leader and his party. It has led to more conflict than integration'[6] (Box 8.1).

Box 8.1 Africa's window dressing

Nation building was an invention that borrowed heavily from European settlement. Up to and including political independence, this entailed many different inconsequential transformations: changing state names to give political and historic legitimacy to its populations; changing capital cities' names and locations, especially with the shift from coastal to inland sites to provide better access; changing flags; changing national currencies, changed monetary policy, and imagery printed on currencies; conscripting troops into the national service; religious and linguistic homogenization through the promotion of national language and religion (this included Swahili as Ugandan dictator Idi Amin's method of Ugandan integration); republicanism, federalism, and centralization to abolish traditional kingdoms; one-party states to ban factionalism and ethnic-based associations; censuses to institutionalize ethnicity and simplify or reduce diversity; land nationalization to promote mobility between regions and break up ethnic homelands, even when these produced landholding inequalities as well as anti-migrant violence; education and curricular policy changes; and not least, the Africanization of political leaders' names.

Source: Bandyopadhyay, Sanghamitra, and Elliott Green, 'Nation-Building and Conflict in Modern Africa', *World Development*, 45, May 2013, pp. 118-19, available at <http://www.sciencedirect.com/science/article/pii/S0305750X12002264>.

IDENTITY OBSESSION

What significance does reference to building a Rainbow Nation have over mere nation building? For starters, when artfully and graphically depicting the core idea of nationhood, it can involve more complexity.

Nelson Mandela's governing African National Congress (ANC) and the governments of his successors have pursued a set of policies 'recognizing commonalties, reducing tensions and promoting the formation of social partnerships among different cultural groups'.[7] But South Africa is deeply divided by race, ethnicity and economic inequality. Those marginalised by apartheid gained little in the 1990s and thereafter from poverty alleviation programmes or Black economic empowerment policies. Many continue to suffer from homelessness, unemployment, deteriorating economic conditions and alienation. As a result, growing economic marginalisation has fuelled discontent among South Africa's poor and 'constitutes the biggest threat to the formation of a cohesive national identity in South African society'.[8]

177

Identities in South Africa – Black, Coloured, Indian, White – have muddied the waters. One research project found that the most salient ethnic differences were based, inescapably, between African and White groups, with Coloured and Indian fitting in between.[9] Twenty-five years after Black-majority rule, racism remains at the heart of inequality and disparity. Irregular immigrants arriving in the country are an additional identity marker. So 'the main challenge to nationhood in post-independence Africa has been how to balance the recognition of ethnic groups with the imperatives of the envisaged nationhood'.[10]

The country has been populated by different communal groups but state boundaries are arbitrary, drawn up by colonial powers, and are not congruent with patterns of ethnic settlement. Moreover, weak central governments had been the rule across Africa. Ian Lustick has observed how 'the belief that African borders are immutable, and thereby excluded from calculations about how Africans can respond to the exigencies of their existence, appears to be breaking down'. Today 'Africa faces, among its other woes, the possibility of cascading patterns of fragmentation and attachment.'[11] But for South Africa, it is the opposite curse: strong government ruling over large and diverse populations.

The collapse of the Soviet bloc occurred two years before White-ruled South Africa had run its course. The existence of empire furnishes an obvious point of comparison: 'The South African state formed in 1910 was a British empire in microcosm and, without apartheid, was always likely to show the same fissiparous tendencies of the Russian empire without communism.' The consequence in each case was that 'Ethnic politics, so long obscured or concealed, suddenly mattered a great deal.'[12]

Few modern political systems have ever been based so exclusively on ethnic categories as South Africa under apartheid. Democracy had been crushed after 1948 under the political domination of the National Party (NP). Through 'petty apartheid' legislation, the government divided the population along strict racial categories – White, Indian/Asian, Coloured and Native (later Bantu or African). Mixed marriages were banned and strict forms of segregation in residency, education, employment and amenities were enforced.[13]

When President F. W. de Klerk announced his proposal for democratic reforms and a post-apartheid constitution in 1990, it was to the ANC and its imprisoned leader, Mandela, that he turned. Privileged by this overture, the ANC leadership, many of who were Xhosa, did not include a Zulu representative. Yet ever since the rule of King Shaka in the early nineteenth century (discussed below), Zulus have constituted a large, historic, influential ethnicity.

Mandela's political skills were put on display when he read a poem in a

178

court about to free him about the great Zulu king: 'Suddenly there were no Xhosas or Zulus, no Indians or Africans, no rightists or leftists, no political or religious leaders. We were all nationalists.'[14] Mandela took this story to heart and applied it in the transition period when racial and ethnic rivalries between Blacks and Whites, and between Blacks and Blacks, were palpable.

For South Africa experts, Xhosa and Zulu 'occupy polar positions on some key questions of ethnic identity, ideology, organizational affiliation, leadership preferences, and strategic inclinations'. More than that, 'one of these groups is significantly overrepresented and the other underrepresented in the leading extra-parliamentary opposition organizations'.[15] Given Zulu grievances of unfair representation, the new democracy's first challenges were to deflect the threat of separatism; the collapse of the USSR had taught them that.

Differences separate the two communities but language is not one. They speak languages that belong to the Bantu language group, as do the other seven African languages given official constitutional status (Afrikaans and English are recognised but are not Bantu). Zulus are concentrated in South Africa's most populous province, KwaZulu–Natal, while Xhosas have mostly settled on the Cape. But political differences are profound and may display different political cultures. Path dependence, in which cultures follow roads taken earlier, had much to do with this: 'The Xhosa-speakers of the Cape were the most politically aware Africans in the country, having grown up within a relatively liberal environment in which a qualified franchise had long been available.... Zulu-speakers were conservative, even parochial, by comparison.'[16] Another difference was political participation. At the time that the Union of South Africa was created in 1910, there were already 12,000 Blacks and Coloureds registered as voters in the Cape, but only a handful where Zulus were concentrated in Natal. Some Xhosa nationalists concluded that Zulus lagged behind them in democratic culture and it seemed natural that Xhosa should inherit the fledging democracy.

The shift from White-minority to Black-majority rule was cemented in the 1996 constitution. It asserted that South Africa 'belongs to all who live in it' – a truism that, at the least, replaced the apartheid system. It established nine non-ethnically defined provinces, all of which had Black-majority populations except for the Western Cape. The constitution recognised traditional indigenous leaders and the principle of autonomy for all groups. A commitment to protecting national minorities was evidenced in the state's recognition of eleven official languages and the 2003 creation of the Commission for the Promotion and Protection of the Rights of Cultural, Religious and Linguistic Communities.

Black-majority rule eliminated the homelands and, with them, fiefdoms of power and patronage beholden to homeland rulers. These had first been set up under the 1953 Bantu Authorities Act to train the Bantu for self-government while moving them from White-populated areas and denying them citizenship. No extended sense of nationhood was envisaged by this Act. The semi-autonomous kingdom of KwaZulu subsequently developed into an 'independent' KwaZulu in 1972. It consisted of forty-four pockets of land on both sides of the Tugela river – a 'polka-dot state' in the words of Mangosuthu Buthelezi, head of the Zulu nationalist organisation Inkatha Freedom Party (IFP). It was a fraction of the size of Shaka's kingdom but IFP leaders used the bantustan to hand out patronage.

Building an inclusive democracy did not go so far as to embrace a federal system, in contrast to Russia. Provincial chief executives were appointed by the central government but the constitution in theory precluded asymmetrical arrangements that would give special status to the Zulus. The South African government refrained from giving national minorities special rights.

More than anything, the elimination of apartheid entailed reversing racism directed against Blacks and Coloureds. An ambitious programme called Black Economic Empowerment (BEE) tried to overcome racial disparities in wealth and income by promoting Black ownership and control of the economy. The creation of Black-owned and Black-controlled enterprises was a pillar in developing small, medium and micro-enterprises. Other policies committing the government to a proactive role in encouraging economic deracialisation included programmes to promote affirmative action in employment, giving Black enterprises preferential treatment with regard to acquiring stakes in the economy, and crafting incentives for public participation in BEE. These programmes produced a small if budding Black business class.

Shortly after his release from prison in 1990 after serving twenty-seven years, Mandela visited Durban in KwaZulu–Natal. He was hailed by tens of thousands of Zulus but had still not met Buthelezi; the latter did not regard him as the conquering hero the West did. But Mandela agreed to make concessions to the Zulus. The key one was formal recognition of KwaZulu and of its king in the constitution. One British newspaper praised Mandela for being duplicitous:

> It is almost reassuring to note among the blemishes on his track record the reneging on solemn promises made to the Inkatha Freedom Party before the previous elections to invite foreign mediation in the problem of endemic violence in KwaZulu–Natal.[17]

The two Black communities had pursued different strategies under apartheid. The ANC waged an armed struggle against the government in the hope of making South Africa ungovernable. Inkatha concentrated its efforts on a negotiated solution. After the transition, Inkatha allied itself with opponents of change, ranging from bantustan leaders to representatives of the White

180

Box 8.2 Mandela's method

Nation building was spearheaded by Mandela, for whom national reconciliation was the priority for his presidency. He drew the National
Party and the Inkatha Freedom Party into the Government of National
Unity. He accepted FW de Klerk as one of his deputy presidents.
He undertook a series of grand symbolic gestures for reconciliation
– from having tea with the wives of apartheid-era heads of state to
embracing the Springbok emblem for the national rugby team; from
visiting former President PW Botha to insisting on the inclusion of elements of the old national anthem in the new one; from overseeing the
adoption of eleven official languages for the country to retaining the
services of white bureaucrats and security officials among his staff.
And he both promoted and attracted new metanarratives to replace
the dominant ones of the old regime – these new narratives fore-
grounded concepts like the 'rainbow nation', the 'new' South Africa,
'the struggle', 'truth and reconciliation', 'the people' and 'Madiba
magic'.

Source: *The Nelson Mandela Foundation: Race and Identity in 2015*, 15 April
2015, available at <http://mg.co.za/article/2015-04-15-the-nelson-mandela
-foundation-race-and-identity-in-2015/>.

Afrikaner right. This discredited Inkatha more than did the ANC's acceptance of Soviet and Cuban backing and its inclusion of communist leaders
within its ranks during the anti-apartheid struggle (Box 8.2).

A South African expert has concluded that 'it was naive for liberals,
Marxists or other anti-racists to imagine that once white domination had
been overthrown an ethnic Zulu nationalism would not seek to fill the power
vacuum within its own area.'[18] But the 1994 elections exploded the myth of
a united Black nation assuming the colours of the Rainbow Nation. A theory
held that 'To recognize nationalism below the level of an inclusive Black
nationalism is to run afoul of an important South African taboo.'[19]

ELECTIONS AND NATIONHOOD

Democratic elections boost nationhood sentiment by encouraging citizen
participation. To be sure, as nationhood entails belonging, elections themselves are not sufficient for its creation. Anyway, South Africa's first general
elections in 1994 steered a path not towards nationhood but towards political
violence.

It is simplistic to describe the ANC as a multiethnic movement and Inkatha as essentially Zulu. But it is also true that in the 1994 elections Inkatha appropriated the history of the Zulus as its own. The ANC emphasised a future that all Blacks in South Africa might build together.

Inevitably, the ANC–Inkatha rivalry resulted in violent clashes: between 1990 and 1994 nearly 15,000 people were killed, two-thirds of them in KwaZulu–Natal. Many Black townships became war zones as Inkatha prepared anti-ANC demonstrations. ANC officials, in turn, vilified Buthelezi as a Zulu nationalist who undermined the building of a new South Africa. Buthelezi

> was a mass of paradoxes, a Christian who honored African tradition and an avowed democrat who yet clearly distrusted the ballot. Urbane and charming, with connections in the boardrooms of Western corporations, he could, in a moment, turn from avuncularity to the language of tribal war.[20]

The results of the elections produced the expected ANC victory. Mandela became the country's first Black president. But Inkatha shared some of the spoils: it gained 10.5 per cent of the vote nationwide, and it won 43 seats compared with 252 for the ANC and 82 for the Nationalists. It received 3 of 27 cabinet posts. Buthelezi was appointed to the cabinet and Inkatha entered into a power-sharing agreement with the ANC. In the KwaZulu–Natal legislature, Inkatha defeated the ANC handily by 50 to 32 per cent.

Following his victory, Mandela began an all-out campaign to promote a single South African identity. He preached national reconciliation and sought an end to political violence. In 1996, he achieved success on both fronts when the Truth and Reconciliation Commission was established under Archbishop Desmond Tutu. Political violence seemed to be coming to an end.

But there was also a warning of trouble to come. Claims were being made that southern Africans from other countries were foreigners stealing the fruits of democracy. Already in 1994 the Minister of Home Affairs cautioned that 'aliens who are pouring into South Africa' would be competing for resources, a discourse circulated across society and shared by policy makers across party lines.[21]

Mandela remained highly critical of his Inkatha coalition partner. In a speech to South Africa's parliament in 1995, he now claimed that more than 20,000 Blacks had died in KwaZulu–Natal in the past ten years and he blamed Buthelezi for fomenting violence: 'Chief Buthelezi has made a public call to Zulus to rise against the central government and has said if we do not get the right to self-determination it is not worth being alive.'[22]

In 1999, prior to South Africa's second elections, the ANC–Inkatha quarrel seemed to be patched up. Thebi Mbeki had replaced Mandela as

ANC head and Inkatha itself was transformed. Its new logo displayed a family of elephants that symbolised unity in diversity. This resembled nationhood at its best.

Inkatha now stressed a pan-South African programme, reputedly outdoing the ANC. It claimed that South Africa was 'deeply troubled: By unemployment. By crime. By poverty. By disease. By corruption. By a breakdown in the social fabric. By a lack of discipline. By a lack of respect for others. By indolence.'[23]

The ANC's overwhelming victory in 1999 was tempered by its one regional loss, in KwaZulu–Natal, to Inkatha. The ANC gained 66 per cent of the national vote, approaching a two-thirds majority. Inkatha obtained 9 per cent of the vote (34 seats) and fell behind the 10 per cent (38 seats) registered by the Democratic Party, formerly the Progressive Party, which had been the one White parliamentary voice against apartheid. The vote in KwaZulu–Natal was close: the IFP edged out the ANC by 40.5 to 39.8 per cent.

The ANC's message proclaiming a single South African identity received further backing in the 2004 elections. It captured 70 per cent of the vote (and 279 of the 400 seats). Inkatha's support was down to 7 per cent (28 seats). More surprising was that for the first time the ANC defeated Inkatha on its home turf: the ANC received 47 per cent of the vote (38 seats) compared with the IFP's 37 per cent (30 seats).

There seemed to be no stopping the ANC juggernaut. Buthelezi complained that the party was aiming to create a single-party state. After these elections, the IFP left the coalition government after ten years. More serious grievances were heard, with the UN's Human Development Index reporting that South Africa was faring poorly. The honeymoon period was over and social inequality had not been reduced.

ZULU AS HISTORIC NATION

Given its White minority government and relative prosperity, South Africa was not a typical Third World country. But it did share many problems with other countries on the continent, such as ethnic divisions.

As noted above, Zulu and Xhosa have long contended for becoming South Africa's elite. Do Zulu historical grievances, land claims, sense of oppression and other moral declarations appear justified, then? Given that Zulu King Goodwill Zwelithini's definition of the Zulu nation in a 1991 speech was 'Brothers born of warrior stock', has the Zulu quest for homeland not ruled out separation from the South African state?

During the European conquest of southern Africa, most native groups succumbed without a fight. Some were rewarded with a measure of political

183

independence, like the Sotho in Lesotho, the Swazis in Swaziland and the Tswana in Botswana. But the Zulu resistance to colonial rule was fierce. It cost more British soldiers' lives than the British conquest of India did.

The Zulu state emerged from single ethnic stock (or *ethnos*) – the Nguni-speaking Bantu. North of the Tugela river where KwaZulu is now located, the heartland of the Zulu kingdom and its most prestigious clans were to be found. South of the river lies Natal, home of what are regarded as inferior *kaffir* Zulus.

Before his death in 1828, Shaka transformed Zulus from a relatively unimportant tribe in southern Africa into the strongest native empire in African history. He assumed the chieftaincy in 1816 and defeated many of the Zulus' more powerful neighbours. At its zenith, the Zulu Empire contained more than 2 million subjects. Shaka's unbending rule inevitably engendered conspiracies against him, and one led by his two half-brothers succeeded in killing him. Before he died, Shaka's last words of prophetic doom were: 'The whole land will be white with the light of the stars, and it will be overrun by swallows.'[24]

In 1843 a British-imposed treaty turned Natal into a colony. This marked the start of a period of British expansion in southern Africa. Lord Carnarvon, who had helped engineer a Canadian dominion out of British North American territories in 1867, was sent from the Colonial Office to settle disputed claims in South Africa. One historian wrote: 'Since 1874, Carnarvon had pondered how the jumble of ethnic and political blocs that made up the subcontinent – British colonies, Boer republics, and Bantu kingdoms – could be neatly composed into a South African confederation.'[25] To engineer this Dominion, in 1877 the British annexed Transvaal and its capital, Pretoria. The pretext was that they wished to save the Boer population from a Zulu attack.

The annexation of Transvaal led to two Anglo-Boer wars, each driven by rival resource claims. In 1886 the discovery of gold, more precious than diamonds, on the Witwatersrand upped the stakes and marked a caesura, suddenly transforming South Africa into the world's largest gold producer. This was the catalyst for the Second Boer War in Transvaal, a region controlled by Dutch-speaking Afrikaners. About 25,000 Dutch Afrikaners died, mostly in concentration camps. It also was costly to the British, claiming 22,000 lives, and for Africans too: 12,000 lives.[26]

Integral to its imperial policy, the British set out to demilitarise and incorporate Zululand into the South African confederation. The conditions stipulated in the British ultimatum to the Zulu King in 1879 were that the Zulu army was to be demobilised and a British resident diplomat was to have final political authority. When the King refused, the British army (which included 10,000 Zulu-speaking levies) marched into Zululand.

British forces were taken by surprise by the mobile Zulu army of 25,000 warriors, greater than any put together by Shaka. In 1879 at Isandlwana, they were overrun, suffering heavy casualties. In London, Prime Minister Benjamin Disraeli was stricken by the bad news emanating from Zululand and commented laconically: 'A wonderful people, the Zulu. They beat our generals, they convert our bishops, and they write *finis* to a French dynasty' (a reference to Louis Napoleon, French Prince Imperial, who was cut down by Zulu warriors).[27]

Zulu mobility and valour proved no match for European firearms. Later in 1879, at Ulundi, Zulu forces were crushed, the capital burned and the King taken away in chains. In 1886 Zululand was converted into a British colony. As with Kosovo Polje for the Serbs, the Alamo for Americans, and the Plains of Abraham for Quebeckers, Zulus regard this lost battle as a defining moment in their national history.[28] But as one historian mused, 'How different it would have been if, after the conquest, Britain had extended the same protective wing over Zululand that it did to three other large ethnic groups in the region' – the Tswana, Sotho and Swazi.[29]

Zulu fortunes were revived when Buthelezi rose to leadership in the 1960s.[30] He founded *Inkatha ya KwaZulu* ('Ring of the Zulu') as a cultural movement. Sensing a nationalist backlash, he changed the name to *Inkatha ye Nkululeko ye Sizwe* ('Ring of the Nation'), thereby mimicking the ANC's multiethnic imagery. But essentialism remained: 'Inkatha's dominant "tradition" involves Zulu ethnicity (an ethnic populism) which depends in content, structures and agents on the apartheid system.' Buthelezi's ethnic exclusivism fed racially inciting politics.[31]

Inkatha benefited from the ban under apartheid on African nationalist parties. When Ulundi was chosen as the Zulu homeland capital, it worked to the IFP's advantage and was a cause for celebration: 'Within the heartland of KwaZulu, Buthelezi and Inkatha have "captured" monuments and historical sites to define territory, both physically and symbolically.'[32] During the Soweto uprising of June 1976, Zulus in the township did not support the general strike, intended to cripple the White-run economy. Reprisals against Zulus, cast as collaborators, followed. The dearth of protests against apartheid in KwaZulu and Natal at this time raised Blacks' suspicions about Buthelezi's connivance with the racist regime.

Not all Zulus supported Buthelezi's policies. Many living in the townships of Durban and in rural areas around Pietermaritzburg preferred the ANC. For the Zulu establishment, however, the adversary was made up of not only political opponents but also 'Zulus who rejected the version of politicized ethnicity propounded by the Inkatha leadership and the Zulu king'.[33] This strategy also had the most clout: 'Those who politicised and mobilised Zulu ethnicity also controlled pensions, land allocation and education; signed work-seekers' permits; and approved bottle store licences.'[34]

Rather than outright independence, Zulu King Goodwill Zwelithini established a reconstituted multiracial Zulu state with constitutional ties to South Africa. He enjoyed the support of the traditionalist group in the royal court. The rapprochement between Goodwill and Mandela in 1995 led to the issuing of an invitation to Mandela to attend a sacred Zulu ceremony commemorating Shaka. This reconciliation was also to foreshadow the election of Jacob Zuma, a Zulu, to the South African presidency in 2009. But what followed was an explosion of xenophobia against southern African Blacks that was blamed on Zuma and the Zulu King.

Xenophobia without racism

If apartheid capitalised on differences in race, culture and gender, after 1994 the Rainbow ideology supported nation building. Its emphasis was on sameness rather than difference, and its stress was on fighting racism. Its main idea was that, instead of race, gender and class mattering, only the human race counts – a grandiose if noble sentiment.

The notion of belonging is central to South Africa's debate. One writer contends that 'People are inclined to measure their exclusion from the justice of an authority by what they don't have when their needs are not taken into account.' Accordingly, 'This phenomenon of creating outsiders is real.'[35] In its place a policy of inclusion becomes crucial:

> Leadership in democracy is about a demonstrable change in behavior that focuses on being seen and believed to be inclusive. This will help to recast a sense of nationhood we don't enjoy now, in spite of our having a Constitution, a territory, a Parliament, a flag, a defense force, a currency and a football team.[36]

Whether migrants to South Africa feel they belong or not serves as the litmus test of nationhood. How many have arrived since apartheid? Figures range from 2 million (BBC) to 5 million (New York Times). The 2011 census found that 2.2 million were born outside the country and made up 4.2 per cent of the population of 52 million. Of these, 1.7 million were not citizens in 2011. Officials were doubtful that the immigrant population had more than doubled to the New York Times' claim of 5 million.[37] But one issue was clear: 'The segregation, discrimination, hatred and prejudice that characterize the history of the past were shifted to foreigners residing in South Africa.'[38]

Many reasons are given for the outbreak of xenophobia in the country. In 2016, on South Africa Heritage Day, Deputy President and incoming ANC leader Cyril Ramaphosa reiterated how the country was creating a new and united society made up of Blacks and Whites. Unofficially campaigning to take over from the scandal-plagued Zuma, he cautioned that the country would not prosper if extreme inequality, joblessness and exploitation of the poor were to continue: 'The spirit of *ubuntu* needs to permeate everything we do,' he insisted, referring to the Bantu term signifying humanity. *Ubuntu* signifies not just humanity towards others but the belief in a universal bond of sharing that connects all humanity. It approximates my understanding of nationhood. Ramaphosa added: 'By paying closer attention to indigenous knowledge, traditional ways of mediating conflict, and African restorative justice, we stand a better chance of ending the unacceptably high levels of violence in our society.'[39]

But traditional ways might have little impact on the country's gargantuan racial and economic problems. In 2016 the National Planning Commission sketched all

the scars of apartheid – racial profiling, race-based discrimination and their continuing impact in a range of sectors, the triple discrimination experienced by African women, and gender inequality in broad terms; the accentuating of ethnicity, poor education access, joblessness and inadequate wages for labor.

Naledi Pandor, Minister of Science and Technology and member of the ANC national executive, added that 'Attaching the unifying symbol of nationhood to these examples could help promote social cohesion in South Africa. Our country has not fully achieved cohesion.'[40]

The post-apartheid Rainbow Nation was failing even as a national brand. If branding means modifying people's perceptions (as noted in Chapter 1), it is about not only pride but profit too. Perceptions of South African racism and xenophobia have taken a toll on foreign direct investment. So Ivor Chipkin's suggestion of exploring post-apartheid 'democratic imagery' may be a preferable strategy.[41]

A symbol of colonial racist rule was provided by the statues erected in an earlier era: above all, those of Cecil Rhodes – British businessman, mining magnate, Prime Minister of the Cape Colony from 1890 to 1896, and ardent advocate of British imperialism. An official ANC statement in 2015 asserted that 'For too long, deep-seated and institutionalized resistance to transformation has been the hallmark of many sections of our society and this untenable situation must change.' Nationhood found its way into this symbolic issue: 'As a nation we must find each other, in the absence of emotive racial polarization, to build and unite around symbols that are an embodiment of the values and ethos of a democratic South Africa and the overarching principles of reconciliation and a common nationhood.'[42] To cheering crowds, Rhodes's statue was taken down in Cape Town, but not in Oxford.

Former President Thabo Mbeki had insisted that reconciliation required the construction of common nationhood and social bonds. This could abolish disparities in the quality of life of South Africans, putting an end to the existence of a country of two nations. For Mbeki, 'reconciliation and nation building is defined by and derives from the material conditions in our society which have divided our country into two nations – one Black and the other White.'[43] Southern African immigrants had a stake in such nationhood.

Early incidences of xenophobia occurred in the 1980s when hostilities in neighbouring countries led to possibly 350,000 immigrants fleeing to South Africa. The first concerted attacks on foreigners in the country took place in 2008 in Alexandra and Johannesburg, and a second surge in 2015 began in KwaZulu–Natal then spread to Johannesburg. This phenomenon was exceptional. For Audie Klotz, 'The commonplace conflation of xenophobia with racism does not capture the South African situation, where anti-foreigner sentiments among Africans primarily target other Africans. Instead, attackers have frequently charged that outsiders are stealing the fruits of democratization.'[44]

Rather than racist explosions, Klotz emphasised how 'ascriptions appear to be tied mainly (though not exclusively) to nationality, rather than religion or ethnicity. And democratization has coincided with what appears to be a new form of anti-immigrant violence.' Thus, even though they had an extended history of cross-border mobility and social integration, Zimbabweans turned into a target of the attacks precisely because they had different nationality.[45] But local residents also went after foreign immigrants from Mozambique and even far-off Somalia and Nigeria.

In order to evaluate the country's xenophobia, a measure was introduced in 2014 called the South African Reconciliation Barometer. Contrary to Klotz's thesis, it revealed increasing hostility across racial lines. Resentment on both sides had been growing, with Whites blaming Blacks for the government's failures, and Blacks pinpointing Whites' continued wealth and asking what had changed since apartheid ended.[46] But immigrants introduced a different dimension to the equation.

The director of the African Centre for Migration and Society minimised fears:

> Xenophobic attacks are no great mystery. There have been a lot of misconceptions about what's behind them such as threatened hyper-masculinity.... However, the understanding that these violent attacks are South African versus foreigner should rather be regarded as foreign shopkeepers competing with South African shopkeepers.[47]

Another reporter's attitudes also banalised xenophobia: 'We are peevish and intolerant against our own African brothers and sisters. We are gradually sinking into hyper-nationalist paranoia and self-righteousness.' South Africans are envious: 'The stereotypes are nasty: They are stealing our jobs. They are drug dealers. They take our women. They force our local shops out of business with cut-rate prices.' Xenophobia is an 'us and them' syndrome, though with murderous consequences.[48] Foreigners are cast as *makwerekwere*, a derogatory term for the hostile other and onomatopoeia for a 'babbler', someone who speaks unintelligibly.

Yet a different South African analyst highlights how media coverage increased stereotyping of foreigners:

> Existing explanations in terms of economic crises, political transition, relative deprivation, or remnants of apartheid all contain an element of truth but are not in themselves sufficient. Proclamations from politicians coupled with media reporting on drug syndicates, prostitution and human trafficking, all feed and in turn feed off a popular perception that migrants are bad for South African society and its economy.[49]

Arguably the most original and compelling understanding of South African xenophobia is offered by cultural anthropologist Jason Hickel. He believes that 'people often draw evocative connections between their ideas about foreigners and their ideas about witchcraft, or, in IsiZulu, *ubuthakathi*'. Focusing on the racial disturbances of May 2008 in Cato Manor, on the outskirts of Durban, Hickel links the misfortune (*amashwa*) of poverty, joblessness and inability to marry as the product not of chance but of human subjects who exhibit morally questionable behaviour: 'Just like witches, immigrants are said to participate in forms of accumulation that are considered immoral and anti-social, enriching themselves at the expense of others.'[50]

In KwaZulu–Natal, the most powerful witches are said to be foreign ones: 'witches from places like Mozambique bring exotic herbs that South African healers do not know about, and therefore cannot counteract'. In addition, Nigerians in particular (as the stereotype has it)

> are thought to be heavily involved in illicit trade in drugs, arms, and human organs. They are also accused of trafficking in goods that are considered to be fake, like counterfeit designer clothes and pirated DVDs. They are regarded as shadowy masters of the black market, capable of marshaling arcane techniques to secure wealth from hidden sources.[51]

Hickel thus links xenophobic violence to a quasi-universal urge to establish order against encroaching chaos, where economic activity blocks social reproduction, and anti-social individuals disrupt fertility by accumulating capital at the expense of others.

Victims feel they have lost their grip on the most fundamental means of social reproduction.[52] They critique 'policies that have demolished formal-sector employment and left people to fend for themselves in a precarious informal economy and rely on state patronage'. This is where the immigrant makes an appearance:

We might say the figure of the immigrant represents the ideal neoliberal subject: individualized, kinless, uprooted, cheap, flexible, enterprising, maximizing, and risk-taking. Residents of Cato Manor refuse to celebrate this kind of personhood, and cast it as cultureless, dangerous, unstable, and destructive; in sum, as bare life, devoid of the characteristics that make a person fully human.[53]

It may be a mischaracterisation, then, to label political violence as xenophobia since it draws false equivalences between concepts of otherness found in different locations in the world. 'Xenophobes in each of these contexts are anxious about different kinds of issues and respond to them in different ways.'[54] But this explanation offers little consolation to the immigrant to South Africa who has been excluded from nationhood, let alone brutalised.

NOT BELONGING – AGAIN

In 2016 South African media reported on a measure that looked at the risk of genocide. The notion that discrimination was based on nationality or witchcraft was conveniently discarded. *Genocide Watch* announced that the country had reached a dramatic phase: it was at stage six on a ten-point scale of international genocidal risk.[55]

At this point, the NGO reports, 'extremists drive the groups apart', 'hate groups broadcast polarizing propaganda', 'extremist terrorism targets moderates', 'moderates from the perpetrators' own group are the first to be arrested and killed', 'leaders in targeted groups are the next to be arrested and murdered', 'laws erode fundamental civil rights and liberties' and 'targeted groups are disarmed to make them incapable of self-defense'. This paints a grim picture of genocidal risk. More cautious analysts have dismissed its value.[56]

But if the level of xenophobia is measured, South Africa may be one of the most egregious cases documented in international surveys. Detailed analysis of attitudes towards migrants conclusively demonstrated resounding hostility to foreigners. Jonathan Crush and his collaborators found that, compared to citizens of other countries, South Africans were least open to outsiders and were determined to impose the largest number of restrictions on them. Thus the proportion of people wanting strict limits or a total prohibition on immigration rose from 65 per cent in 1997 to 78 per cent in 1999. About 50 per cent supported or strongly supported the deportation of foreign nationals including those living legally in South Africa. Three-quarters backed a policy of deporting anyone not contributing economically to South Africa. Research concluded that 48 per cent of South Africans saw migrants from neighbouring nations as a criminal threat; 29 per cent believed they were carriers of disease; and 15 per cent reported losing jobs to foreigners.[57]

These tendencies had already been signalled by the Southern African

Migration Project (SAMP). In 2001 it showed that 21 per cent of South Africans wanted to ban the entry of foreigners into the country. The 2006 SAMP survey discovered that the average South African scored four on a scale of xenophobia (zero is extremely xenophobic, ten not xenophobic at all).[58] A separate survey, Afrobarometer, confirmed that in 2011 45 per cent of South Africans strongly did not want foreigners to live in the country because they took away jobs.[59] In 2015 it found that 68 per cent observed that the government was managing immigration very or fairly badly. Strangely, 59 per cent asserted that the government unified South Africans into one nation fairly or very well.[60]

Crush and Sujata Ramachandran offered a summary of their findings. Xenophobia denialists believe that attacks on migrants and refugees are simply acts of criminality, not xenophobia, and they shift blame to the state's dereliction of its duties: in particular, the failure to control borders and deal with the foreign threat. In similar fashion, former President Mbeki blamed racist outbursts on individual prejudices, not the country's inequalities.

Xenophobia minimalists, on the other hand, argue that the phenomenon constitutes an epiphenomenon, or symptom, of a deeper malaise and does not get at the root causes of violence. They view violence as the signifier of a broader, deeper social crisis linked to intense competition for scarce resources – jobs, homes, services. It leads to a predisposition to resort to violence.

Finally, xenophobia realists are steeped in discovering the many sources of the phenomenon. They base their findings on a systematic representative sampling of the population; SAMP is an example. Realists put their faith in such periodic surveys, which 'provide unequivocal evidence of deep-rooted and pervasive hostility and animosity towards migrants and refugees in the country'.[61]

How much reliability, validity and overall objectivity are provided by multifaceted research projects? For an alarmist organisation like Genocide Watch, Whites, Boers, immigrants and police are at risk of genocide while Marxist racists and xenophobes are the potential murderers. The survey ignored the basic fact that attacks on Black African immigrants were aimed at their disproportionately larger, more vulnerable presence in the informal sector. By contrast, they have less visibility in the formal segment of the national economy. Media attention also zeroes in on confrontations with foreign workers employed in South African mines. As is often the case, media coverage can serve as both an enabler of and a solution to South Africa's xenophobia.

OF KINGS AND PRESIDENTS

It goes without saying that political rulers do have agency in producing or reducing xenophobic violence. Academic research has given South Africa a low risk of genocide for the period 2016–20, though the country has ranked 110 of 149 countries in its Politicide survey.[62] NGOs such as Genocide Watch, by contrast, can make unsubstantiated claims: for example, Zulus are responsible for political violence against Whites, Boers and the police. Idle chatter about xenophobia can itself be a call to ethnic violence.

The South African government has not distinguished itself in managing immigration. In 2015 it responded to xenophobic fears by proposing a Refugee Amendment Bill that would have rolled back the rights of refugees. Applicants for work permits would be evaluated according to whether they could support themselves for four months – while prohibiting them from working.[63]

The People's Coalition Against Xenophobia persuaded a court to overturn this policy. 'To equate crime to the presence of undocumented people in our society is not tackling xenophobia, it is legitimizing xenophobia,' it wisely stated. But the government's reaction was simple: 'we have to tackle xenophobia by getting rid of illegal immigrants.'[64]

In autumn 2015 South African authorities succeeded in deporting 15,000 undocumented immigrants to their home countries. The cost was prohibitive since they had to provide transportation for people – no small matter when it entailed people from Malawi, with which South Africa had no common border. As Klotz observed, therefore, 'In South Africa, we witness this irony in deportation policies: government portrays itself as protecting citizens from foreigners, despite minimal effect on migration, which reinforces xenophobic discourses.'[65]

Zulu King Goodwill contributed to stoking xenophobic attacks when, in 2015, he warned foreign nationals to go home, even describing them as 'lice'. In his defence, he claimed that xenophobia was being used to embarrass Zulus and their monarch: 'The people who are doing this have one thing in mind – they want Africans to fight each other. No one should kill.' Thousands of foreigners were displaced, creating tension with other countries on the continent.[66]

President Zuma survived scandals and impeachment votes while holding office. When combined with inept immigration policies, his term weakened his political legitimacy. At the end of 2017 he was replaced as ANC head and, shortly afterwards, as South African President by Ramaphosa. Ramaphosa was born in Soweto, had been Mandela's original choice for president and now had the powerful ANC machinery behind him. A trade union boss of the National Union of Mineworkers (NUM), his influence

192

had been critical in negotiations ending apartheid and moving the country towards democratic elections.

Independently wealthy, Ramaphosa has stood for racial equality and workers' rights. His exhortation that 'The spirit of *ubuntu* needs to permeate everything we do' offers possibilities of belonging. It may even reflect a disposition towards nationhood, if that is the consensus in South Africa.

Notes

1. Isaacs-Martin, Wendy, 'National Identity and Distinctiveness: Developing a Common Identity in a Nation State (with References to South Africa)', *Africa Insight*, 2012, 42, no. 2, pp. 169–83.
2. Bandyopadhyay, Sanghamitra, and Elliott Green, 'Nation-Building and Conflict in Modern Africa', *World Development*, 45 (May 2013), p. 108, available at <http://www.sciencedirect.com/science/article/pii/S0305750X12002264>.
3. United Nations High Commissioner for Refugees, *'The World in Numbers'*, available at <http://popstats.unhcr.org/en/overview>.
4. Cited by West, Gerald O., *The Stolen Bible: From Tool of Imperialism to African Icon* (Leiden: Brill, 2016), p. 326.
5. 'South Africa's National Symbols', *Brand South Africa*, 15 September 2016, available at <https://www.brandsouthafrica.com/people-culture/arts-culture/south-africas-national-symbols 2009a>.
6. Bandyopadhyay and Green, 'Nation-building'.
7. Stinson, Andrew Todd, 'National Identity and Nation-Building in Post-Apartheid South Africa', MA thesis in Political and International Studies, Rhodes University, Grahamstown, South Africa, 2010, p. 3.
8. Ibid., p. 4.
9. Adams, Byron G., Fons J. R. Van de Vijver and Gideon P. De Bruin, 'Identity in South Africa: Examining Self-Descriptions across Ethnic Groups', *International Journal of Intercultural Relations*, 36, no. 3, May 2012, pp. 377–88.
10. Ramutsindela, Maano, 'Down the Post-Colonial Road: Reconstructing the Post-Apartheid State in South Africa', *Political Geography*, 20, no. 1, January 2001, p. 70.
11. Lustick, Ian S., *Unsettled States, Disputed Lands* (Ithaca, NY: Cornell University Press, 1993), p. 1.
12. Taylor, Stephen, *Shaka's Children: A History of the Zulu People* (London: HarperCollins, 1995), p. 339.
13. Beinart, William, and Saul Dubow, 'Introduction: The Historiography of Segregation and Apartheid', in William Beinart and Saul Dubow (eds), *Segregation and Apartheid in Twentieth-Century South Africa* (London: Routledge, 2003), pp. 1–24.
14. Mandela, Nelson, *Long Walk to Freedom* (London: Little, Brown and Company, 1994), p. 188.
15. Horowitz, Donald L., *A Democratic South Africa: Constitutional Engineering in a Divided Society* (New York: Oxford University Press, 1991), p. 61.
16. Taylor, *Shaka's Children*, p. 299.
17. Brink, André, 'Mandela a Tiger for our Time', *The Guardian*, 23 May 1999, available

at   <https://www.theguardian.com/world/1999/may/22/southafrica.nelsonmandela 4 June 1999>.

18. Hastings, Adrian, *The Construction of Nationhood: Ethnicity, Religion and Nationalism* (Cambridge: Cambridge University Press, 1997), p. 164.

19. Horowitz, *A Democratic South Africa*, p. 130.

20. Taylor, *Shaka's Children*, p. 2.

21. Cited by Audie Klotz, 'Borders and the Roots of Xenophobia in South Africa', *South African Historical Journal*, 68, no. 2, 2016, p. 192.

22. 'Buthelezi Accused of Fanning Unrest', *Glasgow Herald*, 4 May 1995.

23. Cited by Inkatha website, available at <http://www.ifp.org/za/emainfesto.htm>.

24. Cited by Taylor, *Shaka's Children*, p. 102.

25. Ibid., p. 204.

26. 'Second Boer War Records Database Goes Online', *BBC News*, 24 June 2010, available at <http://www.bbc.com/news/10390469>.

27. Cited by Brian Roberts, *The Zulu Kings* (London: Book Club, 1974), p. 348.

28. On the Zulu view of the 1879 war, see John Laband, *Kingdom in Crisis: The Zulu Response to the British Invasion of 1879* (Durban: University of Natal Press, 1992). On the peace that followed the war, see Jeff Guy, *The Destruction of the Zulu Kingdom: The Civil War in Zululand, 1879–1884* (London: Longman, 1979).

29. Taylor, *Shaka's Children*, p. 288.

30. Mare, Gerhard, and Georgina Hamilton, *An Appetite for Power: Buthelezi's Inkatha and the Politics of Loyal Resistance* (Johannesburg: Rava, 1987).

31. Mare, Gerhard, *Ethnicity and Politics in South Africa* (London: Zed Books, 1993), p. 103.

32. Ibid., p. 78.

33. Ibid., p. 60.

34. Ibid., p. 67.

35. 'The House that SA Didn't Build', *News24*, 2 February 2015, available at <http://www.news24.com/Archives/City-Press/The-house-that-SA-didnt-build-20150429>.

36. Ibid.

37. Wilkinson, Kate, 'Do Five Million Immigrants Live in South Africa?', *Mail & Guardian*, 6 May 2015, available at <https://mg.co.za/article/2015-05-06-do-5-million-immigrants-live-in-sa>.

38. Ejoke, Ufuoma Patience, and Kelechi Johnmary Ani, 'A Historical and Theoretical Analysis of Xenophobia in South Africa', *Journal of Gender, Information and Development in Africa*, 6, nos 1–2, 2017, p. 164.

39. Nkalane, Michael, 'Spirit of Ubuntu Needed Nationwide', *Cape Times*, 11 April 2016, available at <http://www.iol.co.za/capetimes/news/spirit-of-ubuntu-needed-nationwide-2072555>.

40. Pandor, Naledi, 'Challenge to Build New South Africanness', *Sunday Independent*, 4 October 2015, available at <http://www.iol.co.za/sundayindependent/challenge-to-build-new-south-africanness-1924675>.

41. Chipkin, Ivor, *Do South Africans Exist? Nationalism, Democracy and the Identity of 'The People'* (Johannesburg: Wits University Press, 2007).

42. Kodwa, Zizi, cited in 'ANC Backs Removal of Statues but ...', *IOL*, 7 April 2015, available at <http://www.iol.co.za/news/politics/anc-backs-removal-of-statues-but--1841761>.

43. 'Thabo Mbeki Backs ANC Call to Criminalise Racism', *Sowetan Live*, 16 March 2016, available at <http://www.sowetanlive.co.za/news/2016/03/16/thabo-mbeki-backs-anc-call-to-criminalise-racism>.
44. Klotz, 'Borders', p. 180.
45. Ibid., p. 181.
46. 'Make the Rainbow Real', *Mail & Guardian*, 12 December 2014, available at <https://mg.co.za/article/2014-12-11-editorial-make-the-rainbow-real>.
47. 'Inequality and Poverty Drive Xenophobia', *Mail & Guardian*, 8 April 2016, available at <https://mg.co.za/article/2016-04-07-inequality-and-poverty-drive-xenophobia>.
48. Mkhondo, Rich, 'The Impact of Xenophobia to SA the Brand', *IOL*, 23 April 2015, available at <http://www.iol.co.za/business-report/opinion/the-impact-of-xenopho bia-to-sa-the-brand-1849127>.
49. Masenya, Malesela J., 'Afrophobia in South Africa: A General Perspective of Xenophobia', *Bangladesh e-Journal of Sociology*, 14, no. 1, January 2017, p. 86.
50. Hickel, Jason, 'Xenophobia in South Africa: Order, Chaos, and the Moral Economy of Witchcraft', *Cultural Anthropology*, 29, no. 1, 2014, pp. 108–9.
51. Ibid., pp. 112–13.
52. Ibid., pp. 119–20.
53. Ibid., p. 121.
54. Ibid., p. 122.
55. 'Racism in South Africa,' available at <http://www.genocidewatch.org/images/South_Africa_09_03_30_the_perfect_storm.pdf>.
56. 'No Genocide Risk in SA', *Dailynews*, 9 September 2016, available at <http://www.iol.co.za/dailynews/opinion/no-genocide-risk-in-sa-2070108>.
57. Crush, Jonathan (ed.), *The Perfect Storm: The Realities of Xenophobia in Contemporary South Africa* (Cape Town: Institute for Democracy in South Africa, 2008).
58. Cited by Ejoke and Ani, 'A Historical and Theoretical Analysis', pp. 170–1.
59. Afrobarometer Round 5 Survey in South Africa, 'South Africa Round 5 Questionnaire: 2011', available at <http://www.afrobarometer.org/countries/south-africa/south-africa-round-5-questionnaire>.
60. Afrobarometer Round 6 Survey in South Africa, 'Summary of Results for South Africa: 2015,' p. 51, available at <http://afrobarometer.org/sites/default/files/publica tions/Summary%20of%20results/saf-r6-sor.pdf>.
61. Crush, Jonathan, and Sujata Ramachandran, *Xenophobic Violence in South Africa: Denialism, Minimalism, Realism* (Cape Town: SAMP, 2014), Migration Policy Series No. 66, Southern African Migration Programme, pp. 1–3, available at <http://imrc.ca/wp-content/uploads/2014/09/Xenophobic-Violence-in-South-Africa.pdf>.
62. Goldsmith, Benjamin E., and Charles Butcher, 'Atrocity Forecasting Project Update: New Forecasts for 2016–2020, & Evaluation of our Forecasts for 2011–2015', Australian National University, Department of Politics and International Relations, 23 March 2016.
63. Dludla, S'duduzo, 'Anti-Xenophobia Coalition to Try to Stop Refugee Amendment Bill', *TMG Digital*, 18 June 2016, available at <http://www.sowetanlive.co.za/ne ws/2016/06/18/anti-xenophobia-coalition.-to-try-to-stop-refugee-amendment-bill>.
64. 'South Africa Court Halts Migrants' Deportation', *BBC News*, 12 May 2015, available at <http://www.bbc.com/news/world-africa-32712125>.
65. Klotz, 'Borders', p. 182.

66. Letsoalo, Matuma, 'King Zwelithini Blames "Third Force" for Violence', *Mail & Guardian*, 21 April 2015, available at <https://mg.co.za/article/2015-04-21-king-zwelithini-blames-third-force-for-violence>.

CHAPTER NINE

Peru – Indígenas, Mestizos, Criollos

MIGRATION AND SOCIAL CLASS

In 2015, the net migration rate in Peru – the number of immigrants who arrived minus that which left – was –1.6 migrants per thousand population. It ranked about 130th in the world as a receiving country, indicating that the vast majority of the world's states took in more immigrants than did Peru. Net migration rate numbers had deteriorated: –3.4 in 2010, a mammoth –4.3 in 2000, a decline to –1.8 in 1990 and a more evenly balanced –0.8 in 1970 (Table 9.1). Even if the 2015 figure was less than half of that in 2000, Peru still suffers from the largest net population loss of the countries studied in this book.[1] This can signify a brain drain as well as a business drain.

Unlike in many other states, too many international immigrants are not an issue. With low legal and little illegal in-migration, the proposition that Peruvian nationhood has not changed one way or the other is self-evident (Table 3.1).

Out-migration existed in Peru since Spanish colonisation of the Inca empire, then named the Viceroyalty of Peru, began in 1572. Ironically, the attraction of returning to Spanish roots has been an option. During the twentieth century, Peruvian nationals were attracted to destinations that historically have been sending regions. The phenomenon accelerated in the twenty-first century when the US became the favoured destination.

The number of Peruvians who emigrated to different parts of the world is approximately 3 million. Beginning in the 1960s, migration to Europe, especially Spain, surged: it amounted to 137,000 in 2009, only to drop back to 84,000 when Peruvians preferred the US. In 2014 emigrants to the US from South America chiefly comprised Colombians (707,000, or 25 per cent of immigrants), followed by Peruvians (449,000, or 16 per cent), Ecuadorans (424,000, 15 per cent) and Brazilians (336,000, 12 per cent). They accounted for about three-quarters of the total US immigrant population from South

America. Italy, Germany, the Netherlands, Canada and Australia have also emerged as other destinations for Peruvians.[2]

Closer to home, Peruvians made up 35,000 (20 per cent) of migrants living and working in Chile: that is, less than one-tenth of its US diaspora. They worked predominantly in wealthier areas of Santiago as *empleadas* and *empleados* (household help) and were typically of indigenous background. By contrast, Peruvians in Argentina numbered far more, over 100,000. At first, Peruvian elites sent their children to be educated as doctors, lawyers and other professionals, overwhelmingly in Buenos Aires. But as numbers climbed and indigenous groups became more common than supposedly pure-blood *Criollos*, a xenophobic backlash occurred.

Except for Peruvians who return to the country, few foreigners permanently reside there. Their total is only 65,000, of which 15 per cent are Argentines and 10 per cent US Americans (only 6,000). The British diaspora accounts for 5,000. Even if Venezuelans furnished with temporary work permits in 2017 are counted, nationhood will expand very little (Table 9.1).

For politicians, immigration is regarded as a bad word in much of South America: it causes more problems than it solves. The Ministry of the Interior is responsible for immigration policy but no coordinated initiative to increase numbers exists. Besides there are few entry points through which would-be immigrants can arrive. If we examine the synopses of programmes of political parties, called *Planes de Gobierno*, infrequent references are made to immigration.

Following Augusto Pinochet's military coup, Southern neighbour Chile passed a draconian law on immigration in 1975, designed to keep out subversives, undesirables and exiles that the ruthless dictator had expelled. The law primarily defined immigrant categories through the lens of national security and served as deterrent to dangerous elements like terrorists. This legislation was not copied in Peru even though the country experienced its own internal terrorist threat. The immigration-sceptic approach has been unshaken. Peru

Table 9.1 Net migration rate: Arriving immigrants versus departing emigrants (migrants per thousand population)

	India	**Peru**	Russia	South Africa	UK	US
2015	−0.4	**−1.6**	1.4	3.0	3.1	2.9
2010	−0.5	**−3.4**	3.0	2.5	6.6	3.3
2000	−0.1	**−4.3**	3.1	1.4	1.7	6.3
1990	0.0	**−1.8**	1.3	−0.7	0.4	2.8
1970	−0.1	**−0.8**	−0.9	1.8	0.3	1.5

Source: 'World Data Atlas', *Knoema*, available at <https://knoema.com/atlas/topics/Demographics/Population/Net-migration-rate?baseRegion=PE>.

198

also realises that people come here as tourists, not migrants escaping hardship or persecution.

Discrimination based on origin, race or ethnicity is prohibited. Peruvian presidential elections have revealed a host of diverse candidates running for office. Alejandro Toledo, President of Peru from 2001 to 2006, was confronted for being a *Cholo* (*Mestizo* or mixed blood) but Alan García, President from 1985 to 1990 and 2006 to 2011, was not categorised that way.[3] Then President Ollanta Humala, who ruled from 2011 to 2016, openly campaigned as a *Cholo*. His successor, Pablo Kuczynski, elected in 2016, broke the twenty-first-century streak of ruling *Cholos* and was of German–Polish and French descent. Earlier a *Chino* (of Japanese descent), Alberto Fujimori, ruled the country from 1990 to 2000 but was ousted on corruption charges. Peru furnishes a leading example of a country where ethnic or racial background has significance, but political collusion between those at the top of the political system is at least as relevant.

An Office of Registration of Identity (RENIEC) is responsible for granting citizenship. A Ministry of Social Inclusion even claims to welcome immigrants. Yet diversity is not prized but is seen as creating chaos. South American travellers can enter Peru, and most other South American countries, using only national identity cards. As a result, Peruvians who work in Argentina, Chile and Ecuador have few formalities to meet when registering for work. More rigorous are regulations regarding professional positions.

When outside their country, Peruvians are 'inclined to adapt to the receiving societies rather than maintain existing ties with their country of origin'.[4] When Peruvians overstay their visas in South America, many await the next amnesty to extend their visits. In some respects the Southern Cone resembles the EU in terms of passport-free travel.

Failing to attract migrants from other countries to replace Peru's émigrés generates a fall in the numbers who could take part in nationhood. A measure that ostensibly eases admittance to Peru for a select group of foreigners was approved in 2017: a special temporary visa for Venezuelans seeking to escape the humanitarian crisis in their country was issued. Some 30,000 Venezuelans applied for the visa, which included a temporary work permit.[5] But even this visa spotlights the temporary nature of denizenship in Peru.

Factors that contributed to Peru's emigration-sending trend included an economic crisis beginning in the late 1970s that produced hyperinflation. More significantly, the war with *Sendero Luminoso* ('Shining Path') in the 1980s resulted in the death or disappearance of up to 100,000 Peruvians. With few economic opportunities available, many looked to emigration abroad as a solution. From the 1970s, Peruvians of all social groups were prepared to move to the US, Spain, Chile, Japan and elsewhere.

In the 1990s GDP fell and incomes declined, which hit the middle and lower-middle classes hard, even as the Maoist insurgency by Shining Path continued. Like many cosmopolitans, upper-class Peruvians of European descent often disassociated their place of origin with the notion of home. They stressed their class status rather than their national identity. Emigrants from the urban middle class, predominantly *Mestizos*, more frequently associated home with their place of origin. Ironically, however, in their adopted places of residence, ethnic or minority migrants regarded their identity as being on equal terms with Peruvians of *Mestizo* and European descent.[6] Aspirationally, their status was boosted by emigration.

Immigration for *Cholos* of mixed blood was motivated by the need to escape discrimination at home: 'migrants classified as *Cholos* and subject to cultural prejudices in Peruvian society often emigrate to elude racial and social discrimination as much as to achieve social and economic mobility'.[7] Such poorer groups migrated to neighbouring countries such as Argentina, Chile and Bolivia in the south, or Ecuador and Colombia in the north, where residence visas and work permits were not required. But the very poorest sectors, in the high Andes or on the Amazonian plain, were among those who had the fewest chances to emigrate.

With more than 3 million Peruvians on the move, remittances back home have grown to one of the largest totals in cumulative terms; national revenue from remittances has increased to over US $21 billion dollars. But for one migration specialist, 'Peruvian emigration has not resulted in strong transnational or diasporic relations', particularly when compared to Caribbean, Central American and Mexican migrations headed to the US. Indeed, a diasporic consciousness among Peruvians is not even imminent.[8]

INDIGENEITY

A distinctive migration phenomenon has governed Peruvian society. Related to poverty, it has induced the indigenous population to take a chance on life in the city. This phenomenon overlaps with rural to urban, village to *barrio*, sierra to coast patterns.

Non-Spanish-speaking indigenous groups make up the bulk of this trend, which occurs wherever indigenous people are drawn to the *barrios* to try their luck. *Barrio* is translated as neighbourhood, but the Urban Dictionary simply calls it the hood or ghetto – the poor, ethnic part of town. It is a word used less frequently in Peru.

As discussed in Chapter 3, indigenous groups, known also as first peoples, aboriginals, the native population or autochthonous peoples, are ethnic groups descended from and identifying with the original inhabitants of a pre-settler territory. They are distinguished from groups that have more recently occupied, colonised or settled the area.

In Peru's case internal migration from the highlands to the coast overwhelmingly dominates migration patterns. Such movement may accomplish the nationhood-conjuring trick of enlarging the nation by incorporating hitherto marginal groups into it. Whether Peru suffers from the affliction of two solitudes – indigenous peoples on the one hand, as opposed to *Peninsulares* and other settlers on the other – the transgressive behaviour of indigenous migrants may result in far-reaching mixing and mingling.

Indigeneity is itself complex. Peru counts between 50 and 100 indigenous groups. Most notable and numerous are the highland Quechua speakers: about 4.5 million people living in Peru speak Quechua and 8 million identify themselves as Quechua. This was the original language of the Incas, which was disseminated across wide expanses of the Andean highlands that make up western South America. In total, somewhere between 8.5 and 11 million people speak closely related dialects of Quechua. It is the most widely spoken surviving Indian language of the Americas. This language group, spreading across national borders that exist between Peru, Bolivia, Ecuador and Colombia, makes individual nations nonsensical. Ethnic kinship can map these regions better than borders.

In Peru Quechua is recognised as a co-official language; in Bolivia it functions as the second national language. In the Peruvian and Bolivian highlands, 90 per cent of people are said to understand Quechua, 80 per cent are fluent in it and 50 per cent speak it as their only language. *Mestizos* in rural and even urban areas are familiar with it. Invariably, however, Quechua is associated with lower-class Indian peasantry.

Another indigenous group is made up of Aymara speakers. Totalling only 500,000, they are an entrepreneurial group also located in the highlands and concentrated in high-altitude regions near Puno and Lake Titicaca. Furthermore, indigenous peoples live in the Amazon jungle, especially in the region around Iquitos. Because of their remoteness and insular smaller communities, they make up as many as sixty diverse ethnic groups speaking seventy languages. Their territorial swathe is enormous, however: 1.2 per cent of the Amazonian population occupies over 58 per cent of Peru's territory.

All of these indigenous languages and cultures are officially recognised, making up *las culturas indígenas*. To be sure, Spanish remains the common language, the *lingua franca* of *Criollos* who proclaim their *sang pur*. They live far away from the highlands, form social elites and dominate coastal culture.

CASTA REPRESENTATIONS

Social life in the New World has been meticulously documented through the prism of an intriguing art form. In 1746 Andrés Arce y Miranda, a creole attorney from Puebla, Mexico, criticised a series of paintings that became known as the *cuadros de castas*, widely called *casta* paintings today. This art admirer worried that depictions of racial mixtures would send back to Spain the ruinous message that *Criollos* – Mexican-born children of Spanish parents – were sullied by unclean mixed blood. *Casta* paintings, from which Spaniards inferred much about the New World, first appeared around the mid-eighteenth century. They were still in demand on the art scene in 1821, when the majority of Spain's American colonies were becoming independent.

To date, over a hundred series of *casta* paintings (the term is less used in Peru than Mexico) have been discovered and documented. They represent a wide gamut of different racial mixtures: from the offspring of unions between Spaniards and Indians, or *Mestizos*; Spaniards and Blacks, or *Mulattos*; and Blacks and Indians, or *Zambos*. They were premised on the notion that each race carries a distinct kind of blood. Inescapably, pure Spanish blood was most closely linked to civilisation and wealth, Black blood to slavery and degeneracy.

Casta painting cycles typically begin with the depiction of a liaison between a 'pure' Spaniard and a 'pure' African or Indian mate. This dalliance results in the birth of a *Mulatto* or *Mestizo* child. Further racial and ethnic mixtures take on ever more complex proportions. Racial taxonomies include outlandish labels such as *no te entiendo* ('I don't understand who you are'), *lobo tente en el aire* ('wolf, hold yourself in mid-air') and *Español con India sale Mulato* ('Spaniard with Black makes *Mulatto*'). The intermingling of Spanish settlers with South American Indians and also imported African slaves became the focal point for genealogical study and research.

Classical *casta* paintings are made up of a standard series of sixteen canvases. They depict a man, woman and child arranged according to hierarchies of race and status. Their dress and occupation are highlighted. Paintings make clear that only certain rights, occupations and institutions were open to the offspring of Spaniards. Spanish males are portrayed as men of leisure or professionals, Blacks and *Mulattos* as coachmen, Indians as food vendors, and *Mestizos* as tailors, shoemakers and tobacconists. Females, *Mulattas* and *Mestizas*, are represented as cooks, spinners and seamstresses. Spaniards and their Indian or African brides sport rich European costumes; deprived *Lobo–Mestizo* couples wear plain or ragged dress.

Some *casta* series focus on the representation of racial mixtures as well as material culture and dress styles. Others give background information to the Spanish art collector about the flora and fauna peculiar to the New World: avocados, chilli peppers, pineapples, prickly pears, parrots, armadillos.

While *casta* paintings depict imagery of ethnic offspring of mixed marriages, they say little about lived experiences of people in the New World. The majority of paintings were produced in Mexico but Peru had an equal fascination with ancestry. One was even commissioned by the Viceregency of Peru to be included in the natural history collection of the future King Charles IV of Spain.[9] Its overall purpose was to illuminate for the Viceroyalty the extraordinary ethnic diversity of the country.[10]

Criollo elites were obsessed with the socio-racial hierarchy prevalent in colonial society that privileged White Spanish elites. Colonial social life was presented in idealised terms. In contrast, beggars, vagrants and drunks were denigrated, even though they had populated travellers' and colonial bureaucrats' accounts of the native population. Viewers could gaze upon scenes of prosperity and domesticity where subjects were engaged in productive labour, consumption and commerce. Positive images of Mexico and Peru under Spanish imperial rule were self-aggrandising.[11] They elaborated on relations of social power and control prevalent in the colonies, invariably favouring those of pure blood.[12]

Indeed, Spanish fixation on purity of blood evolved into an elaborate caste system depicting colonised South America. Four primary groups were identified: *Peninsulares* – Spanish-born Whites. They were followed by *Criollos* – also of Spanish and White descent but who had been born in South America. Then came the *Índios*, a catchall term for any member or descendant of an indigenous group. The bottom of the caste ladder were *Negros* – Black Africans and their descendants brought over for slavery.[13] But some Peruvians are cynical about this rigid idealised hierarchy. Some self-deprecatingly invoke a famous Peruvian saying: *el que no tiene de Inga tiene de Mandinga* – that is, every Peruvian has either indigenous Inca or African blood.

In colonial times, *Peninsulares* held all the positions of power and influence. *Criollos* made up the professional and business classes. *Mestizos* were the working class in the towns and cities, doing menial jobs that the elite felt they could not trust to *Índios* and *Negros*. *Índios* often slaved in the mines while *Negros* toiled in the low-lying coastal farms that provided food for the country.

This elaborate caste system persisted in colonial Peru until the wars of independence began in 1820. At that time Peru remained a feudal society in racial and social terms. Independence for Peru and the rest of Spanish America would see the abolition of slavery and the caste system, but colonial racial ideology has taken longer to dissipate.

In independent Peru educated *Criollos* stood to gain most. They were entrusted with the highest positions of authority. They also exploited the liberalisation of trade that Madrid had previously monopolised. On the other hand, Spain knew that the best way to control a country with so many social strata like Peru was by setting sections of society against each other. That was how in 1821, at the time of independence, a population of Whites totalling about 150,000 controlled a population of over 1 million.

March to the Cities

In 1959 Chabuca Granda composed a national anthem for Peru that was not to be. A composer and singer who popularised *Criollo* waltzes mixing in Afro-Peruvian rhythms – then an unfashionable genre of Peruvian music – she rewrote the first stanza of the hymn to insert the historical encounters, tragic and heroic, experienced by Peru.

In place of the 1821 national hymn – an opera-influenced epic march chosen by General José de San Martín, founder of the independent Peruvian state – Chabuca Granda's stanza idolised Túpac Amaru, the last Indigenous Neo-Inca monarch (or Sapa Inca), who had been recognised as head of state by the Spanish but who was nevertheless hanged in Cusco in 1572. It conjured up the imagery of both Indigenous and pure-blood Peruvians searching for a single ideal, perhaps a conception of nationhood.[14]

> Glory founded in millennia of history
> Was shaped into the national sentiment
> And it was the shout of Túpac Amaru
> Which alerts, which demands
> And which impels, towards liberty.
> And the Creole and the Indian embrace
> Yearning for a single ideal.

The stanza was never performed as part of the anthem. Forthrightness rarely figures in the composition of truthful national anthems.

In an anthropological study that has become a Peruvian classic, José Matos Mar has described the role of an expanding state – *el estado desbordado* – and an emergent national society in Peru. The description is, again, consistent with my understanding of how nationhood can be employed. There is a catch, however: it concerns the rush of migrants originating not from another country but in what he calls the Other Peru: rural, provincial, communitarian, segregated, forgotten by history. For Matos Mar, the Other signifies Indigenous Peru.[15]

The author has argued that Indigenous migrants have helped construct a true national society made up of multiethnic communities. They have moved from the Andes to the coastal cities, and above all, Lima. Evidence for this is that Lima rapidly expanded and in 2015 accounted for 8.3 million of the country's total population of over 31 million. Society, state and nation are conflated as a result of this migration process and these concepts have become liminal. As is the case with immigration-receiving countries such as the UK and US, then, outsiders have forged a new identity even though they originate in Inca, Viceregency and independent Peru – not from the outside.

For years, Matos Mar asked himself, the question was whether Peru constitutes a national society and, in contrast to other Latin American countries, formed a nation–state. Profound social exclusion and cultural marginalisation had characterised highlands Peru in particular. But beginning in the 1990s, the migrant population from all of its provinces, including the Amazon, undertook the process of modernisation.

At the time of independence in 1821, no one could have foretold that the power of culture and the process of integration would transform a society where most of the population lived along the coast. The war with Shining Path had been an exception, and the process of gradual, progressive, peaceful social mobilisation produced what the author termed the popular expansion of society.

In 1532, at the time of the Conquest, Peru's diverse and scattered populations had reached 7 million. After its gradual decimation between 1620 and 1821, it hovered at between 1 and 1.2 million. In the 1940 census, the population was 65 per cent rural, 35 per cent urban. In that year its diversity was already notable: 53 per cent White and *Mestizo*, 46 per cent *Índios*, 0.5 per cent Black, 0.7 per cent Asian.

Rapid modernisation and an urban revolution, noted Matos Mar, resulted in 2010 in a new society: 74 per cent urban and 26 per cent rural. In terms of regional breakdown, the population was now 63 per cent coastal, only 28 per cent highland and 9 per cent jungle. In Lima, where 31 per cent of the population was concentrated, and elsewhere on the coast such as Trujillo, where 750,000 lived, the country had become socially remodelled. Arequipa, Peru's second largest city of about 830,000, also experienced significant in-migration, though it was exceptional since it lay in the highlands. Peru had become genuinely multiethnic, pluricultural and multilinguistic.

As with foreign-born migration, key to the integration of highlands peoples is integration. Arriving Indigenous groups have become crucial to economic development and social transformation: 'Their social and cultural impact helps re-create and inspire positive regional and local identities, undergird existing cultural pluralism, achieve a national identity, and serve as staunch defenders of national sovereignty.'[16]

To be sure, the Other Peru could not be overlooked. Internally displaced people profoundly affected by the war from 1980 to 2000 had been attracted by the need to create ethnic citizenship for all Peruvians – not solely originating from caste lines. The major conflict regions of the war had been the centre and south of the country, particularly in the area around Ayacucho. Indigenous peoples 'were the main victims of the terrible confrontation between *Sendero Luminoso* and the armed forces and police'.[17] In those regions as many as 600,000 peasants fled their homes in order to save themselves and their families. Some migrated to nearby towns and provincial capitals, others to large coastal cities like Lima.[18]

Apart from the war, high poverty levels were the principal cause of out-migration from the Andes and the Amazon basin. Internally displaced people were already poor and came from rural areas: that is, those that had fewer than 100 houses grouped contiguously.[19]

Finally, population movements were triggered by any one of seven securiti-sation factors. These were:

1. economic
2. food-related
3. sanitation-related
4. environmental
5. personal
6. communal
7. political.[20]

These were the incentives to move, and mass migration to the cities, the author reported, has proved to be a blessing in disguise: unheard-of develop-ment and modernisation have ensued.

INTEGRATING INTO URBAN CULTURE

Quechua speakers may be a part of Peru but they may not be of it. And that may be the way that many Indigenous people like it. Matos Mar, himself Quechua, believed that migration from the Andes to Lima and other cities on the Pacific coast was not a simple demographic movement. It amounted to an unstoppable tide that triggered radical social change while disre-garding Peru's oligarchic political and economic structures. The 8 million migrants who left the Andes between 1940 and 2010 built shantytowns, then later brick houses, and paved streets in their *barrios*. They forged a new *Mestizo* culture and created jobs for themselves in an informal, unregistered economy.

In the last printing of *Desborde popular*, Matos Mar was even more opti-mistic about the fruits of urban mobility. In 1940 Lima had just over 600,000 inhabitants; by 1995 its population had increased to 7 million. Urbanisation, globalisation, rapid economic growth for two decades, improved communica-tions and transport systems, and political decentralisation had at last forged a nation. Even the Other Peru – the unofficial land from which migrants moved – had now generated economic modernisation, the rise of a diverse middle class and the spread of local democracy. The move from countryside to city transformed the descendants of often-illiterate *campesinos* into citizens who were asserting their political rights.

To be sure, the emergent nation may have destroyed much of the older political order but it failed to create new political institutions or effective political parties. The critique has been, then, that the emergent nation, on the road to nationhood, has not yet become a developed country.[21]

Anthropologist Rodrigo Montoya Rojas has taken up Matos Mar's narrative.[22] Migrants have arrived from all over Peru. Lima today is a metropolis of many cultures and languages, and it has also become Andeanised. Basing his studies largely on extensive fieldwork with Andean migrants in Villa El Salvador, a district located south of metropolitan Lima, Montoya Rojas raised questions about the relations governing culture and power, Indigenous movements in the city, and the future of Quechua culture in Peru.

The author examined the experience of *ayllu* integration, a movement asserting the presence of Quechua culture in the highlands but now also being transposed to coastal towns. *Ayllu* constitute a pre-colonial Andean communal system that represents an indigenous model of local government. Not only do they still exist after centuries, but also they are in the process of being re-energised in Quechua and also Aymara communities distant from the highlands. Thus at one end are Andean highland *ayllu*, on the other those forged by migrants in a place like Villa El Salvador, just south of of Lima, who wish to preserve the sense of indigenous culture. 'In the case of the first generation of migrants, Quechua culture in Lima is partially reproduced and recreated.'[23] But it tends to be lost after that, only reproducing fragmentarily. Even later generations, though, are able to identify with the culture, particularly with the music, singing, dance and spirituality, if not speaking the language.[24] The endless question is, then, how authentic such a culture is.

The reproduction of Andean culture by different generations of migrants is key in the author's reflections. He emphasises the sacredness of authority that recognises the Incas as 'Son of the Sun'.[25] Quechua culture comprises 'a people who claim their culture and their language as a way of defending against the aggression of the dominant culture'.[26]

As with many anthropologists who regard culture as inseparable from language, Montoya Rojas highlights the importance of the Quechua language for the reproduction of its culture. The relationship between language and culture is just about one to one. He also advances a sharp distinction between the two Andean cultures, Quechua and Aymara.[27] Whereas coca chewing is seen as a powerful symbol of cultural identity for Quechua, Aymara are perceived as more capitalistic and their members stereotyped as hard workers.

But in the massive mobility pursued by Indigenous peoples, Montoya Rojas anticipates that Quechua, alongside Aymara and speakers of Amazon basin languages, can organise politically to defend cultural rights. A negative development that affects Quechua culture is the expansion of Castilian as *lingua franca*. Related to this is the decline in Indigenous monolingualism and the lure of greater bilingualism. A final problem (which was noted in the US case) is 'religious warfare waged by Protestant sects'. In this struggle between Indigenous Quechua communities and modernity, Montoya Rojas sees this as an 'uneven battle'.[28]

EXTRANJEROS

It is clear that racial mixing began when the Spanish conquistadors overran the Inca Empire in the sixteenth century. But it is a little-known fact that it continued when successive waves of African slaves, indentured Chinese labourers, and migrants from Japan and Europe were inserted in Peru. As depicted in *casta* paintings, even today socio-economic cleavages follow racial lines. So an Indigenous woman may only ever work as a maid, and a Black man can only aspire to serve as a hotel doorman. In turn, a Japanese citizen, or his daughter, can hope to be president of the country.[29]

Afro-Peruvians frequently came to Peru from the slave port of Buenaventura in Colombia. The last time a racial variable was included in the census to identify Afro-Peruvians was in 1940. Currently, efforts are under way to include this group in national statistics. In 2009 Peru became the first country in South America to apologise to its African-descended population for centuries of abuse, exclusion and discrimination. Yet when it comes to legislative action to combat racism and promote equal opportunity, the country is considered one of the most backward nations in the Americas. Indigenous and African descendants in Peru earn 40 per cent less than mixed-race people. Most Black Peruvians, who make up around 10 per cent of the population, are trapped in poverty. In poor neighbourhoods of Lima such as La Victoria, racial stereotypes of Blacks as an underclass are dominant.

In a study of Piura, where Spanish conqueror Francisco Pizarro founded the third Spanish city in South America and the first in Peru, 26 per cent of Afro-Peruvian children were not enrolled in school in 2012. Surveys indicate that half of Afro-Peruvians complained they were insulted at least once on the street. Four out of ten felt discrimination in their workplace or in other public spaces.

Nearly as demoralising is the widespread stereotype of Afro-Peruvians. One respondent insisted that 'When I say I don't dance, don't cook and don't play an instrument, people say "how could you be Black? You are a fake!"'[30] But in recent years Afro-Peruvians have seen a revival in their culture, especially music and dance; renowned singer Susanna Baca is an exemplary case. A poetic style known as *decima*, a form exemplified in the work of Afro-Peruvian poet Nicomedes Santa Cruz, is another example.

Impressive anthropological research on an Afro-Peruvian community located in northern coastal Peru has been conducted by Tanya Golash-Boza. She emphasises that her subjects 'do not see themselves as part of a broader community of people descended from African slaves'.[31] In her study of the town of Ingenio, she found an unexpected lack of attention to Afro-cultural difference. Afro-Peruvians gave primacy to other ways of framing their lives and using other lenses: as Peruvians, *Criollos*, agricultural workers, men and women, mothers.

Local perceptions of Blackness did not deny there was racial or skin colour discrimination. Nor did these perspectives buy into the discourse of Afro-Peruvian 'sameness' found in the mantra 'We are all Peruvians.' Progressive changes by political leaders in South America's recently uncovered multi-cultural contexts now favoured communities that were bearers of cultural specificity having a clearly demarcated status as ethnic group. But claims based primarily on racial grievances would not succeed, as they rarely have in the other instances of Negritude examined in this book.[32]

A last group I wish to examine in this chapter is the category of *Chinos*. As early as the sixteenth century, Asian coolies were brought to Acapulco, Mexico, from Manila. The Spaniards termed this diverse community of Asians *los Índios chinos*, even though they originated not only from China but also Japan, Philippines and Indonesia, *inter alia*. When they were sent to Peru they were simply called *Chinos*. Owning a *Chino* coolie displayed high status. It is a term used to this day despite the fact that many are of Japanese descent. Former President Fujimori and daughter Keita are referred to as *Chinos*.

The Peruvian image of Japanese, many who were deported during World War II, has been positive. Oddly, the social hierarchy considers *Chinos* a part of Peruvian nationhood in a way that Indigenous and Black Peruvians are disputable.

UNTYING THE GORDIAN KNOT

Social hierarchies in the six countries studied in this book are frequently rigid. This *reality* contrasts with the *rhetoric* of political leaders, which typically conveys a politically liberal message. To be sure, the reality has hardened as a result of electoral failings of etablishment parties in recent elections. These encompass many European countries, the US, India, South Africa and other states not discussed here: notably, Turkey, Egypt, Myanmar, the Philippines and other would-be exclusionary ethnocracies.

A key obstacle in crafting national belonging is the socio-political hierarchies that ordinary citizens adopt. Sometimes they may disregard the importance of immigrants to their lives through the use of stereotypes based on their social class rather than performance criteria. Nationhood cannot be built if, having made crucial steps in integrating into host societies, immigrants are not accorded a fuller sense of belonging. A crucial step, then, in evolving into a nation enlarged through consensus-based immigration is to hotwire appreciation of migrants in the minds of citizens. Fashioning nationhood in this way permits political socialisation to begin at an early stage and it may pre-empt the need to struggle with racism and xenophobia subsequently.

NOTES

1. 'World Data Atlas', *Knoema*, available at <https://knoema.com/atlas/topics/Demographics/Population/Net-migration-rate?baseRegion=PE>.
2. Organization of American States, 'Continuous Reporting System on International Migration in the Americas – SICREMI', 2012, available at <http://www.migracionoea.org/index.php/en/sicremi-en/34-sicremi/publicacion-2012/paises-en/546-sintesis-historica-de-la-migracion-internacional-peru.html>.
3. Interview with Carlos Alza Barco, Pontificia Universidad Católica del Perú, 15 August 2012.
4. Paerregaard, Karsten, *Peruvians Dispersed: A Global Ethnography of Migration* (Lanham, MD: Lexington Books, 2008), p. 237.
5. 'Permiso Temporal de Permanencia para Ciudadanos Venezolanos', Decreto Supremo No. 023-2017 IN, *Migraciones Perú*, 31 July 2017, available at <https://www.migraciones.gob.pe/index.php/ptp-venezolanos/>.
6. Paerregaard, *Peruvians Dispersed*, p. 199.
7. Ibid.
8. Ibid., p. 232.
9. Deans-Smith, Susan, 'Casta Paintings', *Not Even Past*, available at <https://notevenpast.org/casta-paintings/>.
10. The major Peruvian *casta* collection is held by the Museo Nacional de Arqueología, Antropología e Historia del Perú.
11. *Colonial Latin American Review*, 9 November 2011, available at <http://www.tandfonline.com/doi/abs/10.1080/10609160500314980>.
12. Ramirez, Yasmin, 'New World Orders: Casta Painting and Colonial Latin America', *Artnet*, 1996, available at <http://www.artnet.com/magazine_pre2000/features/ramirez/ramirez12-02-96.asp>.
13. Gaughran, David, 'Colonial Peru, the Caste System, and the "Purity" of Blood', *South Americana*, 20 March 2012, available at <https://southamericana.com/2012/03/20/spain-peru-and-the-purity-of-blood/>.
14. Porcari, César Colomba, 'El Himno según Chabuca', *Caretas*, no. 1884, 27 July 2005, Lima, pp. 56–58, available at <https://sites.google.com/site/himnonacionaldelperu/chabuca-granda-y-el-himno-nacional-del-per>.
15. Matos Mar, José, *Perú: Estado desbordado y sociedad nacional emergente* (Lima, Peru: Universidad Ricardo Palma, Centro de Investigación, 2011), pp. 30–2.
16. Ibid., p. 555.
17. Montoya Rojas, Rodrigo, *Porvenir de la cultura quechua en Perú: Desde Lima, Villa El Salvador y Puquio* (Lima: Fondo Editorial de la Universidad Nacional Mayor de San Marcos, 2010), p. 559, available at <www.scielo.org.pe/pdf/anthro/v29n29/a16v29n29.pdf>. See also Rodrigo Montoya Rojas, *Destinies of the Quechua Culture in Peru* (Eastbourne: Sussex Academic Press, 2018).

18. Ministerio de la Mujer y Poblaciones Vulnerables (MIMP), Nicolás Zevallos Trigoso (ed.), *Desplazamientos internos en el Perú* (Lima: Organización Internacional para las Migraciones, 2015), p. 34.
19. Ibid., p. 40.
20. Ibid., pp. 50–5.
21. Bello, 'The Migrant Nation', *The Economist*, 22 August 2015, available at <https://www.economist.com/news/americas/21661802-urbanisation-peru-has-brought-citizenship-also-host-problems-migrant-nation>.
22. Montoya Rojas, *Porvenir*, reviewed by Luis Florentino Andrade Ciudad (Pontificia Universidad Católica del Perú) in *Anthropologica*, 29, December 2011, pp. 255–9.
23. Montoya Rojas, *Porvenir*, p. 16.
24. Ibid., p. 541.
25. Ibid., pp. 484–5.
26. Ibid., p. 528.
27. Ibid., p. 428.
28. Ibid., pp. 557–8.
29. Collyns, Dan, 'Peru's Minorities Battle Racism', *BBC News*, 13 June 2010, available at <http://www.bbc.com/news/10205171>.
30. 'In Peru, Black Is an Invisible Color', *World Bank*, 14 October 2013, available at <http://www.worldbank.org/en/news/feature/2013/10/14/Peru-negro-color-invisible>.
31. Golash-Boza, Tanya, *Yo Soy Negro: Blackness in Peru* (Gainesville, FL: University Press of Florida, 2011), p. 115.
32. Review of *Yo Soy Negro* by Stanley R. Bailey, *Social Forces*, 93, no. 3, 27 November 2012.

Select bibliography

Richard Alba and Nancy Foner, *Strangers No More: Immigration and the Challenges of Integration in North America and Western Europe* (Cambridge: Cambridge University Press, 2015).

Benedict Anderson, *Imagined Communities: Reflections on the Origin and Spread of Nationalism* (London: Verso, 1983).

Melissa Aronczyk, *Branding the Nation: The Global Business of National Identity* (New York: Oxford University Press, 2013).

Étienne Balibar and Immanuel Wallerstein, *Race, Nation, Class: Ambiguous Identities* (London: Verso, 1991).

Zygmunt Bauman, *Europe: An Unfinished Adventure* (Cambridge: Polity Press, 2004).

Zygmunt Bauman, *Retropia* (Cambridge: Polity Press, 2017).

Reinhard Bendix, *Nation-Building and Citizenship* (Berkeley, CA: University of California Press, 1977).

Seyla Benhabib, *The Claims of Culture: Equality and Diversity in the Global Era* (Princeton, NJ: Princeton University Press, 2002).

Homi K. Bhabha, *The Location of Culture* (London: Routledge, 1994).

Paul R. Brass, *Ethnicity and Nationalism: Theory and Comparison* (Newbury Park, CA: Sage, 1991).

Rogers Brubaker, *Citizenship and Nationhood in France and Germany* (Cambridge, MA: Harvard University Press, 1992).

Christopher Caldwell, *Reflections on the Revolution in Europe: Immigration, Islam and the West* (New York: Anchor, 2010).

Margaret Canovan, *Nationhood and Political Theory* (Cheltenham: Edward Elgar, 1998).

Dipesh Chakrabarty, *Provincializing Europe: Postcolonial Thought and Historical Difference* (Princeton, NJ: Princeton University Press, 2000).

Partha Chatterjee, *The Nation and its Fragments: Colonial and Postcolonial Histories* (Princeton, NJ: Princeton University Press, 1993).

Partha Chatterjee, *Nationalist Thought and the Colonial World: A Derivative Discourse* (London: Zed Books, 1986).

Amy Chua, *Political Tribes: Group Instinct and the Fate of Nations* (New York: Penguin Books, 2018).

Amy Chua, *World on Fire: How Exporting Free Market Democracy Breeds Ethnic Hatred and Global Instability* (New York: Anchor Books, 2004).

Frantz Fanon, *Black Skin, White Masks* (New York: Grove Press, 1994).

Elena Fiddian-Qasmiyeh, Gil Loescher, Katy Long and Nando Sigona (eds), *Oxford Handbook of Refugee and Forced Migration Studies* (Oxford: Oxford University Press, 2014).

Andre Gunder Frank, *ReOrient: Global Economy in the Asian Age* (Berkeley, CA: University of California Press, 1998).

Azar Gat, *Nations: The Long History and Deep Roots of Political Ethnicity and Nationalism* (Cambridge: Cambridge University Press, 2012).

Liah Greenfeld, *Nationalism: Five Roads to Modernity* (Cambridge, MA: Harvard University Press, 1993).

Montserrat Guibernau, *Belonging: Solidarity and Division in Modern Societies* (Cambridge: Polity, 2013).

Montserrat Guibernau, *Nations Without States: Political Communities in a Global Age* (Cambridge: Polity Press, 2000).

Ted Robert Gurr, *Peoples Versus States: Minorities at Risk in the New Century* (Washington, DC: United States Institute of Peace Press, 2000).

Adrian Hastings, *The Construction of Nationhood: Ethnicity, Religion and Nationalism* (Cambridge: Cambridge University Press, 1997).

Eric Hobsbawm, *Nations and Nationalism Since 1780: Programme, Myth, Reality*, 2nd edn (Cambridge: Cambridge University Press, 1992).

Jane Jenson, *Defining and Measuring Social Cohesion* (London: Commonwealth Secretariat, 2010).

Christian Joppke, *Is Multiculturalism Dead? Crisis and Persistence in the Constitutional State* (Cambridge: Polity, 2017).

Elie Kedourie, *Nationalism*, 3rd edn (London: Hutchinson, 1966).

Hans Kohn, *Nationalism: Its Meaning and History* (Huntington, NY: Robert E. Krieger, 1982).

Will Kymlicka, *Multicultural Odysseys: Navigating the New International Politics of Diversity* (Oxford: Oxford University Press, 2007).

Michèle Lamont, *The Dignity of Working Men: Morality and the Boundaries of Race, Class, and Immigration* (Cambridge, MA: Harvard University Press, 2002).

Mark Lilla, *The Once and Future Liberal: After Identity Politics* (New York: Harper, 2017).

Sylvia McAdam (Saysewahum), *Nationhood Interrupted: Revitalizing* nêhiyaw *Legal Systems* (Saskatoon, SK: Purish Publishing, 2015).

Mamdani Mahmood, *Good Muslim, Bad Muslim* (New York: Doubleday, 2004).

Nasar Meer, *Key Concepts in Race and Ethnicity* (Thousand Oaks, CA: Sage, 2014).

Helen O'Nions, *Asylum – A Right Denied? A Critical Analysis of European Asylum Policy* (London: Routledge, 2014).

Liav Orgad, *The Cultural Defense of Nations: A Liberal Theory of Majority Rights* (Oxford: Oxford University Press, 2015).

Anne Phillips, *Multiculturalism without Culture* (Princeton, NJ: Princeton University Press, 2007).

Sasha Polakow-Suransky, *Go Back to Where You Came From: The Backlash Against Immigration and the Fate of Western Democracy* (New York: Nation Books, 2017).

Robert Rowthorn, *The Costs and Benefits of Large-scale Immigration* (London: Civitas, 2015).

Olivier Roy, *Holy Ignorance: When Religion and Culture Part Ways* (New York: Columbia University Press, 2009).

William Safran (ed.), *The Secular and the Sacred: Nation, Religion and Politics* (London: Frank Cass, 2003).

William Safran and Jean A. Laponce (eds), *Language, Ethnic Identity and the State* (London: Routledge, 2005).

Peter W. Scholten and Ilona van Breugel (eds), *Mainstreaming Integration Governance* (London: Palgrave Macmillan, 2018).

Hugh Seton-Watson, *Nations and States: An Enquiry into the Origins of Nations and the Politics of Nationalism* (Boulder, CO: Westview Press, 1977).

Gayatri Chakravorty Spivak, *Nationalism and the Imagination* (New York: Seagull Books, 2010).

Claude M. Steele, *Whistling Vivaldi: How Stereotypes Affect Us and What We Can Do* (New York: W. W. Norton, 2011).

Raymond Taras, *Liberal and Illiberal Nationalisms* (Basingstoke: Palgrave, 2002).

Raymond Taras, *Xenophobia and Islamophobia in Europe* (Edinburgh: Edinburgh University Press, 2012).

Raymond Taras and Rajat Ganguly, *Understanding Ethnic Conflict*, 4th edn (New York: Longman, 2010).

John Taylor and Helen Lee (eds), *Mobilities of Return: Pacific Perspectives* (Canberra: Australian National University Press, 2018).

Index

Canada (*cont.*)
immigration policies, 141
integration, 74
minority population, 23
nation branding, 11
refugee policies, 141–2
two solitudes of, 16
casta paintings, 201–3
Césaire, Aimé, 35
Chakrabarty, Dipesh, 5
Chatterjee, Partha, 5, 153
Chaudhuri, Nirad, 170
Chebel d'Appolonia, Ariane, 37
Chechyna, 88–9
Chile, 198
Chua, Amy, 10, 132
Churchill, Winston, 113, 157, 158, 159
citizenship
and nationhood, 138
Peru, 198
civic nationalism
and assimilation, 21–2
contrasted to ethnic nationalism, 20–1
in Russia, 89, 90
climate change
capitalism and, 164
carbon dioxide concentrations, 164
flooding, Bangladesh, 167
and migration flows, 163, 165–7
pollution-related deaths, 164
Coates, Ta-Nehisi, 144, 145
colonialism
in Africa, 175–6, 178, 183–4
in America, 125
the British in India, 151–3
and British nationalism, 111–12
casta paintings and the socio-racial hierarchy, 201–3, 208
'doctrine of discovery', 55, 56
French federation with its colonies, 35
humanist ideology and, 5
impact on modern-day nationalisms, 5
independence movements, 17
post-Empire population in Britain, 102, 103
cosmopolitanism, 15
Crouch, Colin, 112
Crush, Jonathan, 191
cultural appropriation, 59
cultural defence policies, 23–4
cultural nations, 20–2, 32, 42
Czerny, Fr. Michael, 53

Davis, Mike, 158
de Klerk, F. W., 178, 181
de Tocqueville, Alexis, 131
Denmark, 67–8
Desai, Kiran, 162

Disraeli, Benjamin, 155
diversity
commodification of, 11
multiculturalism models for, 7, 16
social diversity in Peru, 198
super-diversity, 52
Du Bois, W. E. B., 34, 145
Dugin, Aleksander, 87
Durkheim, Émile, 19

economic migrants
and asylum seekers, France, 13
from Peru, 199–200
Enlightenment, 5, 125
ethnic identities
constructivist approach to, 19
and nation-building, 18
ethnic nationalism, 20–1
ethnicity
casta paintings, 201–3, 208
ethnic divisions in free market democracies, 10
ethnic-based politics, South Africa, 178–9
ethno-nationalism, Russia, 83–4, 87–8, 97–8
inclusion of ethnic groups within nationhood, 14–15
kinship and, 21–2
in relationship to religion, 33
ethnocentrism, 37
Eurasianism, 86–7
Eurocentrism, 4–6
Europe
Muslim experience in, 118–19
public opposition to Muslim immigration, 39–40
European Court of Human Rights (ECHR), 66
European Network Against Racism (ENAR), 14–15
European Union (EU)
Brexit, 103–6, 112, 119–21
free movement of people, 103–4
migration levels to Britain, post-Brexit vote, 119–21
Posted Workers Directive, 94

famines, 158–9
Fanon, Frantz, 34
Farage, Nigel, 119
Ferrante, Elena, 3
Foner, Nancy, 62, 64
France
asylum seekers vs economic migrants, 13
colour-blind Republican model, 37
concept of nationhood, 6
federation with the colonies, 35
Francafrique, 35–6

immigration policies
American, 75, 135–7, 139
Canada, 141–2
Great Britain, 75
India, 75
Peru, 75, 198–9
Russia, 75
South Africa, 75, 175, 192
India
Adivasis (Scheduled Tribes), 58
Bengal Famine, 158–9
BJP (Bharatiya Janata Party), 161, 168–70
British colonialism of, 151–3
climate change and migration flows, 165–7
Hindu nationalism, 151, 156–7, 159–62, 168–70
Hindu-Muslim conflict, 167, 168, 169
historical immigration, 76
immigration policies, 75
immigration to, 151
Indigenous peoples in, 165–6
migration from, 151
mobility and dam construction, 165
modern day separatist movements, prevention of, 162–3
modern Indian nationalism, 152, 153–4, 156
Muslim League (India), 157–8, 159–60
Muslim 'minorities', 151
Muslim separatism, 154, 156–60
national anthem, 151
net international migration, 77
net migration rate, 198
partition, 157–8, 159–62, 163
pollution-related deaths, 164
Rashtriya Swayamsevak Sangh (RSS), 161, 162
secular nationalism, 168
the *Sepoy* (or Soldiers') Mutiny, 154–6
spiritual nationalism, 154, 156
Indigenous peoples
Adivasis (Scheduled Tribes), India, 58
Australia, 58
defined, 54, 200
in Europe and Russia, 58
Far East, 58
First Nations, Canada, 54–7, 59
in India, 165–6
jus soli concept and, 53–4
language rights, 44, 46
nationhood and, 58–60
Native Americans, 57
of North America, 54
in Peru, 200–1, 204–7
pre-Columbian Indigenous peoples, 57
Inkatha Freedom Party (IFP), 181–3, 185
integration
in Australia, 71–3

in Austria, 65–6
in Belgium, 66
in Canada, 74
defined, 51–2
in Denmark, 67–8
in Germany, 66–7
within nationhood, 2, 16
in Norway, 68
in Sweden, 68–72
see also belonging
interculturalism, 7, 16
intermarriage
attitudes towards in Russia, 95
kinship and, 21–2, 138
rates in the US, 144
intersectionality theory, 143
Ishiguro, Kazuo, 58
Islam *see* Muslims
Islamophobia, 32, 36

Jefferson, Thomas, 126–7
Jenson, Jane, 62
Jinnah, Muhammad Ali, 151, 157, 160
Johnson, Lynton Kwesi, 113

Kedourie, Elie, 17
King, Thomas, 55
kinship
ethnicity and, 21–2
intermarriage and, 21–2, 138
Klein, Naomi, 164
Klotz, Audie, 188, 192
Kohn, Hans, 18, 42, 109
Kurz, Sebastian, 46, 65–6
Kwesi Johnson, Lynton, 113
Kymlicka, Will, 46

labour markets, 15
Lagrange, Hugues, 37–8
language
Aymara speakers, Peru, 44, 201, 207
Bantu, South Africa, 179
within the cultural nation, 20, 32, 42
diglossia, 45
English fluency among ethnic minorities in Britain, 115
and English nation-building, 108, 109
French language, 43
of Indigenous peoples, 44, 46
language bias compared to religious discrimination, 46–7
linguistic communities, 17–18, 19–20
majority vs minority languages, 44–5
mandatory Russian language tests, 92–3
and nation-building, 42–3
and political control, 42–3
in post-colonial America, 127–8, 129–30
prejudice against, 42–6

EU representative:
Easy Access System Europe
Mustamäe tee 50, 10621 Tallinn, Estonia
Gpsr.requests@easproject.com

www.ingramcontent.com/pod-product-compliance
Lightning Source LLC
Chambersburg PA
CBHW050353270326
41926CB00016B/3725